MULTICULTURAL EDUCATION SERIES

James A. Banks, Series Editor

D0092074

Un-Standardizing Curriculum

Multicultural Teaching in the Standards-Based Classroom

Christine E. Sleeter

Teachers College, Columbia University
New York and London

Published by Teachers College Press, 1234 Amsterdam Avenue, New York, NY 10027

A portion of Chapter 5 originally appeared in *Rethinking Schools* magazine, Fall, 2004. For more information: www.rethinkingschools.org.

Library of Congress Cataloging-in-Publication Data

Sleeter, Christine E., 1948–
    Un-standardizing curriculum : multicultural teaching in the standards-based classroom / Christine Sleeter.
        p. cm.—(Multicultural education series)
    Includes bibliographical references and index.
    ISBN 0-8077-4622-3 (cloth : alk. paper)—ISBN 0-8077-4621-5 (pbk. : alk. paper)
    1. Multicultural education—United States—Curricula—Planning.
    2. Multicultural education—Study and teaching—United States.   I. Title.
    II. Multicultural education series (New York, N.Y.)

    LC1099.3.S589 2005
    370.117—dc22   2005048583

ISBN-13   ISBN-10
978-0-8077-4621-9 (paper)   ISBN 0-8077-4621-5 (paper)
978-0-8077-4622-6 (cloth)   ISBN 0-8077-4622-3 (cloth)

Printed on acid-free paper

Manufactured in the United States of America

12   11   10   09   08   07   8   7   6   5   4   3   2

Contents

Series Foreword

The nation's deepening ethnic texture, interracial tension and conflict, and the increasing percentage of students who speak a first language other than English make multicultural education imperative in the 21st century. The U.S. Census Bureau (2000) estimated that people of color made up 28% of the nation's population in 2000 and predicted that they would make up 38% in 2025 and 47% in 2050. In March, 2004, the Census revised its projections and predicted that by 2050 people of color and Whites would each make up 50% of the U.S. population (El Nasser, 2004).

American classrooms are experiencing the largest influx of immigrant students since the beginning of the 20th century. About a million immigrants are making the United States their home each year (Martin & Midgley, 1999). More than seven and one-half million legal immigrants settled in the United States between 1991 and 1998, most of whom came from nations in Latin America and Asia (Riche, 2000). A significant number also come from the West Indies and Africa. A large but undetermined number of undocumented immigrants also enter the United States each year. The influence of an increasingly ethnically diverse population on the nation's schools, colleges, and universities is and will continue to be enormous.

Forty percent of the students enrolled in the nation's schools in 2001 were students of color. This percentage is increasing each year, primarily because of the growth in the percentage of Latino students (Martinez & Curry, 1999). In some of the nation's largest cities and metropolitan areas, such as Chicago, Los Angeles, Washington, D.C., New York, Seattle, and San Francisco, half or more of the public school students are students of color. During the 1998–1999 school year, students of color made up 63.1% of the student population in the public schools of California, the nation's largest state (California State Department of Education, 2000).

Language and religious diversity is also increasing among the nation's student population. In 2000, about 20% of the school-age population spoke a language at home other than English (U.S. Census Bureau, 2000). Harvard professor Diana L. Eck (2001) calls the United States the "most religiously diverse nation on earth" (p. 4). Islam is now the fastest-growing religion in the U.S. Most teachers now in the classroom and in teacher education programs are likely to have students from diverse ethnic, racial, language, and religious groups in their classrooms during their careers. This is true for both inner-city and suburban teachers.

An important goal of multicultural education is to improve race relations and to help all students acquire the knowledge, attitudes, and skills needed to participate in cross-cultural interactions and in personal, social, and civic action that will help make our nation more democratic and just. Multicultural education is consequently as important for middle-class White suburban students as it is for students of color who live in the inner-city. Multicultural education fosters the public good and the overarching goals of the commonwealth.

The major purpose of the *Multicultural Education Series* is to provide preservice educators, practicing educators, graduate students, scholars, and policy makers with an interrelated and comprehensive set of books that summarizes and analyzes important research, theory, and practice related to the education of ethnic, racial, cultural, and language groups in the United States and the education of mainstream students about diversity. The books in the *Series* provide research, theoretical, and practical knowledge about the behaviors and learning characteristics of students of color, language minority students, and low-income students. They also provide knowledge about ways to improve academic achievement and race relations in educational settings.

The definition of multicultural education in the *Handbook of Research on Multicultural Education* (Banks & Banks, 2004) is used in the *Series*: Multicultural education is *"a field of study designed to increase educational equity for all students that incorporates, for this purpose, content, concepts, principles, theories, and paradigms from history, the social and behavioral sciences, and particularly from ethnic studies and women's studies"* (p. xii). In the *Series*, as in the *Handbook*, multicultural education is considered a "metadiscipline."

The dimensions of multicultural education, developed by Banks (2004) and described in the *Handbook of Research on Multicultural Education*, provide the conceptual framework for the development of the books in the *Series*. They are: *content integration, the knowledge construction process, prejudice reduction, an equity pedagogy,* and *an empowering school culture and social structure.* To implement multicultural education effectively, teachers and administrators must attend to each of the five dimensions of multicultural education. They should use content from diverse groups when teaching concepts and skills, help students to understand how knowledge in the various disciplines is constructed, help students to develop positive intergroup attitudes and behaviors, and modify their teaching strategies so that students from different racial, cultural, language, and social-class groups will experience equal educational opportunities. The total environment and culture of the school must also be transformed so that students from diverse groups will experience equal status in the culture and life of the school.

Although the five dimensions of multicultural education are highly interrelated, each requires deliberate attention and focus. Each book in the series focuses on one or more of the dimensions, although each book deals with all of them to some extent because of the highly interrelated characteristics of the dimensions.

The national focus on creating high academic standards and holding educators accountable for student achievement is having mixed results in the nation's schools. Many of the standards-based reforms were created to respond to the requirements of the No Child Left Behind Act (NCLB) that was led by President George W. Bush and enacted by Congress in 2001. However, many states had initiated standards-based reforms prior to the passage of the NCLB Act.

Some researchers and educational leaders view the reforms required by the NCLB Act as promising. A study by Roderick, Jacob, and Bryk (2002) indicates that performance improved in low-performing schools after the implementation of standards-based reform. Some school leaders in high-minority, low-achieving schools have applauded the NCLB Act because it requires school districts and states to disaggregate achievement data by poverty, race, ethnicity, disability, and limited English proficiency. These administrators believe that the disaggregation of achievement data has helped to focus attention on the academic achievement gap between Whites and students of color such as African Americans, Mexican Americans, and Native Americans.

The NCLB Act and related reforms have evoked a chorus of criticism from other researchers and school reformers (Meier & Wood, 2005). The critics of the Act argue that standards-based reforms driven by the NCLB Act have had many negative consequences on the curriculum and on school life. They contend that these reforms have forced many teachers to focus on narrow literacy and numeracy skills rather than on critical thinking and the broad goals of schooling in a democratic society, led to an overemphasis on testing and less focus on teaching, and deskilled (Giroux, 1988) and de-professionalized teachers. Amrein and Berliner (2002) analyzed 18 states to determine how high-stakes tests were affecting student learning. They concluded that in all but one of their analyses student learning was indeterminate, remained at the same level before high-stakes testing was implemented, or went down when high states testing policies were initiated.

In this insightful and practical book, Sleeter makes an important distinction between *standards* and *standardization* and describes why she supports standards but is opposed to standardization. Standards—which describe quality—can be used by teachers to help students attain high levels of academic achievement. Standardization has adverse affects on students, teachers, and schools because it leads to bureaucratization and to a focus on low-level knowledge and skills that can be easily measured by norm-referenced tests.

Sleeter describes how standards can guide effective and culturally responsive school reform. However, she explicates the ways in which attempts to implement standards have often gone astray and lead to standardization, which has resulted in inflexible curricula and teaching strategies, teaching which violates the home cultures and languages of students, and contributed to the de-professionalization of teaching.

Teachers face a dilemma when they try to teach in culturally responsive ways as well as help students to acquire the knowledge and skills needed to perform successfully on state and national standardized tests. If they ignore the tests low-achieving students will become further marginalized within schools and society and the existing social, political, and economic structures will be reproduced (Willis, 1977). They may also put their own professional reputations and status at risk because of the punitive sanctions that teachers can experience in many school districts if the test scores of their students do not increase between testing cycles.

How can teachers navigate this difficult terrain? How can they teach in culturally responsive ways in schools that are driven by testing and standardization? The purpose of this visionary and needed book is to help teachers construct answers to these questions and to teach in culturally responsive ways in schools that are driven by state and national standards. Sleeter sets forth the conceptual, ideological, and theoretical issues that teachers need to consider in order to teach imaginatively in standards-driven environments. However, one of the strengths of this book is that she goes beyond theory and illustrates how reflective teachers can teach in standard-driven schools with specific concepts, lessons, and units that she observed in the classrooms of eight creative teachers.

Sleeter's rich experience as a practitioner and her rigorous scholarship are blended skillfully in this important and helpful book. She draws upon her years of public school teaching, her experience as an innovative teacher educator, and her incisive and significant scholarship (Sleeter & Bernal, 2004) to create a book that classroom teachers will welcome because of the possibilities it creates for them. Scholars and educational researchers will appreciate this book because it exemplifies how they can navigate and enrich the worlds of practice and scholarship.

James A. Banks
Series Editor

REFERENCES

Amrein, A. L., & Berliner, D. C. (2002). High-stakes testing, uncertainty, and student learning. *Education Policy Analysis Archives, 10*(18). Retrieved February 14, 2003 from http://epaa.asu.edu/epaa/v10n18/.

Banks, J. A. (2004). Multicultural education: Historical development, dimensions, and practice. In J. A. Banks & C. A. M. Banks (Eds.), *Handbook of research on multicultural education* (2nd ed., pp. 3–29). San Francisco: Jossey-Bass.

Banks, J. A., & Banks, C. A. M. (Eds.). (2004). *Handbook of research on multicultural education* (2nd ed.). San Francisco: Jossey-Bass.

California State Department of Education (2000). On line [http://data1.cde.ca.gov/dataquest]

Eck, D. L. (2001). *A new religious America: How a "Christian country" has become the world's most religiously diverse nation.* New York: HarperSanFrancisco.

El Nasser, H. (2004, March 18). Census projects growing diversity: By 2050: Population burst, societal shifts. *USA Today*, p. 1A.

Giroux, H. A. (1988). *Teachers as intellectuals: Toward a critical pedagogy of learning.* Granby, MA: Bergin & Garvey Publishers, Inc.

Martin, P., & Midgley, E. (1999). Immigration to the United States. *Population Bulletin, 54* (2), pp. 1–44. Washington, DC: Population Reference Bureau.

Martinez, G. M., & Curry A. E. (1999, September). *Current population reports: School enrollment-social and economic characteristics of students* (update). Washington, DC: U.S. Census Bureau.

Meier, D., & Wood, G. H. (Eds.). (2005). *Many children left behind: How the No Child Left Behind Act is damaging our children and our schools.* Boston: Beacon.

Riche, M. F. (2000). America's diversity and growth: Signposts for the 21st century. *Population Bulletin, 55* (2), pp. 1–43. Washington, DC: Population Reference Bureau.

Roderick, M., Jacob, B. A., & Bryk, A. S. (2002). The impact of high-stakes testing in Chicago on student achievement in promotional gate grades. *Educational Evaluation and Policy Analysis, 24* (4), 333–357.

Sleeter, C. E., & Bernal, D. D. (2004). Critical pedagogy, critical race theory, and antiracist education: Implications for multicultural education. In J. A. Banks & C. A. M. Banks (Eds.), *Handbook of research on multicultural education* (2nd ed. , pp. 240–258). San Francisco: Jossey-Bass.

U.S. Census Bureau (2000). *Statistical abstract of the United States* (120th edition). Washington, DC: U.S. Government Printing Office.

Willis, P. (1977). *Learning to labor: How working class kids get working class jobs.* New York: Columbia University Press.

Acknowledgments

This book would not have been written, nor taken the form that it has, without the wisdom, help, and support of several friends and colleagues. My friend and editor at Teachers College Press, Brian Ellerbeck, encouraged me to take on this project before I had even begun to think about it, and stuck with me through my uncertainty over its initial shape, its intended audience, and an earlier draft that obscured too many main ideas. His thorough reading and feedback made this a much stronger book than it would have been otherwise. I also thank my valued friend and colleague James Banks, who encouraged my writing of this book and invited it into his series. He offered considerable helpful and detailed feedback. His suggestions on an earlier draft strengthened this book considerably.

Several other close colleagues gave helpful suggestions along the way, as well as asking hard questions. Their interest and knowledge helped to guide me as I struggled to narrow down why I was writing the book and for whom. I extend my sincere thanks to Peter Murrell, Noni Mendoza Reis, and Bob Hughes for their comments and suggestions on earlier drafts, and occasional conversations as I was trying to figure out key issues.

The Visible Knowledge Project at Georgetown University, and its California State University–Monterey Bay affiliate, helped to fund a self-study of my Multicultural Curriculum Design course, which included videotaping much of the course for one semester. My indomitable videographer Cathy White helped out greatly by both videotaping and sharing with me her analysis of one semester of the course. My campus colleagues in the Visible Knowledge Project encouraged me to pursue several of the ideas in this book; thanks particularly to Rina Benmayor, Cecilia O'Leary, and Renee Curry.

I am deeply appreciative to the teachers who allowed me to study them as they took my Multicultural Curriculum Design course, and who taught me a good deal about multicultural curriculum in the process. I am especially indebted to the eight teachers who invited me into their classrooms and allowed me to construct portraits of their work. They have a special place in my heart and are truly amazing teachers!

Finally, I thank my cherished "dog-walker and driver," Joe Larkin, for his constant support as I worked on this project. Your work as a teacher and your thoughtful development and use of multicultural curriculum in your own courses inspired many of the ideas in this book. You also kept me grounded, and your belief in me kept me going.

Introduction

One evening as I was completing this book, I was talking with friends, one of whom is an elementary teacher in California. In the course of a conversation about a proposed project to infuse arts into the schools, my friend said that, although she loved the idea, her school as well as others she was familiar with would be unable to participate because there was no room in their highly prescribed curriculum. She explained that California's primary-grade teachers spend about 3½ hours each day using a state-approved, scripted reading–language arts curriculum package and 70 minutes each day on math, again using state-approved curriculum materials that match state curriculum standards. Since science achievement is now being tested, they also must teach to the science standards, and they have required daily minutes for physical education. Social studies (not yet tested) is worked in as teachers find time. While they would love to infuse the arts, they have virtually no time in which to do so. This conversation reflected a challenge I have experienced when working with multicultural curriculum in California: the ever-increasing degree to which curriculum has been prescribed at the state level with the result that teachers have less and less space for anything except what is prescribed.

I chose to write this book primarily for teachers for three main reasons. First, in addition to being a scholar and an author, I have also been a teacher for over 30 years. This book evolved from my work learning to design and teach multicultural curriculum, which began while I was teaching public school in Seattle in the early 1970s. At that time, although I lacked the language, conceptual frameworks, and content depth to do this well, I was interested in learning and teaching multicultural content in various disciplines. Multicultural curriculum fascinates me because it involves learning about diverse peoples and ideas through lenses of immigrant and historically marginalized communities. As I moved from public school to university teaching, I gradually developed a framework that has helped me—as well as many K–12 teachers—work with curriculum in a substantive and meaningful way.

A second reason I wrote this book mainly for teachers is that teachers have asked me to do so. Most teachers I work with are currently under

1

tremendous pressure to bring up test scores. It is true that low expectations for students of color and students from poverty communities, buttressed by taken-for-granted acceptance of the deficit ideology, has been a rampant and persistent problem for a long time (Perry, Steele, & Hilliard, 2003). It is also true that large numbers of teachers, especially White teachers, are complicit; therefore, empowering teachers without directly addressing the deficit ideology may well aggravate this problem. At the same time, many teachers are becoming frustrated as they see their work shift from engaging students in interesting academic pursuits (or learning how to engage them more effectively) to marching students through content that will appear on tests. Many are frustrated by dwindling support for language diversity and near silence about cultural diversity and equity as principles around which to build curriculum, schooling, and society at large. Experienced teachers are also frustrated by directives that often ignore their expertise and insights. Teachers ask for help figuring out how to carve out space for culturally relevant and engaging curricula in a standards-based environment. Many teachers also want external audiences to see the dilemmas and frustrations that heavily standardized curricula and tests create.

Third, many teachers experience fairly little professional development in learning to plan curriculum. Preservice teachers routinely learn basics of planning lessons and units, but once certified and hired, many are afforded little systematic continued development of their curriculum-planning skills. Some teachers are left to their own devices to hone their ability to plan curriculum (and some never learn to do so very well); others are handed information-packed textbooks to cover and scripted packages that leave little space for their own professional input. Currently, many beginning teachers see the curriculum standards *as* the curriculum itself. When studying beginning teachers in Massachusetts, Kauffman and colleagues (2002) found that standards documents offered teachers lists of topics and skills students should learn—too many to teach well. The pressure to raise test scores made these teachers very anxious about covering everything; teachers felt they were running frantically from one topic to the next, but couldn't skip topics because they might show up on tests. Classroom materials were only partly aligned to the standards, increasing teachers' anxiety about content coverage. Most new teachers had been given little help planning curriculum, so in that pressured and high-anxiety context, they appreciated scripted curricula that told them what to do. However, it seems to me that if teachers are central to what happens in classrooms, it is vital that teachers be supported in learning to plan and teach intellectually sound curricula that engage their own students.

This book focuses on curriculum for two main reasons. First, culturally relevant and intellectually rich curriculum has the potential to improve student learning, as examples throughout this book will show. Second, to the extent that curriculum reflects public knowledge and knowledge frameworks that young people learn, multicultural curriculum is a valuable resource for educating citizens for participation in a multicultural democracy. Knowledge itself is embedded in social power relations. Curriculum, and who gets to define it, is political because knowledge in a multicultural democracy cannot be divorced from larger social struggles. It is a medium through which a society defines itself and forms the consciousness of next generations. In Pinar's (2004) words, "The school curriculum communicates what we choose to remember about our past, what we believe about the present, what we hope for the future" (p. 20). It has long mattered because, "at stake was nothing less than the nation's definition of itself" (Zimmerman, 2002, p. 73).

But efforts to offer all children an intellectually rich curriculum have become conflated with standardizing what everyone should know, thereby reducing the diverse funds of knowledge with which next generations have awareness or familiarity. *High standards* and *standardization* are not the same, yet they have been treated as if they were. The word *standard* refers to level of quality or excellence. For decades, people have advanced standards as a tool for attempting to improve services or outcomes, such as standards for air quality, fairness in journalism, or basic funding for public services. Standard setting is not a new idea and has been used by progressives as well as by conservatives (Sherman & Theobald, 2001). The curriculum planning framework developed in this book uses and advocates for standards, not standardization.

Performance standards specify how well students are expected to master a given body of knowledge or skills. For example, distinguishing among performances that are inadequate, proficient, or excellent provides a yardstick for communicating how well students have learned. Meier (2002) pointed out that making such distinctions requires developing good judgment: "Standards in their genuine sense have always depended on the exercise of that suspicious quality of mind—our fallible judgment—and training ourselves, as Jefferson recommended, to the better exercise of such judgment" (p. 132).

Content standards specify what students should know (Lewis, 2000) and have become the basis for determining what students should be tested over and how performance should be measured. As the publication *High Standards for All Students* explained,

> Content standards define what all students should know and be able to do. They describe the knowledge, skills, and understanding that students should

have in order to attain high levels of competency in challenging subject matter. . . . [Content standards] allow every student, every parent, and every teacher to share in common expectations of what students should know and be able to accomplish. (U.S. Department of Education, 1994, p. 2)

However, it is quite possible to set performance standards, yet not establish detailed content standards. *Standardization* is a consequence of standard setting when attempts to improve student learning become bureaucratized and curriculum is defined in detail in terms of what is measurable and is established at state or national levels. This book focuses on equity and diversity in curriculum and particularly on what teachers can do to "un-standardize" knowledge in their own classrooms, while working toward high standards of academic learning.

This book illustrates possibilities and spaces teachers have for designing and teaching multicultural curriculum through vignettes of eight classroom teachers. Classroom observations and interviews with them, however, revealed not only possibilities but also constraints and challenges teachers face when working with multicultural curriculum in the context of the standards movement. So, while this book presents a curriculum design framework and highlights possibilities of teacher agency, it also examines constraints on that agency, particularly in the context of California, where the book was written and the teacher vignettes took place.

Chapter 1

Standards, Multicultural Education, and Central Curriculum Questions

In 1997, when I was presenting the conceptual framework for California State University–Monterey Bay's Master of Arts in Education program to a group of county-level administrators, I recall them blanching when I mentioned constructivist learning (at the time, I was unaware of debates about "fuzzy math"[1]). When they heard about the program's emphasis on multicultural curriculum, they told me that this is not what the schools needed; instead the schools needed pedagogy that would close the achievement gap. They were looking for knowledge and insights to help address an important equity issue—student learning in very diverse communities—yet, paradoxically, regarded equity frameworks and diverse funds of knowledge as irrelevant.

STANDARDS AND DIVERSE FUNDS OF KNOWLEDGE

As a society, we do not collectively seem to know how to educate a diverse population well. Nor do we collectively seem to know how to approach many other challenges that relate directly to equity and diversity, such as distributing resources in ways that work for diverse communities or communicating across lines of difference without regarding the differences themselves as a problem. Parker (2003) asked a fundamental question: "How can we live together justly, in ways that are mutually satisfying, and which leave our differences, both individual and group, intact and our multiple identities recognized" (p. 20)? The answers, I believe, lie *within* diversity rather than outside of or despite it. The main problem is learning to value points of view and accumulated knowledge that is not dominant and has been routinely excluded from the mainstream. As Apple (1999)

5

pointed out, "Curriculum is itself part of what has been called a selective tradition. That is, from the vast universe of possible knowledge, only some knowledge gets to be official knowledge" (p. 11). That narrowing of what it is possible to know results in paradoxical situations such as trying to address an equity issue—the achievement gap—with only a limited range of conceptual tools for understanding why it exists in the first place.

Differences systematically serve as a basis for distributing resources and opportunities inequitably, which can make the standards movement appear to be a helpful solution. For many equity-minded educators, setting clear standards for all students is a way of minimizing the degree to which race and class structure inequitable access to an academically challenging curriculum. As Thompson (2001) maintained, standards-based reform "departs radically from the tracking and sorting carried out by the factory-style school of yore." He argued that standards-based reform promotes equity by including students, parents, and teachers in a shared understanding of goals, and by making goal attainment public. Expectations are no longer a secret, and schools can no longer fail to educate with impunity. J. B. Hunt, governor of North Carolina (2003), agreed that one virtue of standards-based reform is its transparency, making publicly visible exactly what is expected of students, how they will be assessed, and how they are doing. By making curriculum standards transparent and results visible, students would no longer be subjected to disjointed or unchallenging curriculum that does not prepare them for public life and the workplace, nor be subjected to teachers who do not teach.

There are beginning to be reports that in some schools, students demonstrate more learning on tests because of standards-based reform. For example, based on a study of reading and math performance in Chicago Public Schools, Roderick, Jacob, and Bryk (2002) found improved achievement in the lowest performing schools, particularly those that serve African American students. Because standards provide a public goal that can be used as a tool to strength curriculum and instruction, equity advocates such as Haycock and Craig (2002) advise administrators to use standards to reshape curriculum and instruction in their own schools.

Paradoxically, the use of standards-based reform as a way of eliminating inequity has resulted in homogenizing the curriculum, even while classrooms in the United States have become more diverse. Many educators today assume that curricula are now sufficiently multicultural and that this is no longer an important issue. However, based on a historical analysis of textbook controversies, Zimmerman (2002) observed that we now have "a history of many colors but one idea, culturally diverse yet intellectually static" (p. 15). Glickman (2000/01) characterized standardized curriculum as the institutionalization of a "single definition" of a well-educated person, when what we need in a democracy that faces immense challenges is a "marketplace of ideas and a diversity of perspectives" (p. 49).

Diverse funds of knowledge means that everyone does not learn the same things. Allowing for development of diversity in expertise can serve as an intellectual resource for constructive participation in a multicultural democracy and a diverse world. It is to our benefit that we do *not* all learn the same thing, beyond the basic skills. Helping next generations acquire intellectual resources of diverse communities, including those that have been historically silenced, can enable creative dialog and work, out of which we might better address problems that seem intractable. Examples of such problems are as follows:

- As U.S. citizens, we severely shortchange our ability to communicate with the rest of the world when we insist that communication be done in English because most of us are not bilingual, that schoolchildren learn English only, and that languages other than English be "overcome" rather than nurtured. If we began to expect that everyone master at least two languages (including English), our collective ability to communicate with the rest of the world would be greatly strengthened.
- Many citizens of the United States worry about youth learning values that prize excess materialism rather than spiritual development. Mainstream citizens are often unaware of strong spiritual roots within many non-European indigenous and immigrant communities, from whom all of us can learn.
- The dominant way of life in the United States is at odds with the preservation of the natural environment. It might be necessary to human existence, over the long run, to learn from, rather than discarding, bodies of human wisdom, which have arisen outside the so-called Western tradition, that can give insights about living sustainably with the earth.
- Many people feel powerless to make changes in society, yet there are long histories of struggle that show how people working collectively have made changes in the past. Familiarity with these histories can inform current efforts.
- Historically, there have been various ways of constructing egalitarian social and economic systems, and political systems that are more democratic than our own. The more we know about multiple alternatives, the better we can improve the systems we have currently.

In these examples I do not mean to suggest replacing one set of standards with another, but rather I am suggesting that we question the wisdom of standardizing what everyone teaches and learns. Nor am I calling for dismantling traditional knowledge. Rather, I am advocating for attending to, valuing, learning from, and passing on a much wider array of knowledge than that which resides in traditional bodies of school knowledge only. As Pinar (2004) argued, what is at stake right now, in a context that has converted intellectual inquiry as a goal of teaching to fixation on "bottom-line" test score production, "is control of the curriculum, what teachers are permitted to teach, what children are permitted to study" (p. xii). Thus the "why" of multicultural curriculum is that it reflects and teaches diverse funds of knowledge both as a social resource and as a handmaiden to intellectual inquiry.

There is no single "how" of multicultural curriculum. The framework that is developed in this book offers a way of planning that takes into consideration a variety of factors, including academic achievement. Even teachers whose work is closely defined by content standards and testing can usually find spaces for adapting, modifying, or developing intellectually rich multicultural curriculum. This book's framework for multicultural curriculum design is situated within four central curriculum questions.

CENTRAL CURRICULUM QUESTIONS

Curriculum theorists and designers have long wrestled with several central, persisting questions (e.g., Apple, 2004a; Bellack & Kliebard, 1977; Beyer & Liston, 1996; Kliebard, 1982; Taba, 1962). I have synthesized them into the following four, which form a skeletal structure for this book (as delineated at the end of this chapter):

1. What purposes should the curriculum serve?
2. How should knowledge be selected, who decides what knowledge is most worth teaching and learning, and what is the relationship between those in the classroom and the knowledge selection process?
3. What is the nature of students and the learning process, and how does it suggest organizing learning experiences and relationships?
4. How should curriculum be evaluated? How should learning be evaluated? To whom is curriculum evaluation accountable?

These questions are partly normative: answers rest on value judgments and moral stands. Whose answers prevail, ultimately, is a political matter. Kliebard (1995) emphasized that "the curriculum at any time and place becomes the site of a battleground where the fight is over whose values and beliefs will achieve the legitimation and the respect that acceptance into the national discourse provides" (p. 250).

Kliebard (1982) identified four main groups that emerged in twentieth-century debates over these questions: the *humanists*, "guardians of an ancient tradition tied to the power of reason and what they regarded as the finest in the Western cultural heritage" (p. 23); the *developmentalists*, who believed curriculum should derive from the interests and growth of the child; the *social efficiency educators*, who believed the curriculum should be standardized around the needs of an industrial society; and the *social meliorists*, who saw the curriculum as a way of preparing citizens to address social issues. Each group holds a different conception of what curriculum is for and how it should be selected, organized, and evaluated. While humanists emphasize developing powers of reason and developmentalists focus more broadly on the development of the whole child, social efficiency educators and social meliorists take their purposes from needs of society. Social efficiency educators generally ground their view in needs of an expanding capitalist economy; social meliorists place human social problems at the center of concern. These divergent groups and struggles for legitimation continue, as will be examined later in this chapter.

It is deceptively easy, however, to shift from questions of value and ideology, to questions of method. In his classic book *Basic Principles of Curriculum and Instruction*, Ralph Tyler (1969) proposed principles and process for curriculum planning that turned the central questions listed above into four sequential steps:

1. What educational purposes should the school seek to attain?
2. What educational experiences can be provided that are likely to attain these purposes?
3. How can these educational experiences be effectively organized?
4. How can we determine whether these purposes are being attained? (p. 1)

Although the first question is normative, Tyler assumed that once it is answered, we can get on with the business of following sequential planning steps.

In fact, reducing normative and philosophical questions to technical matters leads to the reduction of curriculum to what is measurable. Short (1986) explained that "measured" curricula "take as their key design feature the reduction of their intended outcomes to pre-specified elements, which, when 'taught' and 'learned,' can be measured, and on which a definitive report of 'results' can be made public" (p. 6). In his analysis of nine different "fully articulated, carefully explained and argued" curriculum designs from the past (p. 3), he noted that none advocate reduction of curriculum to what can be measured. Rather, "all advocate rich, expansive, evocative curricula in which educative consequences that are valued, sought, and achieved are seldom fully known [until] after the curriculum is activated and engaged by pupils" (p. 7).

The reduction of ethical questions to measurement truncates a reasoning loop that silences alternative points of view. As Apple (2004a) pointed out, "in the quest for orderliness, the political process by which often competing visions of purposes deal with each other and come to some sort of understanding is virtually ignored" (p. 105). Beyer and Liston (1996) offer a broader definition of *curriculum* than the content standards–textbook–test trilogy common to today: "Curriculum is the centerpiece of educational activity. It includes the formal, overt knowledge that is central to the activities of teaching, as well as more tacit, subliminal messages—transmitted through the process of acting and interacting within a particular kind of institution—that foster the inculcation of particular values, attitudes, and dispositions" (p. xv).

Beyer and Liston's definition incorporates the hidden curriculum, which is what students actually learn through the ongoing, repetitive processes of the classroom—its "daily grind" (Jackson, 1968). Horn (2003) defined the *hidden curriculum* as the "unrecognized and sometimes unintended knowledge, values, and beliefs that are part of the learning process in schools and classrooms." It includes not what teachers plan, but rather what students learn, often unconsciously, by how they experience the school and classroom. As Sambell and McDowell (1998) explained, "the hidden curriculum is expressed in terms of the distinction between 'what is meant to happen,' that is, the curriculum stated officially by the educational system or institution, and what teachers and learners actually do and experience 'on the ground,' a kind of de facto curriculum." Although there may always be unplanned space between what teachers intend and what students learn, this broader conception of curriculum offers teachers a wider array of planning considerations than only the content in textbooks, curriculum guides, standards, and tests.

The standards movement and multicultural movements address the four key curriculum questions differently, and in some respects they clash. This is because they have different social origins, and they conceptualize curriculum, diversity, and equity differently.

The Multicultural Movements and Curriculum

In the United States the civil rights movement spawned multicultural education, building on previous movements. James Banks (1996) traced its early roots to the ethnic studies movement of the early twentieth century, and particularly to the work of African American scholars. Lei and Grant (2001) also connected multicultural education to the cultural pluralism movement of the 1940s and the progressive education movement, in which John Dewey was a major figure. Cherry Banks (2005) examined parallels between multicultural education and the intergroup education movement of the 1920s–1950s.

The U.S. Supreme Court decision in *Brown v. Board of Education* (1954) and the civil rights movement opened the door for groups who had been excluded from schools, or from decision making about schools, to speak. Gay (1983) described the ensuing process of movement building:

> The arenas of activity moved from courtrooms and the southern states to the northern ghettoes and the campuses of colleges and schools. The ideological and strategic focus of the movement shifted from passivity and perseverance in the face of adversity to aggression, self-determination, cultural consciousness, and political power. (p. 53)

As Gay noted, when schools were initially desegregated, parents and community leaders of color began to demand that the curriculum reflect their communities, and that teachers expect the same level of academic learning of their children as they did of White children. While schools staffed by White teachers generally regarded the cultures and language backgrounds of children of color as deficient, advocates and scholars from communities of color and language-minority communities argued that culture and language are strengths on which learning can and should be built. The civil rights movement ushered in a vibrant proliferation of movements for equity. The women's movement challenged patriarchy in its myriad forms; the bilingual education movement questioned the hegemony of English, given the rich diversity of languages globally as well as within the United States. Later, the disability rights movement and the gay/lesbian movement challenged legalized and institutionalized assumptions about normalcy.

Multicultural education has served as an arena for working on school-related equity and social justice issues from vantage points of multiple historically marginalized communities. Within its larger discourse about comprehensive reform of schools, one can identify at least four related strands of work on curriculum that multicultural educators address: access to quality curriculum, textbook content, relevance of curriculum to students, and models of curriculum transformation. Embedded in all of these strands are visions of a rich curriculum that will enable young people to examine ways in which a diverse country has struggled to live up to its own ideals of justice, freedom, and equality.

Desegregation and related court cases (such as *Lau v. Nichols*) were driven by demands by communities of color and language-minority communities for access to quality curriculum. Curriculum serves as a gatekeeper regulating who gets access to which opportunities in and beyond high school. Schools have served historically to sort students for a stratified labor market by means such as tracking and by linking academic expectations and school quality with the socioeconomic status and racial composition of neighborhoods in which schools are located (Anyon, 1981; Oakes, 1985). By challenging school segregation, biased testing, biased college admission processes, all-English curricula, tracking systems, biased special education placements, and so forth, communities of color and low-income communities sought access to rich curricula, full educational opportunity, and the same opportunities afforded White affluent English-speaking children.

Similarly, the women's movement fought to remove gender-based barriers to high school and college courses, college admission, athletics and scholarships, and other education opportunities. The mainstreaming movement, later called the inclusion movement, fought to open up access to the least restrictive educational environment for students with various forms of disabilities, and to change processes by which schools create disabilities through institutionalized assumptions about normalcy. These various struggles not only sought to remove barriers to access to quality curriculum, but also questioned core assumptions about knowledge, the hierarchical structure in which opportunities are embedded, and subtle ways schools continued to exclude and silence. For example, advocates of bilingual education have pressed educators to reconsider assumptions that children need to learn English *before* proceeding to academic learning, and that knowledge in languages other than English has minimal value.

Equal access to quality education for all students has been an ongoing struggle, yet to be realized. For example, the Educational Testing Service (ETS) identified three categories of factors that continue to advantage White students. Early development factors include birth weight, possibility of lead poisoning, and nutrition—health factors that reflect social policies that protect middle-class White children more comprehensively than children of color or poor White children (Barton, 2003). Home learning environment factors include being read to, amount of TV watching, parent availability and support, student mobility, and parent participation; some of these also relate to a social context, such as access to jobs. School environment factors include rigor of the school curriculum, teacher preparation, teacher experience and attendance, class size, availability of appropriate classroom technology, and school safety. The ETS report, across the board, found minority students disadvantaged relative to

White students in all 14 of the conditions and experiences conducive to student achievement.

In California two recent investigations reported similar factors that systematically reduce access to learning for students who are poor, students of color, and English-language learners (Gándara, Rumberger, Maxwell-Jolley, & Callahan, 2003; Oakes, Blasi, & Rogers, 2004). These include reduction of bilingual education programs, and inequitable access to the following: credentialed teachers; teachers with professional training for teaching English learners; forms of assessment that capture what language-minority students can do and that help guide classroom instruction; meaningful instructional time when students are in school; sufficient textbooks, computers, and other materials for students; materials that English learners can understand; and functional school facilities.

Textbooks have been the subject of analysis and advocacy for over a century (Zimmerman, 2002). Gay (1983) noted that "textbook analyses that appeared from the 1930s through the 1960s reported similar results for African Americans, Hispanics, Native Americans, and Asians. In fact, textbooks continued to report ethnic distortions, stereotypes, omissions, and misinformation as recently as the mid-1970s" (p. 54; see also Anyon, 1979; Britton, Lumpkin, & Britton, 1984; Hahn & Blankenship, 1983; Powell & Garcia, 1988; Tetreault, 1983, 1984). For at least 3 decades, advocates have argued that textbooks should be representative and accurate, not only for the sake of being truthful but because the quality of school experiences for students from historically oppressed communities is severely compromised when textbooks either omit their communities entirely or portray them in distorted and derogatory ways. However, as Banks (1993) noted, "because of the number of constraints and influences on the development of textbooks, school knowledge often does not include in-depth discussions and analysis of some of the major problems in American society" (p. 12). Textbooks continue to be a flash point of controversy because they inculcate narratives about who we are, how we came to be, where we are going, and whose knowledge counts, issues that are taken up in subsequent chapters of this book.

Multicultural education advocates argue that curricula, more broadly construed, have been too often irrelevant to students from historically marginalized communities. Starting on college campuses during the 1960s, youth demanded ethnic studies courses that related to their own experiences. Gay (1983) explained, "The student activists, abetted by the efforts of textbook analysts and by the new thinking about cultural differences, provided the stimulus for the first multiethnic education programs" by using strategies of civil rights activists such as sit-ins and boycotts (p. 54). Ethnic studies, women's studies, and later gay/lesbian studies scholarship burgeoned as programs were created, and faculty who were hired to teach in them found themselves needing to unearth subjugated knowledge in order to teach it. For example, Cortés (2002) describes his own experience in Chicano studies during the early 1970s, when "the demand for ethnic studies 'experts' was enormous; the supply was minimal. Learning on the run had taken on new dimensions" (p. 11). Now, 30 years later, a wealth of research and theory in the various disciplines in ethnic studies, women's studies, disability studies, gay/lesbian studies, and other critical studies offers depth and substance to the quest for curriculum relevance and wholesale revision (Kumashiro, 2002).

Multicultural education advocates also argue that building curriculum and pedagogy on the cultural frames of reference and linguistic strengths of students from historically oppressed communities shows promise for improving student learning (Au, 1990; Gay, 2000). For example, based on a study of effective teachers of African American students, Ladson-Billings (1994) articulated a theory of culturally relevant pedagogy in which teachers intentionally connect teaching to the lived experiences and knowledge frameworks of their students and students' communities. Research in dual-language learning shows that language-minority students in well-constructed dual-language programs outperform control group students in English-only programs on standard achievement tests (e.g., Cabazon, Nicoladis, & Lambert, 1998).

By the 1980s and onward, alternative models and approaches to curriculum design had been advanced (Gay, 1995). For example, Watkins (1993) sketched Black curriculum frameworks that had developed historically. Tetreault (1989) elaborated on phases of the integration of women into curriculum, ranging from womanless to transformed curriculum. Sleeter and Grant (2003) developed theoretical bases for five different approaches to multicultural education with specific implications for curriculum that share similarities with Banks's (1991b) four models. Cummins (1986) distinguished between empowering and disempowering models of curriculum and assessment for language-minority students, and Darder (1991) developed a model of bicultural critical pedagogy for the classroom. Britzman (1995) elaborated on a theory of queer pedagogy, and Kumashiro (2002) developed a model of antioppressive education. All of these offer guidance for adapting or building curriculum in ways that make constructive use of the wealth of knowledge coming from scholarly inquiry in the various "studies" (such as African American studies or postcolonial studies).

Now that I've given this brief history, I can discuss how the multicultural education movement frames the four central curriculum questions listed earlier in the chapter.

1. *What purposes should the curriculum serve?* Multicultural movements have defined the main purpose of curriculum as social improvement. In part, this means improvement of the lives of peoples who have been marginalized on the basis of race, ethnicity, language, social class, disability, and other identities. Social improvement includes addressing the poor quality of schooling children from historically oppressed communities have received. Multicultural movements situate underachievement within a range of equity issues, arguing that creating equitable conditions for learning will close achievement gaps. Different theorists and constituents define somewhat differently the central issues needing to be addressed (e.g., attitude change versus structural change) and the primary focal group (e.g., racial groups, women, people with disabilities). However, they share a goal of social improvement for equality and justice, and a belief that education should fuel democratic action. Broadly speaking, multicultural movements challenge the United States to live up to its ideals of justice and equality, believing that this country has the potential to work much better for everyone. As tomorrow's citizens, children in schools should learn academic tools and disciplinary knowledge resources from vantage points of multiple communities. Further, young people should develop some sense of solidarity across differences that enables working toward closing the gap between the nation's ideals and its realities.

2. *How should knowledge be selected, who decides what is most worth teaching and learning, and what is the relationship between those in the classroom and the knowledge selection process?* A central concern of multicultural movements has been opening up what counts as knowledge and who gets to decide. Scholars and educators point to countless ways in which "objective truth" has not been objective at all, but rather has consisted of "grand narratives" that are based on experiences and concerns of elites into which everyone is folded. Such narratives are presented as if they were universal and objective. Further, knowledge and the knowledge selection process relates directly to power. As Collins (1998) put it, "despite their commitment to truth, many of the truths produced by anthropology, biology, sociology, political science, history, and other academic disciplines manufactured consent for colonialism, imperialism, slavery, and apartheid" (p. 197). Gallegos (1998) emphasized that the "politics of interpretive location" is bound up with "a much larger contest over resources, space, legitimacy, and the interests of peoples" (p. 235). Rather than nailing down consensus over what everyone should learn, multicultural movements have opened up diverse funds of knowledge and arenas for research, debate, and dialog.

3. *What is the nature of students and the learning process, and how does it suggest organizing learning experiences and relationships?* Multicultural movements directly challenge deficit perspectives about children from historically marginalized communities, and ethnocentric assumptions about what "normal" children are like. Educators assert, with some research support, that honoring and building on children's connections to their cultural and linguistic roots and their community-based identities provides the best base for academic learning. This is, in fact, a process that White middle-class students usually experience in school. By attending to what students in one's own school and classroom already know, the learning processes they developed at home, and the language structures they already have, teachers can help students acquire new knowledge and language more effectively than when these cultural assets are ignored (Au, 1990; Gay, 2000; Heath, 1983; Jordan, 1992; Moll & Gonzalez, 2004; Reyes, Scribner, & Scribner, 1999).

4. *How should curriculum be evaluated? How should learning be evaluated? To whom is curriculum evaluation accountable?* Multicultural movements, which have arisen largely through grassroots community activism based on problems parents and community leaders from historically marginalized communities have had with schools, have emphasized accountability to communities. They have emphasized that expectations for children be held high and that means of evaluating student learning be fair and broad enough to actually capture what children know and can do. Historically, standardized testing has not been designed to do that, and even revamped paper-and-pencil tests are usually inadequate as the sole means of evaluating learning (Darling-Hammond, 1994). Ultimately, communities should be included in the process of deciding curriculum and evaluation.

The Standards Movement and Curriculum

Particulars of today's standards-based reform movement are new, but its fundamental ideas are not. Readers might remember "back to basics" movements in the 1950s and the 1970s, or the competency-based education movement of the 1970s. Like the current standards movement, they were concerned with raising student achievement by specifying exactly what all students should know, then teaching to those specifications. And, like the standards movement today, they usually framed academic achievement as a different (possibly competing) matter from democratizing curriculum.

Historically, standards-based reform goes back to the beginning of the twentieth century, when early curriculum theorists conceptualized the school as a factory producing workers for the needs of society, as Ellwood Cubberley expressed in 1916:

> Our schools are, in a sense, factories in which the raw products (children) are to be shaped and fashioned into products to meet the various demands of life. The specifications for manufacturing come from the demands of twentieth-century civilization, and it is the business of the school to build its pupils according to the specifications laid down. (cited by Beyer & Liston, 1996, p. 19)

Like Cubberley, many of his contemporaries believed that curriculum should be organized scientifically for efficiency, with learning objectives derived from social and economic needs. Curriculum should then be standardized based on those objectives, and student learning measured against them. Teachers should be told exactly what to teach to create maximum continuity as students proceed from one grade level to the next. As Beyer and Liston (1996) observed, "The teacher became cast as a manager of personnel (students) and materials (texts, other curriculum materials), and as an overseer of a process of production (the achievement of minute and pre-specified objectives) that in some ways was as disconnected from her own interests and values as it was from students'" (p. 22).

Genesis of the current standards-based reform movement is often traced to the publication of *A Nation at Risk* in 1983 (National Commission on Excellence in Education), which launched a round of highly visible national discussions that framed the main purpose of schools as regaining U.S. economic competitive advantage internationally. Many reports published during the 1980s argued that U.S. students were increasingly failing to learn the skills and knowledge the United States needed for economic competition. This wave of reports expressed concerns of the business community that technological advances and global restructuring were transforming the nature of production and work and that the United States would need to develop many, many more workers for demands of this new economy. These new workers would need to master skill sets such as "technological visualization; abstract reasoning, mathematical, scientific, and computer expertise; knowledge of specific technologies and production techniques; [and] individual initiative" (Berliner & Biddle, 1995, p. 141).

On the heels of the reform reports were a barrage of highly visible conservative critiques of multiculturalism (e.g., A. Bloom, 1989; Ravitch, 1990; Schlesinger, 1992). These critiques targeted curricular changes and policies that had been instituted in schools and universities, charging that multiculturalism was damaging education and social cohesion. They cast multiculturalists as fringe radicals who were undermining fundamental

American political and cultural ideals by appealing to the divisiveness of ethnic cheerleading. They also argued that multicultural curricula were intellectually weak and addressed minority student achievement in damaging ways by appealing mainly to self-esteem rather than hard work and academic challenge (Sleeter, 1995). In this context, the English-only movement gained momentum as well.

The reform reports, as well as the conservative critiques of multiculturalism, depicted schools and U.S. society generally as being in a state of crisis. In response, in the 1980s states began to construct disciplinary content standards and testing programs. California, for example, began this work in 1982 when it elected Bill Honig as state Superintendent of Public Instruction on a platform of reforming schools by raising standards and centralizing curriculum.

For a time there were also efforts to establish national curriculum content standards and tests. In 1989 President G. H. W. Bush and the state governors called a summit to set goals for improving schools. The resulting National Education Goals Panel set about attempting to establish national goals for student learning. Goals 2000: Educate America Act and Improving America's Schools Act, passed in 1994, gave impetus to efforts to establish national curriculum standards in math, science, history, English, and other disciplines. National discipline-based groups began writing standards for each discipline. The National Council of Teachers of Mathematics (NCTM) established a set of mathematics standards that have subsequently been used by most states. National standards documents were drafted in other disciplines as well, but because of philosophical disagreements over what all students should know within the disciplines, attempts to establish national standards waned, and states were left to determine what students should know. To varying degrees, states used national discipline standards documents to inform the writing of their own state content standards. By the mid-1990s, most states had content standards in place and were designing or beginning to implement statewide systems of testing based on them.

Teachers generally have some awareness of the process by which standards in their own state were set, but little or no awareness of the agenda-setting role that has been played behind the scenes by the business community, including the National Alliance of Business and the Business Roundtable. The Business Roundtable (1997) summed up their position as follows:

> We believe the first step to solving our nation's education problems is to substantially raise academic standards and verify achievement through rigorous testing. . . . To those of us in business, it is obvious that large segments

of our education system are failing today. We are the ones, after all, who get the first real-world view of the young people emerging from the American education "pipeline."

The business community had painted the sense of crisis that emerged during the 1980s through the various reform reports (Berliner & Biddle, 1995). In 1989, the Business Roundtable devoted one of its annual meetings to "synthesizing business-led reforms of the 1980s into a high-stakes testing agenda" (Berlak, 2003, p. 35). Standards, assessment, and accountability emerged as the three components most central to its school reform plan (Business Roundtable, 1999). The organization then systematically applied pressure on states in those three areas.

No Child Left Behind, passed by Congress and signed into law in 2001, mandates that states receiving federal funding

> implement statewide accountability systems covering all public schools and students. These systems must be based on challenging State standards in reading and mathematics, annual testing for all students in grades 3–8, and annual statewide progress objectives ensuring that all groups of students reach proficiency within 12 years. Assessment results and State progress objectives must be broken out by poverty, race, ethnicity, disability, and limited English proficiency to ensure that no group is left behind. (U.S. Department of Education, 2001)

Science was added for testing in 2005. By school year 2013–14, the law requires that all students score at or above the proficiency level established by their state. Schools that fail to meet targets not only receive negative publicity and sanctions, but ultimately may be shut down, a consequence beginning to be applied at the time of this writing.

States have responded somewhat differently to this legislation; to illustrate a range of responses, I contrast California with Nebraska. California had been establishing a system of detailed content standards, testing, and accountability targets prior to passage of No Child Left Behind. By 2004, it required an extensive test battery given to all students in Grades 2–11. Content tests in English–language arts and math were given to students in Grades 2–11; history–social science in Grades 8, 10, and 11; and science in Grades 5–11. A norm-referenced test was given to students in Grades 2–8 in reading, language, spelling, and mathematics; and to students in Grades 9–11 in reading, language, mathematics, and science. All 10th graders also took the California High School Exit Examination in language arts and math, which will be required for graduation beginning with the class of 2006. Alternative assessment was made available for students with significant cognitive disabilities. Spanish speakers who had been in U.S.

schools for less than one year or who participated in bilingual programs took the Spanish Assessment of Basic Education (SABE), a nationally normed test that measures basic skills.

In Nebraska, by contrast, curriculum and assessment are controlled at the district level. Although the state established content standards, districts may either adopt them or develop equally rigorous standards of their own. The state also sets a schedule for student assessment, but the assessments are chosen—and some are developed—at the district level, with teacher participation. School districts use a combination of assessments, including norm-referenced tests, criterion-referenced assessments, and locally developed classroom assessments. Districts submit portfolios of assessment practices and procedures for quality review by the state. The only statewide test is a writing test. Districts also participate in other national assessments such as the National Assessment of Educational Progress (NAEP). Nebraska's local control, however, is an exception to the top-down model used in most states.

Thus school reform following the Business Roundtable's model has national authority. But it offers a compelling twist to earlier accountability systems by requiring schools to address historic achievement gaps. Herein lies a connection between multicultural education movements and the standards movement: coming from different social locations and using very different sets of assumptions, both attempt to improve the learning of children from historically oppressed communities. In a letter to Congress, over 100 African American and Latino superintendents emphasized their support for accountability systems that focus directly on this gap, writing that underachievement of students of color and students who live in poverty "has been swept underneath overall averages for too long." They found that accountability systems "give them leverage for moving their systems to action" ("Don't turn back the clock," 2003).

In light of this summary, I now briefly examine how the standards-based reform movement frames the four central curriculum questions.

1. *What purposes should the curriculum serve?* Through the standards movement, the business community and conservative allies have defined normatively what schools should do and what curriculum is for, rendering the other three curriculum questions as technical matters. They define the main purpose of curriculum as making the United States more economically competitive globally by providing the business community with workers for a revamped economy, and making future workers more employable by equipping them with skills employers seek.[2] A much less stated purpose is to reduce dissent and promote cultural and linguistic

assimilation by focusing everyone on the same skills, facts, and traditional discipline-based concepts.

2. *How should knowledge be selected, who decides what knowledge is most worth teaching and learning, and what is the relationship between those in the classroom and the knowledge selection process?* The standards movement assumes consensus about what all students should know and be able to do, and that consensus can be established at the state level objectively by disciplinary "experts." Generally standards are presented as consensus documents, even if their adoption was controversial.[3] It further assumes worthwhile knowledge is measurable on standardized tests. School or classroom level selections of knowledge are to be made *within* the boundaries of a state's content standards, and aligned to them. So, since the degree of specificity of standards varies from state to state, local latitude to select what to teach and learn varies accordingly.

3. *What is the nature of students and the learning process, and how does it suggest organizing learning experiences and relationships?* Implicitly, the standards movement casts children as empty vessels to fill with prescribed knowledge. State standards generally are much more specific about what to teach than they are about children or how teaching might occur. An exception is in the area of reading, for which mandated teaching processes are specified in many state standards. And it is assumed that specific "best" teaching strategies that work in classrooms across the country can be identified through experimental research. Standards documents as well as No Child Left Behind legislation emphasize that all children can learn, implicitly framing children as relatively homogeneous except for differences in achievement level; differences such as those based in culture or language are minimized in standards discussions.

4. *How should curriculum be evaluated? How should learning be evaluated? To whom is curriculum evaluation accountable?* Evaluation of students' learning and of school performance are strongly emphasized in the standards movement, with criterion-referenced standardized tests serving as the main evaluation tool. Schools and teachers are to be held accountable to the state through testing, with the requirement of meeting annual targets, including targets aimed at closing achievement gaps. Schools are also held accountable to parents, in a market-based context. Ultimately, the law encourages parents to seek another school if the one their child attends does not produce reasonably high test scores.

FRAMEWORK FOR MULTICULTURAL CURRICULUM DESIGN

In the context of the recent standards movement, what can teachers do—particularly those who subscribe to the work of multicultural movements? All students can benefit from well-planned, coherent curriculum, and teachers are central to planning the curriculum that students actually encounter. Four decades ago, Taba (1962) questioned the removal of curriculum planning from classrooms and teachers, stating, "The usual method of curriculum revision is to start by revising the 'framework' before experimenting with the more specific parts of a functioning curriculum: the teaching units on specific grade levels" (p. 9). She went on to speculate that "if the sequence in the curriculum development were reversed—that if, first, teachers were invited to experiment with specific aspects of curriculum and then, on the basis of these experiments, a framework were to be developed—curriculum development would acquire a new dynamic" (p. 9).

The remainder of this book develops possibilities,[4] tempered with concern about constraints. The book develops a curriculum framework that can help teachers design multicultural curricula that foster intellectual engagement and democratic activism. In the framework, illustrated in Figure 1.1, curriculum is organized around central ideas, and developed in relationship to transformative intellectual knowledge (knowledge bases of historically oppressed communities), students and their community, academic challenge, classroom resources, and ongoing assessment of learning. In the process, teachers critically examine the impact of their own beliefs on curricular decisions they make. As the arrows suggest, all of the elements interrelate and affect one another.

To explore and illustrate what teachers can do, I developed vignettes of teachers' thinking, planning, and teaching on the basis of my work with two sections of the Multicultural Curriculum Design course I taught during fall 2001 and fall 2003.[5] The two sections included 39 educators; most appear (somewhat in the background) in Chapters 2–9.[6] The educators are highly diverse, including K–12 classroom teachers and beginning college-level instructors. The number of years they had taught varied widely, ranging from a few who had just earned their teaching credential or had just begun instructing at the college level to several who had taught for at least 15 years. Table 1.1 gives a breakdown of the 39 participants in my study according to the level at which they taught, gender, and racial/ethnic identification.

I also selected eight very competent K–12 teachers for classroom visits and developed teaching vignettes based on these visits. Seven of the eight were part of the 39 educators described above. I included one addi-

Figure 1.1. Framework for Multicultural Curriculum Design

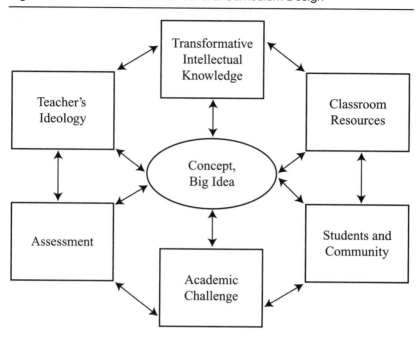

tional teacher who was in the same graduate program but not in that particular course, because the work she was doing in her classroom fit this book so well. When selecting these eight teachers, I tried to make the group as diverse as possible in terms of grade level, student population, and teacher's racial/ethnic background. All eight are women; four teach elementary school, three teach middle school, and one teaches high school. They were teaching in six different school districts, none in the same school. Racially and ethnically, four are White and four are of color; their backgrounds and identities are sufficiently complex that they are described when the teachers are introduced in subsequent chapters rather than here. Although their student populations vary quite a bit, all reflect demographics of the central coast of California.[7]

During 2003–04 I spent 2–8 hours in each of their classrooms in 1–3 visits. I also taperecorded an interview with each teacher; the interviews lasted about an hour. I developed the vignettes working with notes from my observations, transcriptions of the interviews, copies of class papers and other data (either videotapes or journals), and in some cases, master's theses. After I had constructed the vignettes and embedded them within

Table 1.1. Demographic Characteristics of Participants in Study

Characteristics	Number of Participants
TEACHING LEVEL	
Elementary	17
Secondary	12
College/adult	10
GENDER:	
Female	31
Male	8
RACIAL/ETHNIC IDENTIFICATION:	
White	17
Mexican, Mexican American, Latino	9
Greek national	3
African American	2
Biracial (Latino/Filipino, and Indonesian/Italian)	2
Asian American	2
Filipino	1
Kenyan national	1
Chadian national	1
Chinese national	1

earlier drafts of chapters, I sent drafts to the teachers and invited their feedback; all eight responded. Teachers had the option of being referred to by their real first name, or by a pseudonym; seven of the eight elected their real name.

The remaining chapters relate to individual parts of the framework for multicultural design and are nested within the four central curriculum questions discussed earlier in this chapter.

1. *What purposes should the curriculum serve?* Chapter 2 examines how assumptions teachers bring to curriculum planning affect decisions they make. Teachers need to be aware of their own beliefs regarding diverse

communities, the nature of knowledge, and connections between knowledge and its social location; this chapter gives some guidance in developing that awareness. Chapter 3 examines "big ideas" as a tool for designing curriculum for coherence and depth rather than breadth of coverage. Content standards can serve as a source of big ideas, but at the same time, they rest on ideological foundations teachers need to examine.

2. *How should knowledge be selected, who decides what knowledge is most worth teaching and learning, and what is the relationship between those in the classroom and the knowledge selection process?* Chapter 5 explores transformative intellectual knowledge, reinserting sustained consideration of whose knowledge schools teach back into curriculum planning. Guidance is given to help teachers start to investigate and work with transformative intellectual knowledge. Chapter 7 discusses standards in relationship to intellectual challenge and preparation for college, showing strategies teachers can use to plan for intellectual engagement, while developing skills and content knowledge simultaneously.

3. *What is the nature of students and the learning process, how does it suggest organizing learning experiences and relationships?* Chapter 6 explores students and their communities in relationship to curriculum design. Suggestions are given for learning about and connecting with students' community-based knowledge. Then the chapter explores building curriculum in a way that engages students with diverse points of view. Chapter 8 examines the selection and use of teaching resources for classroom use, beginning with a critique of textbooks, then considers selecting resources in relationship to both content and form. Both chapters emphasize curriculum planning for active student engagement with academics.

4. *How should curriculum be evaluated? How should learning be evaluated? To whom is curriculum evaluation accountable?* Chapter 4 examines assessment of student learning. The chapter begins with a discussion of the testing context within which most teachers are working, then considers the design and use of classroom-based assessment in ways that are fair to students and offer guidance for improving teaching and learning.

Finally, Chapter 9 returns to a consideration of multicultural curriculum design in light of very real differences in assumptions between multicultural and standards movements. Teachers face ethical issues when deciding how to navigate crosscurrents of multicultural curriculum and accountability systems. Teachers can learn to construct stronger student-relevant, difference-sensitive, antioppressive curriculum; teachers are also directed to teach to standards and tests, to which students are held accountable. A vignette of a classroom teacher illustrates these crosscurrents and embedded ethical dilemmas.

NOTES

1. In 1985 California had adopted a math framework that "in many ways was the antecedent of the 1989 NCTM [National Council for the Teaching of Mathematics] Standards" (Schoenfeld, 2004, p. 269) in its emphasis on thinking and problem solving. But it was loudly condemned by conservative groups that objected to constructivist pedagogical processes that teach math reasoning in a way that may allow students to come to incorrect answers through computation errors. Constructivism was caricatured in media as "fuzzy math."

2. Notably, the Business Roundtable directly links education with workforce development in its task force Education and the Workforce.

3. California's history–social science framework is an example. Multicultural education critic Diane Ravitch was appointed as its principal writer. Conceptualized around a story of immigration and triumph of the U.S. political system, its writing in the 1980s prompted protests in several communities of color on the basis of its framing everyone as an immigrant and, as a result, downplaying racism, enslavement, and the killing off of indigenous people (Cornbleth & Waugh, 1995; King, 1992; Wynter, 1992). Nevertheless, the California State Board of Education has readopted it three times.

4. The vignettes illustrate a few examples of classroom teaching; readers who are interested in more examples for specific grade levels or subject areas may find *Turning on Learning* (Grant & Sleeter, 2003) useful, since it illustrates how to make curriculum and instruction multicultural through more than 50 before-and-after lesson plans, at K–12 grade levels and in diverse subject areas.

5. The vignettes were supported by a self-study I conducted of my teaching in these two sections. Between 2001 and 2004 I participated in a scholarship of teaching project known as the Visible Knowledge Project, which is a national network of several colleges and universities. The national Visible Knowledge Project is organized through Georgetown University (http://crossroads.georgetown.edu/vkp/). The idea behind "visible knowledge" is exploring how to make complex knowledge more visible to students, using new media. All participants develop a self-study of their own teaching, focusing their investigation on a question related to a course or form of pedagogy; mine examined teachers' learning process in two semesters of Multicultural Curriculum Design.

6. With their permission, I kept copies of most of their papers to use as data reflecting their thinking about issues, their approach to planning, and their responses to some of the activities described in later chapters. During fall 2001 I videotaped about half of the class sessions; during fall 2003 I wrote a detailed

journal describing what happened in each class session immediately after class had ended. Some of these data are used in this book.

7. The K–12 student enrollment of Monterey County, where most of this book's teachers were teaching, was 64 percent Latino, 24 percent White, 4 percent Asian and Pacific Islander, 3.5 percent African American, 3 percent Filipino, 0.5 percent Native American, and 1 percent other; also 39 percent of the students were classified as English-language learners. During school year 2002–03, 57 percent of its public school students were on free or reduced lunch.

Chapter 2

Teachers' Beliefs About Knowledge

To be honest, I never even knew that there was such a thing as European dominant anything! I thought history was what it was, life is what it is, no matter whose perspective you are looking from.
(White elementary teacher, November 23, 2003)

I started thinking, what is making me question my own belief system and what I've always been fed? . . . Reading things like this, and thinking about, well what's causing me to transform? It takes a really powerful example. . . . Hearing something over and over again, you hear it once and you think, aw, yeah, whatever. But you keep hearing it and you start questioning it. . . . But it's like, it has to be something really powerful *like that, or repetitive, in the scope of things, to make people change their minds.*
(Asian American elementary teacher, September 8, 2001)

The teachers above reflected on how difficult it is to see and confront one's basic beliefs about knowledge. The White elementary teacher had always assumed that the version of history in textbooks represented unbiased truth, until she had to critically examine her assumption from vantage points of histories told by subordinate groups. The Asian American elementary teacher viewed learning to recognize her own assumptions as a difficult process since deeply embedded assumptions are not only hard to see but are also useful for ordering one's understanding of everyday life.

Teachers' beliefs about the nature of knowledge have important implications for designing and teaching multicultural curriculum, so I usually start work on curriculum by helping teachers identify and critically reflect on what they take as truth. Developing curriculum that is relevant to and engages students, in contexts in which there is already a considerable amount of prescribed curriculum, requires teachers to judge what is most worth teaching and knowing in order to identify space in which they can invite and work with students' knowledge and interests. Developing multicultural curriculum requires teachers to evaluate knowledge in terms of the sociopolitical context of the community from which it comes, and to judge what difference it makes who authors any given body of knowledge. In addition, developing intellectually rich curriculum requires thinking through not just what facts and information are worth consuming, but also what the intellectual basis of knowledge is. Further, curriculum development requires considering not only how students learn to consume knowledge, but also how they learn to evaluate and produce it. This chapter first explores connections between teachers' beliefs about knowledge and curriculum, then discusses various processes for self-reflection, with some specific examples of how teachers have responded to those processes.

TEACHERS' BELIEFS

Bartolomé and Trueba (2000) recommended that, before teachers can work well with multicultural teaching, they need to develop *ideological clarity*. By this they mean

> the process by which individuals struggle to identify both the dominant society's explanations for the existing socioeconomic and political hierarchy and their own explanations of the social order and any resulting inequalities. Ideological clarity requires that teachers' individual explanations be compared and contrasted with those propagated by the dominant society. The juxtaposing of ideologies, hopefully, forces teachers to better understand if, when, and how their belief systems uncritically reflect those of the dominant society and support unfair and inequitable conditions. (p. 279)

Their words echo those of Freire (1998), who maintained that "I cannot be a teacher if I do not perceive with ever greater clarity that my practice demands of me a definition about where I stand" (p. 93). Even though the work of teachers is structured and constrained institutionally through accountability systems, as well as through other conditions of teachers' work, such as class size (Connell, 1985), teachers have agency to make decisions.

For example, consider two different perspectives about what multicultural curriculum might look like: a cultural difference perspective and an antiracist perspective (see Brandt, 1986, p. 12). The cultural difference perspective focuses on building consensus and understanding about cultural differences, and getting along. The antiracist perspective focuses on challenging racial oppression and exploitation, and reconstructing racist systems to achieve equality of power across racial groups. Since the cultural difference perspective fits with an ideology of the United States as a nation of immigrants, teachers often take it for granted as the only way to frame a multicultural curriculum, without recognizing alternatives. But curriculum based on an antiracist perspective is more likely to reflect points of view about the United States that are articulated by historically oppressed racial groups.

Now imagine a fourth-grade teacher who wants her mostly Anglo student population to develop some appreciation for people different from themselves. She develops and teaches a 2-week interdisciplinary unit on Native Americans that combines social studies, language arts, and art. The unit teaches a little bit about several different Indian tribes historically in terms of geographic location, social structure, and economic activities. Students read stories about Indian mythology and, as art projects, construct totem poles. On the surface, the teacher might believe that Native American people benefit from Anglos having experienced a unit like this, assuming it will lead them to treat Native Americans respectfully. But the unit is structured around a cultural difference perspective the teacher probably takes for granted. (Imagine, for example, teaching this unit but substituting European Americans for Native Americans.) In this case, her curriculum locates indigenous people in history rather than the present, assumes so much simplicity in the histories and social structures of widely diverse indigenous peoples that it actually ends up teaching stereotypes, may assume indigenous knowledge is the equivalent of childlike mythology that can be dipped into but doesn't require serious study, and assumes that culture rather than the politics of conquest and sovereignty is what Anglos should learn. In other words, despite the teacher's good intentions, and even if all of the "facts" in the unit were accurate, its basic underlying ideology is problematic. An antiracist curriculum would start by critically examining conquest and ongoing struggles for sovereignty (Bigelow & Peterson, 1998). A glimpse of what that might look like in a classroom is illustrated in Chapter 6.

Because assumptions guide what teachers do, it is worthwhile to spend time examining the basis on which one makes teaching decisions. Ideological beliefs come partially from prior life experiences. Generally people learn ideologies initially while growing up. Family members tell stories about family history and everyday life to teach how life works, who we are, where we come from, and what kinds of things are possible. Television, other media, and school curricula also teach ideologies through stories and imagery. For example, Gallegos (1998) described huge differences between the ideology about America in the curriculum he experienced growing up, and the ideology he learned from Mexican and Indian family members. "The stories about how the world works that I heard and learned growing up are so radically different from the explanations I learned in institutions that they are almost irreconcilable" (p. 244).

Several years ago I examined teachers' conceptions of multicultural education (Sleeter, 1992). To a large extent, and to a greater degree than they realized, their conceptions were rooted in their life experiences and the communities with which they affiliated. Perspectives of the White teachers tended to differ from those of teachers of color, for example, regarding the centrality of racism to how schools work. Significantly, a White teacher whose perspective was similar to those of the African American teachers had sustained contact with African American adults. Teachers' personal histories with social mobility also informed how they understood multicultural education, particularly the extent to which they subscribed to the meritocratic assumption that everyone needs to pull him- or herself up by the bootstraps. Since ideology is rooted, at least in part, in life experience, uncovering taken-for-granted beliefs entails looking at how one interprets one's life in relationship to that of others.

Epistemological beliefs are assumptions about the nature of knowledge and "reality." They form initially at home and in school, and can develop as one gains education (Schommer, Calvert, Gariglietti, & Bajaj, 1997). Research on teachers' and college students' epistemological beliefs suggests three rough stages that lie along a continuum, through which people can grow (Schommer, 1998; White, 2000). At one end are those who hold *absolutist* beliefs, seeing knowledge as fixed and certain, outside the knower, and established by authority figures. At the other end of the continuum are *reflective* individuals, who see knowledge as situated within the context in which people create it; problems have multiple solutions, and truth claims can be evaluated on the basis of the veracity of evidence on which they rest. In the middle are *relativists*, who reject anchoring knowledge in established authorities, but not knowing how to use any other way to evaluate truth claims, assume that all perspectives are equally valid. At early stages of relativism, people tend to see all knowledge as resting on personal opinion and individual experience.

According to White (2000), roughly half of the adult population holds an absolutist perspective about the nature of knowledge, and only a small proportion holds a reflective perspective. In a study of preservice students, she found most holding a relativist perspective, which she suggested represents a move away from viewing knowledge as fixed and textbooks as absolutely true. As preservice students began to question the knowledge taught by textbooks and authority figures, they seemed to substitute personal opinion and experience for expert authority as the basis for judging truth.[1] White observed that, as college students, most were only beginning to learn to evaluate what is true on the basis of evidence and reasoning rather than personal experience or external authority.

Learning to work with multiple perspectives, multiple frames of reference, and multiple funds of knowledge is at the heart of multicultural curriculum design. So, as a heuristic device to examine teachers' epistemological beliefs and to help them reflect on their own assumptions, I and my colleagues in the Visible Knowledge Project[2] developed an analytical framework that appears in Table 2.1. It describes a rough progression of levels in learning to think complexly about multicultural curriculum, illustrating what teacher thinking might look like at emerging, developing, and accomplished levels. The framework includes four dimensions along which epistemological beliefs can be examined: task definition, perspective taking, self-reflexivity, and locus of decision making. The set of assumptions labeled *Emerging* correspond to what White (2000) characterized as absolutist thinking. Those labeled *Developing* correspond to relativist thinking; and those labeled as *Accomplished*, to reflective thinking.[3]

Every time I teach a multicultural education course, I struggle to help teachers reflect on their own assumptions. The next section discusses processes I have used to help teachers identify and reflect on their ideological and epistemological assumptions. A use for Table 2.1 is suggested in that context.

TEACHERS REFLECT ON THEIR BELIEFS

Throughout the Multicultural Curriculum Design course, I use various strategies that are designed to prompt teachers to reflect on their own beliefs and assumptions. These strategies include: (1) studying the concepts of ideology and epistemology, (2) reading works that are written from multiple ideological perspectives, (3) engaging in structured or semi-structured personal interactions that challenge teachers' thinking, (4) analyzing epistemological and ideological assumptions in documents, and (5) engaging in reflective writing.

Studying Ideology and Epistemology as Concepts

The first day of class in fall 2001, to find out the extent to which teachers were familiar with the concept of ideology, I asked them to write how they would describe the ideology of curriculum they recently taught. Fourteen of the seventeen responded. Three had no idea and wrote statements such as "I'm not sure what I'm being asked." Eight briefly named a core

Table 2.1. Thinking Complexly About Multicultural Curriculum

	Task Definition	Perspective Taking	Self-Reflexivity	Locus of Decision Making
Emerging	• Assumes a "right" way to design and teach curriculum. • Assumes one already understands what multicultural curriculum is, and that "new learning" involves adding onto that. • Ignores, sees as irrelevant, or lacks confidence to examine elements that are puzzling, feel threatening, or seem impractical.	• Assumes there is a body of "correct" knowledge or attitudes to teach. Tends to interpret and dismiss other perspectives or critical questions as opinion, personal criticism, or simply impractical.	• Seldom reflects on one's work. Strives for certainty, assumes that questioning oneself is the same as questioning one's competence. • Seeks approval for one's thinking from authority figures.	• Either looks to external authorities (the state, well-known people in the field, texts) to find out what and how to teach, or ignores them entirely. • Assumes that educational decision making flows from top down.
Developing	• Recognizes more than one "right" way good curriculum could be designed and taught. • Willing to question things one thought one understood, and to explore elements or dimensions that are puzzling or new.	• Willing to consider multiple and possibly conflicting definitions of what is most worth knowing. • Able to acknowledge how one's own viewpoint, identity, and social location shapes one's perspective. • Willing to own one's judgments about what is best for kids.	• Willing to acknowledge uncertainty, at least tentatively. • Occasionally questions self about what is most worth teaching and why. • Recognizes need to attend to practical consequences of one's teaching on students, while maintaining some level of critical questioning.	• Pays attention to external authorities, but also willing to seek input from students, parents, community members, or other teachers. • Explores how to construct decision making in a way that both satisfies authorities and also invites bottom-up decision making.
Accomplished	• Assumes multiple ways of designing and teaching curriculum emanate from diverse ideologies. • Able to own and work with one's ideology. • Continually tries to recognize new dimensions of curriculum, and to figure out the most ethical as well as practical balance among competing demands.	• Actively seeks multiple perspectives. Makes explicit effort to learn from perspectives different from one's own, especially those that have been historically subjugated. • Able to articulate own perspective as one of many. • Able to invite dialog and discussion across divergent perspectives.	• Views uncertainty as tool for learning. • Consistently monitors, questions, and evaluates practical and ethical impacts of one's work on students. • Questions how one's own positionality, experiences, and point of view affect one's work, but can move forward while doing so.	• Negotiates decision making in a way that consciously places well-being of students at the center. • Regularly engages students and their communities in collaborative decision making, while attending to external expectations of students. • Able to take ownership for the consequences of one's decisions.

33

belief that informs their teaching (e.g., constructivism, child-centered learning, multiculturalism) or that informs the dominant curriculum (e.g., English-speaking). While the other three did not actually define ideology, they used the concept correctly, two by critiquing the ideology of California's standards. For example, one of them answered,

> Since we are ~~asked~~ told to teach the CA state curriculum standards, of which there are many, requiring the majority of instructional time, I'd say the ideology of my curriculum conforms largely to conventional academic knowledge, with individual attempts on my part to introduce a differing perspective. (September 7, 2001)

As their responses suggested, most had not encountered the term *ideology* in relationship to their own work and weren't sure what it meant. However, most were able to identify values and theories they preferred, although they wrote little about why they preferred some theories more than others.

Reading about ideology and epistemology offers teachers a language that can help in their own self-reflection. In another course I taught in the same program, teachers studied how four epistemological perspectives formulate what counts as knowledge, and how truth claims are judged. The perspectives are positivism, phenomenology, narrative research, and emancipatory research.[4] Teachers analyzed articles that embody each perspective in order to figure out assumptions authors make about the nature of knowledge and truth.

In Multicultural Curriculum Design, teachers analyzed several definitions of *ideology*, and several short passages in which the concept was used. Then they spent about an hour collectively constructing the following definition as they wrestled with the concept:

> [Ideology is the] formation of a way of looking at the world based on what you have seen, experienced. It's what you were taught. You may or may not be aware of it. It's a window that frames your view of everything. Was formed in your past, is being formed on an ongoing basis. Gives you a way to simplify, interpret what you see and experience. You justify what you do or think with your ideology. What a group holds as truth. (September 7, 2001)

This definition packs a lot of ideas together. While reading about and defining *ideology* and *epistemology* do not necessarily prompt teachers to reflect on their own assumptions, doing so provides language that serves as a useful conceptual tool for other reflective work.

Readings Based on Diverse Ideological Perspectives

Readings that engage teachers directly with various ideological perspectives prompt more direct self-reflection. For example, in one section of Multicultural Curriculum Design we read Macedo's (1994) *Literacies of Power*, which discusses curriculum, ideology, and power, and selections from *Rethinking Schools*, a newspaper written from critical perspectives mainly by classroom teachers. The readings offered a critical language many of the teachers had not encountered in school previously. As is often the case, many of the White teachers found the points of view in some of the readings uncomfortable, while many of the teachers of color found them affirming. A biracial male middle school teacher wrote, "Reading Macedo is like finding out the truth. I don't know whether to cry or to jump with joy." Students also located and read "transformative intellectual knowledge" (Banks, 1993) for units they developed; this process is described in Chapter 5.

Personal Interactions

Various kinds of personal interactions challenge teachers' thinking in relationship to diverse ideological perspectives, particularly when the readings open up perspectives that are usually not part of the curriculum, but that may resonate with students from historically marginalized communities. Personal interactions can prompt considerable self-reflection, but they require planning in order to manage emotional reactions to uncomfortable points of view. To prepare teachers for emotional reactions to discussions that probe core beliefs, we set ground rules near the beginning of the semester. Figure 2.1 distills those I have borrowed from various sources over the years (with apologies to those from whom I have borrowed, for not keeping track of sources).[5]

Various structured reflection discussions appear in subsequent chapters. I start with fairly short, relatively "safe" discussion topics (such as why a teacher in a short story refused to allow a student to write a paper on Malcolm X instead of Martin Luther King, Jr.), and move to hotter topics over the semester (such as why gay/lesbian literature is usually excluded from the K–12 curriculum).

A pair activity involves writing dialog poems that juxtapose two perspectives. Two authors working together select an issue and two different points of view. Although they are not required to draw on personal experiences and life history, authors usually do so. They create the thoughts of two people, each representing a different perspective and lived experience. Sometimes they intersect and other times they

Figure 2.1. Ground Rules for Discussion

1. Keep in mind that differences in perspective are not the problem; the problem is our great difficulty talking across those differences. Also keep in mind that consensus may not be the goal of discussion. Rather, the main goal may be understanding other points of view. In other words, you should seek understanding, not necessarily agreement.

2. It is okay, and often helpful, to speak from your own personal experience. At the same time, recognize that you can't make generalizations from your experience. Your experience is true for you; it may or may not be true for other people.

3. When listening to someone speak from her or his experience, listen and do not deny the validity of that experience. You can ask questions for clarification. But watch for conversation stoppers, such as
"Yes, but...,"
"You must have been misinterpreting what happened," and
"You shouldn't feel like that."

4. Don't interrupt. Wait for the other person to finish, and make sure you actually heard and followed what the other person was saying before jumping in with what you have to say.

5. If you aren't sure you understood what the other person was saying, try paraphrasing what you heard back to the person, and ask if that is what he or she said or meant. Don't simply dismiss or ignore what the other person said.

6. Express disagreement with someone else in a way that acknowledges and respects the point of view that person has articulated. For example, you might say, "I think I see what you are saying. I see the issue differently, though, and here is why."

7. If you feel attacked or threatened by what another person is saying, it's okay to express your feelings, but own them. You can say, "I am feeling XYZ about what you just said," but do not attack the other person with statements like "You are being really biased!" You might also take a short time-out before saying anything.

8. You don't have to disclose anything you do not wish to disclose. If you are feeling threatened or uneasy and would rather keep your thoughts private, you have a right to do so. Recognize, however, that if all of us never disclosed anything controversial, there would be even less understanding of differences than there is now.

diverge. Dialog poems structure personal narrative writing, offering a way of engaging with "otherness out loud," as SooHoo (2004b) put it. "Composing a narrative facilitates an awakening of consciousness. Deeper, penetrating meaning comes from listening to other narratives" (p. 266). Using this activity, teachers have explored conflicting viewpoints about issues such as gay rights, war, isolation of elderly people, isolation of immigrants, monolingualism, discrimination against people with disabilities, ethnicity, and age differences.

Document Analysis

Document analysis is a strategy that helps teachers identify epistemological and ideological assumptions in materials and resources they use. I have teachers work in small groups and analyze specific documents (such as curriculum guides) or Web sites (such as state department of education Web sites). For analyzing these they use questions such as those in Figure 2.2. (In Chapter 5, we briefly examine textbook analysis, which is a related form of document analysis.)

Reflective Writing

Finally, throughout the semester, I structure reflective writings. During one section of Multicultural Curriculum Design, teachers wrote reflections about various teaching dilemmas they had experienced. Then, on the basis of those reflections, they identified some core beliefs and assumptions underlying their thinking. An example of a writing prompt appears in Figure 2.3: Teachers are asked to reflect on how they handled a specific example of curriculum they were told to teach, which they may have questioned from a multicultural perspective. Other dilemmas teachers wrote about included how they handled a political conflict they had experienced when teaching, a conflict between themselves and students over a specific principle or value, and a conflict between preparing students for tests and teaching to students' interests. I emphasized that I was interested in the reasoning underlying their decisions, much more than the decisions themselves.

A prominent theme that emerged in these reflective writings was teacher agency. The international teachers and many of the U.S. teach-

Figure 2.2. Questions to Guide Analysis of Curriculum Documents for Ideology

1. Who produced this document, resource, or Web site (if it is possible to tell)? Can you tell where the authors or producers are coming from?

2. How is this document, resource, or Web site intended to be used? By whom?

3. What is it trying to accomplish? What is its purpose?

4. What key concepts does it use? What problems, issues, and points of view does it direct attention toward? What does it direct attention away from? Whose view of the world does it tend to support? Whose view does it undermine or ignore?

5. How would you describe the ideology of this document, resource, or Web site?

6. Whose knowledge isn't here, that could be here? What is left out?

Figure 2.3. Writing Assignment on a Teaching Dilemma

1. Write what grade level, level of schooling (e.g., primary level, university level), and/or subject area you teach or work in, as a context for the rest of this writing activity.

2. To what extent do authorities such as the state, the national government, the school district, or the college define what you should teach (or what should be taught in the area you mentioned above)? Describe an example of content that is part of the curriculum you teach, or at the level in which you work, that is prescribed by authority figures.

3. How would you evaluate the example above (curriculum that is prescribed by authority figures) from a multicultural perspective, based on your best understanding at the moment of what that means?

4. If you have any concerns about content that is part of the curriculum you are supposed to teach, from a multicultural perspective, you have a value conflict in deciding what to do. Explain how you think you should deal with those concerns and why. Is what you think you should do the same as what you actually do? Why or why not?

ers, particularly the beginning teachers, assumed that their job is to deliver the mandated curriculum, but gradually began to question that assumption. For example, early in the semester a Kenyan teacher wrote, "In the Kenyan system one cannot negotiate what to teach, but you can negotiate how to teach it in a more relevant way that represents students' experience if one has the resources" (October 13, 2003). An early career U.S. teacher wrote, "As a public school teacher, though, you really can't go outside of your prescribed literature and academic standards" (September 30, 2003). Over the semester, as we explored ethical issues about whose knowledge schools teach and possibilities for practice, teachers saw more space for their own agency.

At the end of the semester, the teachers read what they had written regarding the four dilemmas, and described growth in their thinking. They also had the option of analyzing their growth using the framework in Table 2.1, which had already been presented and discussed in class. A few teachers chose to analyze their thinking using the framework; their discussions reflected on their growth from the Emerging to the Developing level. For example, a beginning teacher wrote about her growing recognition that there is no one right way to teach, nor one right way to make curriculum multicultural. Although she did not articulate a basis on which to evaluate alternatives, she recognized her emerging ability to see the existence of alternatives.

The teachers of color wrote quite a bit about how their beliefs were based on life experiences with race and racism. For example, an African American educator wrote:

My grade school years in Los Angeles, during the sixties, were in classrooms with predominantly other African American students, and were taught by many African American teachers and culturally sensitive young White teachers. I recollect the majority of the African American teachers were very strict yet caring. . . . [At the college I attended] most of the students of color were recruited from Los Angeles. We felt ostracized and alienated. Even though I was the valedictorian of my high school class and accepted into X College "With Honors at Entrance," I was treated like an upward bound or affirmative action student. . . . Subsequently, the humiliation and overwhelming dominant ideology . . . forced me to take a leave of absence after three and half years of instruction. I did not return to complete my undergraduate instruction until some 25 years later. (November 24, 2003)

As a result, she is committed to preparing African American high school students for college entrance and success in college. In another example, a Mexican American elementary teacher wrote:

I have a 3½-year-old daughter who is questioning who she is and where she fits into this world. I never thought I would have to answer such difficult questions this early on [in] her development. About a month ago we were spending time singing songs together and reading various books. I have always shared various literatures of different cultures since she was a baby. While in the middle of one of her favorite songs, "Jesus Loves the Little Children," there comes a part where you sing, "Red and yellow, black and white," which represents the races of our world. She immediately stopped and turned to me and asked, "Mommy, why am I not in the song?" I replied with "What do you mean?" She said, "They don't say brown, I'm not in it." (November 23, 2003)

Experiences like this made her determined to create curriculum in which students can see themselves.

The White teachers' writings generally did not address how race informed their beliefs about multicultural curriculum, although several described other formative experiences that placed them in "outsider" roles. For example, Christi, who is featured in Chapters 3 and 4, described being embarrassed about her hippie parents when she was growing up, which sensitized her to other people who might be embarrassed by home. Kathy, featured in Chapter 6, described growing up as a Quaker and feeling like an outsider around non-Quaker peers. She valued her Quaker roots, but had to learn to deal with other people's persistent ignorance about her religion.

Most teachers showed growth in their ability to ask hard questions of themselves. Reflecting on the article "Planting Seeds of Solidarity" (Peterson, 2000/01), a White teacher perceptively realized that her previous attempts to make curricula multicultural were more limited than she had realized:

> Maybe the reason I have felt a sense of freedom in my classroom to pick and choose what I want to teach outside the state-mandated curriculum is because maybe I have never chosen to teach anything meaningful, anything deep, anything socially sensitive that might make the kids want to be part of a solution, to want to change things, to question why or why not. Maybe I have never dared tackle issues such as poverty, racial injustice, social stratification, all kinds of inequities. (November 23, 2003)

FROM SELF-EXAMINATION TO ACTION

Developing epistemological and ideological clarity means identifying the basis on which one makes classroom decisions, where that basis comes from, and whom it serves most strongly. The hardest part is uncovering taken-for-granted assumptions. Kumashiro (2004) argued that what we take as common sense often is, in fact, oppressive, partly because of the degree to which it is taken for granted. Believing that we cannot work against the grain is one of those assumptions. He noted two reasons why it is difficult to uncover and challenge common sense practices in teaching. The first reason is that we often feel pressure to conform. The second reason "is that commonsensical ideas often give us some sense of comfort," if only because they are so familiar that they don't require rethinking (p. xxiii).

Examining the basis of one's thinking does not necessarily mean that one comes to embrace perspectives that run counter to one's own, to see truth as relative, or to see knowledge that is most worth teaching and learning as fluid. A teacher might decide, for example, that students will be best served by learning traditional disciplinary content well, rather than learning adapted or transformed versions of that content. A teacher might decide that some truths are fixed and unchanging, and that questioning truth leads to unfounded relativism. In one study, for example, Powell (1996) compared two teachers in order to examine the relationship between a teacher's epistemology and her or his approach to multicultural curriculum. One of the teachers held a developmentalist approach, seeing students' needs and interests as the basis for curriculum design. This teacher was receptive to replacing some traditional content with content from ethnic studies because she did not bring a fixed idea about what is most worth teaching. Further, she saw students' interests as a legitimate part of curriculum. The other teacher saw curriculum in terms of the structure of his discipline (science), in relationship to which he judged what is relevant to learn and teach. He also judged students' learning abilities in relationship to their mastery of disciplinary content. He could not see the relevance of content that is not already an established part of science, and so he saw multicultural curriculum as fairly irrelevant.

I approach multicultural curriculum design from the vantage point of my own ideological perspective and epistemological assumptions; these underlie this book and my teaching. However, I value questioning and examining a broad range of ideas from a broad range of perspectives. Doing so ultimately supports critical thinking, dialog, and honest engagement with differences.

The remainder of this book examines various elements of curriculum design and illustrates how teachers have worked with and used these elements in their own classrooms. Working with all of the elements—ranging from identifying what is most worth teaching to thinking through how to assess learning, to figuring out how to connect students' experiences with academic ideas—requires making judgments. While this chapter has offered tools and conceptual frameworks for analyzing how one makes judgments, the process of self-analysis is continual. The next chapter examines building curriculum around central ideas that are judged to be most worth learning, or of enduring understanding. While curriculum standards and textbooks give teachers information and concepts to work with, they do not usually identify central concepts worth teaching in specific classroom contexts. How a teacher thinks this question through is a matter of epistemology and ideology.

NOTES

1. It is possible that an impetus of the standards movement was a reaction against educators using personal opinion and experience as a basis for planning curriculum, since the standards movement reasserts the authority of disciplinary experts to determine curriculum. However, it appears that teachers experience this shift to reassert absolutist thinking, rather than helping move them toward reflective thinking.

2. As noted in Chapter 1, this is a national network of several colleges and universities, organized through Georgetown University. On my campus, about eight faculty members participated over several years.

3. I am always somewhat suspicious of stage theories, since they often reflect value judgments that a group of people make regarding what they take to be inferior development of other people. Stage theories also embody a linear conception of growth that does not necessarily reflect human growth patterns. However, distinguishing among levels of competence can serve as a helpful device for communicating what novice performance "looks like" in comparison to more expert performance. As such, it can serve as a useful heuristic device for discussion and self-analysis.

4. *Positivism* is a way of understanding the world that assumes reality exists apart from the knower and can be known through careful processes of data collection. Positivist research attempts to discern patterns in human behavior, and interventions that affect human behavior. *Phenomenology* is a way of understanding that assumes reality cannot be known apart from the knower, and that knowing is always in context. Phenomenological research consists of the disciplined attempt of a researcher to uncover patterns in the meaning making of others and to illuminate human activity rather than discovering generalizable patterns or laws of social activity. *Narrative* assumes that the most unmediated, holistic forms of knowledge are narrated by individuals based on their own experience without interpretation of a researcher or mediator. Through storytelling, people can connect and interpret events in a way that is meaningful to the narrator. Storytelling also acts as a testimony that certain things did happen, regardless of whether those experiences have been verified through other ways of knowing. *Emancipatory knowledge* serves a community's desire to confront relations of oppression, gain self-determination, and uplift the community. It locates knowledge within the social history of knowers and their communities; emancipatory knowledge comes from and is owned by the community using it for its own purposes.

5. Teachers, possibly with their students, should tailor to students' age and maturity level ground rules for discussing controversial issues in their own classrooms.

Chapter 3

Designing Curriculum Around Big Ideas

I stand here with To Kill a Mockingbird *in one hand and a standard that all students must write a persuasive piece of writing. How can this become transformative? Thus a lesson emerges: The students study the Jim Crow laws in a task force and then they write a letter to the city council about abolishing the laws.*

(Christi, high school English teacher, November 23, 2003)

The big idea comes from the third-grade Social Studies California State Standards and deals with how people have used the resources from the local area. I want to focus this idea on how people have used the land in the [local] valley. I got interested in this topic because I am a relatively new immigrant in this community and I wanted to explore how land was used throughout history.

(Elementary teacher, December 15, 2003)

The teachers above wrestled with connecting content standards with substantive, academically rich ideas that interest them and their students. Teachers can use state curriculum standards as a basis from which to plan engaging, standards-conscious, multicultural curriculum. This chapter discusses starting multicultural curriculum planning by identifying *big ideas* on which content and skills can be hung, and which engage students.

At the same time, standards, textbooks, and other curriculum guides structure knowledge around ideological foundations that need to be examined critically. After discussing what it means to organize curriculum around a central idea, this chapter works through a process for identifying a big idea. A vignette of a high school teacher illustrates an example of creatively connecting multicultural content with state standards. But content standards are not ideologically neutral and need to be examined for the ideology they embody. To illustrate, I look critically at ideology embedded in one set of

43

content standards in order to consider how they might shape one's curriculum in ways one may not see or wish.

ORGANIZING CURRICULUM FOR MEANING AND ENGAGEMENT

Probably everyone has experienced curriculum that marches students through textbook pages, workbook activities, and lists of decontextualized skills and bits of knowledge, punctuated periodically by tests. Prior to the standards movement, many teachers would "*begin* with textbooks, favored lessons, and time-honored activities rather than deriving those tools from targeted goals or standards" (Wiggins & McTighe, 1998, p. 8). Now teachers are expected to plan curriculum based on state content standards; increasingly, many teachers also draw curriculum from anticipated test items. If presented with long lists of standards to cover (as they are in California) and batteries of tests their students will be taking, many teachers—especially beginning teachers—turn the standards into the curriculum itself.

Doing this, however, is likely to result in boring, superficial teaching that favors memory work over understanding. Mona, one of the teachers featured in Chapter 7, expressed concern about what she called "robot" education: "The art of interaction and creativity are being shuffled and many times 'lost' in the scurry to meet 'standards' and testing. I have a very big problem with . . . teachers going into other businesses or careers because the reason for educating our students has shifted to 'robot' education" (September 29, 2003).

Readers may have experienced multicultural curriculum as a topic or set of topics that is separate from the regular curriculum. When teachers are beginning to work with multicultural curriculum, rather than developing concepts or skills they already teach through culturally diverse knowledge bases (more about that in Chapter 5), they often see it as separate lessons or extra content to squeeze into an already crowded curriculum. Beginning curriculum planning around central ideas and concepts, then connecting content to them, helps get past the idea of multicultural curriculum as something separate. Pohan (2000) argues that if one analyzes standards through a multicultural lens, one "will begin to see myriad opportunities available" (p. 25).

It makes good teaching sense to start curriculum planning, including multicultural curriculum planning, by identifying the key concepts, or big ideas, around which a unit, lesson, or course of study will be built. Research consistently finds that the most effective teachers plan this way, regardless of subject area, grade level, or community context, and regardless of whether they are working with standards or not. Their planning places students' active engagement with meaningful ideas at the center. As Walker (2003) put it, "The most important principle of classroom activity design is that *the student's actions determine what will be learned*" (p. 262).

For example, in their study of social studies teaching in three fifth-grade classrooms, Brophy and VanSledright (1997) found that "the process of developing powerful curriculum and instruction begins with identification of clear purposes and goals" (p. 258). The best social studies teachers organized curriculum around "key ideas selected for development in depth because they foster progress toward major instructional goals" rather than "parade-of-facts treatments developed primarily in response to content coverage lists" (p. 258). Similarly, when comparing three teachers whose students learned literacy exceptionally well, with six other less effective teachers, Wharton-McDonald, Pressley, and Hampston (1998) found the three most effective teachers planned carefully around their primary goals for student learning. They were able to articulate those goals and to connect and integrate multiple goals in any given lesson. By being clear in their own minds about the central ideas they want students to learn, effective teachers are able explicitly to help students learn to "sift the significant from the insignificant" (Easton, Forrest, Goldman, & Ludwig, 1985, p. 157). Knapp and colleagues (1995) referred to this kind of planned instruction as "teaching for meaning," in which teachers link skills to meaning, placing meaning rather than skills first.

Backward design (Wiggins & McTighe, 1998) is a useful planning process for structuring this kind of curriculum. Backward design starts with reflection on the essential, enduring understandings teachers want their students to learn. Teachers think through what they believe is most worth teaching and what it looks like when one actually "knows" or "gets it." For example, what does it look like when students "know" how people have used natural resources from the local area, as one of the teachers whose words opened this chapter suggested? Does it only mean listing some uses? Does it also mean evaluating various kinds of resource use and being able to set and defend some criteria for evaluation? The clearer a teacher is about what it means to know and what students do when they know something, the more focused and coherent instruction becomes. Wiggins and McTighe emphasized, "Only by framing our teaching around valued questions and worthy performances can we overcome activity-based and coverage-oriented instruction and the resulting rote learning that produces formulaic answers and surface-level knowledge" (p. 27).

Organizing curriculum around big ideas, then engaging students with them in meaningful ways, is actually consistent with standards developed by various professional organizations, including the National Council on the Teaching of Mathematics, the National Council of Teachers of English, the National Council for the Social Studies, and the National Reading Council. Wang and Odell (2002) argued that professional teaching standards generally support student-centered instruction that involves planning for "students' deeper understanding of concepts and relationships of concepts within and across various subjects," challenging students' misconceptions and connecting their learning "meaningfully with their personal experiences and real-life contexts," and placing "students' active discovery of important ideas at the center" of instruction (p. 483).

Wiggins and McTighe (1998) distinguished between content coverage and what they refer to as "uncoverage," as a tool for planning curriculum for depth. *Content coverage* entails delivering to students predigested content that someone else has thought through, wondered about, made sense of. The dots are connected, all students need to do is absorb. However, one cannot "assume that because we [teachers] or the authors of a work have connected the dots, the student now sees the picture" (p. 102). *Uncoverage* involves students "inquiring into, around, and underneath content instead of simply covering it" (p. 98). Students connect dots that were selected based on the central "big idea." Curriculum organized for uncoverage engages students in looking beneath "blanket statements in textbooks" that "hide controversies and difficulties" (p. 107); "students have to *do* the subject, not just learn its results" (p. 99). Shor (1992), for example, designs curriculum around themes (big ideas) that prompt exploration of problems, such as What is history? He argued that although the teacher may select and introduce the theme, the teacher elaborates on it *with* students. Ironically, curriculum that engages students in working through central concepts is used much more in nations that have outscored U.S. students in the Third International Mathematics and Science Study (TIMSS) than in U.S. classrooms. While U.S. teachers tend to present material to students, teachers in Germany and Japan—two countries that outscore the United States—involve students in working with central ideas (Wiggins & McTighe, 1998, p. 43).

In the next section I describe a planning process that I take teachers through as they begin to develop multicultural curriculum. It is illustrated with some reactions of teachers in both semesters of Multicultural Curriculum Design to shifting gears from planning for content coverage to planning for uncoverage.

PLANNING AROUND BIG IDEAS

Drawing from Wiggins and McTighe's book *Understanding by Design* (1998), I created a set of planning questions, which appear in Figure 3.1,

Figure 3.1. Curriculum Planning Guide

1. Write down a potential concept you could teach.

2. Brainstorm what you could teach, or want students to know, related to that concept.

3. Classify the ideas above according to whether they are
    -   worth being familiar with (*W*)
    -   important to know and/or do (*I*)
    -   essential to enduring understanding (*E*)

4. Rewrite the central idea, based on the work you did above. Write this as a central question, where possible.

5. What sociocultural groups' knowledge do you have a good grasp on, related to the "enduring understandings" above? Which do you *not* have much of a grasp on? (Use this to plan for Transformative Knowledge paper.)

6. List 3–6 things you would like students to be able to do with these understandings by the end of the unit. Use Bloom's taxonomy to make sure you include higher levels of thinking.

7. What do you anticipate students already know or can do, related to this central idea? What would you like to know about their existing knowledge, conceptions, or experiences?

8. List key ideas, understandings, and skills students probably don't have that they will need to learn in order to fully comprehend what you've identified as "enduring." (Many of these might be what you classified as "worth being familiar with," or "important to know.") Your unit will need to teach these things.

9. For each of the items above, list at least one potential form of evidence of student learning. This forms the basis of your unit assessment plan.

10. What teaching/learning experiences will help students successfully master the learning outcomes above, given what students already bring?

to help teachers start to plan a multicultural curriculum unit. I spend about 4 hours working through them with teachers. Questions 1 and 2 ask teachers to identify a potential concept to teach, and then to brainstorm what they could teach or what they might want students to know that is related to the concept. The purpose of brainstorming is to begin to identify the various ideas a teacher has in mind in order to think through what is really central. Teachers can use content standards to help with Questions 1 and 2. Although I encourage teachers not to limit their ideas to what is in content standards, the best way to make sure they are teaching to standards is to use them in their initial curriculum planning.

Detailed and voluminous standards documents, however, can make sorting out main ideas challenging. California, for example, has one of the most detailed, prescriptive sets of content standards in the United States (Wixson & Dutro, 1999). Elementary teachers need to work with two reading–language arts standards documents (92 and 93 pages long), a math standards document (73 pages), a science standards document (61 pages), and a history–social science standards document (69 pages). Those who have English-language learners in their classrooms—which are the majority of teachers—also need to use the English-language development standards (96 pages). If they have time, they should also use a visual and performing arts standards document (172 pages). Further, teachers should familiarize themselves with conceptual underpinnings of each of these various standards documents in the subject matter frameworks, each of which spans 250–350 pages. In each discipline and for each grade level, there are long lists of standards. For example, fifth-grade teachers have 44 social studies standards and substandards to cover, many of which are quite complex. One of the 44 standards states that students will "describe the introduction of slavery into America, the responses of slave families to their condition, the ongoing struggle between proponents and opponents of slavery, and the gradual institutionalization of slavery in the South." Even experienced teachers often find sorting through quantities of such standards to be overwhelming. High school teachers seem to experience a little less pressure than elementary and middle school teachers since generally they have only one or two standards documents to attend to. Nevertheless, the sheer volume of standards at every level makes drawing central concepts to teach from standards documents a difficult process.

When I asked the teachers to identify a concept to teach, all of them in both semesters were able to identify a topic, but most had difficulty thinking through where they might go with it. Most identified topics that were far too broad (e.g., women in art, nutrition, the Thirteen Colonies, the nature of light, or the historical and cultural significance of Mexican dance) or vague (e.g., self-awareness, writer's workshop, or appreciation of culture). A few started with concrete ideas they were not yet sure how they might develop (e.g., a book about Cambodian refugees, or a topic in the social studies text). Teachers' difficulties identifying and elaborating on central ideas around which to plan suggested that generally they have not been asked to plan curriculum in this way. It seemed to me that most teachers were used to planning for content coverage rather than for uncoverage.

Regardless of whether their starting point was too broad, vague, or concrete, I asked the teachers next to brainstorm what they wanted their students to know, related to the concept, as a way of helping them flesh out where they might go with it. Some teachers constructed laundry lists of skills and information related to the topic, which they could then sift through to identify the most central ideas. These laundry lists, to some extent, were drawn from lists of standards. Others generated lists of very broad concepts that added to, rather than clarifying, the first concept they had written; this was particularly the case among beginning teachers. A few were not sure what to write, and wrote fairly little. As the teachers shared with each other what they wrote, many began to recognize vagueness in their own conceptualizations, and they helped each other clarify and focus their ideas. If readers work through the questions in Figure 3.1 on their own, I suggest bouncing what they write off other teachers for feedback, since doing this helps to develop more clarity.

Questions 3 and 4 ask teachers to distinguish between knowledge worth being familiar with, important knowledge and skills, and enduring understandings. Wiggins and McTighe (1998) defined *enduring understandings* as "the big ideas, the important understandings, that we want students to 'get inside of' and retain after they've forgotten many of the details" (p.10). I ask teachers to examine all they had written thus far, and classify each item as *W* (worthwhile), *I* (important), or *E* (enduring), in order to figure out the central idea (from items marked *E*) around which other ideas and skills revolve. Items marked *W* are least important and sometimes can be cut in order to provide more curricular space. Teachers are then asked to take the central idea and elaborate on it by identifying which knowledge and skills are important and which, while worth knowing, might be trimmed out in order to develop fewer ideas in more depth. Most teachers struggled with this process, and working through it took time.

This process of classifying ideas is one that teachers can use with standards documents that list a tremendous amount of content to cover. Which standards offer the most essential, enduring concepts to which others can be connected? One of my previous students now helps teachers in California cluster their reading–language arts standards into four key big ideas: accessing information, interpreting information, producing something with it, and disseminating that information (Action Learning Systems, 2002).

Through this work, most teachers gained a much clearer sense of a big idea around which to build a unit. A high school literature teacher from Greece explained later, for example, how this process helped her recognize why her students usually found literature boring: "Designing curriculum backwards was a new and challenging task for me. So far I was selecting a piece of literature from the textbook and then I was trying to find information and resources to analyze it. It is much more interesting and fruitful, though, to decide on your big ideas, set your objectives and then select literature to support your goals" (October, 2001). She recognized why many teachers found working through these first four questions difficult: They were used to starting with material in their textbook, then trying to make that material interesting to students, but I was asking them to start by identifying what they wanted students to learn, and then consider which resources to use.

Over the semester, some of the beginning teachers continued to struggle to identify what they wanted students to learn. Some were concerned about writing objectives in a "correct" form, which got in the way of thinking; when I asked them to talk to me about their proposed unit, they verbalized ideas and goals that often were different from what they had laboriously written. In teacher preparation coursework, teachers commonly learn to write lesson plans, starting with objectives. It seemed that newer teachers had internalized the idea that units need objectives, but didn't yet know general grade-level curriculum well enough to think deeply about its central purposes. More experienced teachers tended to worry less about the form of objectives and more about their purpose.

The remaining questions in Figure 3.1 are addressed in subsequent chapters. Question 5 helps teachers begin to plan for investigating transformative knowledge related to the big idea for their unit, which is discussed in Chapter 5. Question 6 addresses levels of thinking their proposed unit will develop; I use this question to prompt teachers to examine their expectations of students, a subject addressed in Chapter 6. Questions 7, 8, and 10 ask teachers to consider their students in relationship to their central idea (Chapter 7). Question 9 asks teachers what they would look at to assess student learning in relationship to their main goals for the unit (Chapter 4).

Throughout the semester, teachers experienced a recursive process as they explored their big idea through the lenses provided in subsequent chapters, and continually reflected on ideological assumptions underlying their thinking. In the process, their big idea continually developed and sometimes shifted significantly as teachers learned more. Consider here how a high school teacher took the standards and her own goals for students, and derived from them a big idea and learning objectives.

Christi: Curriculum Planning as Pottery

When reading through the current language arts textbook, I noticed there are many gaps in perspectives. There were very few stories about immigrants, people of color, or young people. . . . The textbook represents little else than White European Americans and a tokenism of women of color. . . . The ideology that emerges in the textbook is that hardworking White Americans who rise up are the ideal, but some hardworking women of color who have overcome all manner of challenges to become famous are also ideal and can be accepted sparingly into the canon. If any immigrant is mentioned at all, it is the White European who originally came to America and succeeded through Horatio Alger–like means. (November 30, 2003)

Christi was in her seventh year as a high school English teacher when she enrolled in Multicultural Curriculum Design. She teaches in a California high school that is located between an affluent, predominantly White community and a working-class community that is quite diverse, predominantly Latino and White. Her high school serves students from both communities. For example, students in the class I visited consisted of 20 ninth graders: 1 African American female, 1 Latino male, 6 Latina females, 9 White females, and 3 White males.

Christi is a White woman who had grown up in the working-class, diverse community her school serves. A tall blond with blue eyes, she "couldn't tolerate the racism" she found in the more affluent, White community because she identified with the diverse community. Her concern about racism gave rise to a unit she planned and taught about West Coast immigration.

Christi is very adept at carefully analyzing the state's content standards and the texts she is given, then creatively designing activist-oriented curriculum. She explained how she does it:

> I think that if you ponder and research any book/topic/lesson long enough you can teach it from a multicultural/activist perspective. . . . I do teach what is expected, but I don't dwell on the minute trivia of the literature, but concentrate on the human issues and the social justice issues. I let the book become a tool for looking at larger issues. However, I also teach the essential standards, but I tweak them to suit what I'm doing. (September 29, 2003)

She commented that the English language arts standards were well written, flexible, and reasonable, even though the textbook she was given reflected a different ideology than she wanted to teach. But, like other teachers, she also had to pay attention to tests the students would be taking. She was expected to use the adopted texts, although she could—and did—use additional materials also.

She approached these requirements much like she approached the standards: She took ideas she *wanted* to teach, and figured out creative ways to connect them with what she *had* to teach. She explained to me how she was approaching standardized testing:

I'm creatively trying to figure out ways to—I actually tried to get a grant for this—take the things I'm teaching in context, and then weave in some standardized test kinds of questions, so we're not just going into this whole other realm, but it's still in context. (February 24, 2004)

As she spoke, she was working her hands as if they held a lump of clay. When she realized what she was doing, she laughed and explained:

My parents do pottery for a living, so I see things that are these clay things, because I was always playing with clay as a child, and making things. So that's how I see this, just taking bits of clay and creating something useful out of it. (February 24, 2004)

Christi's analogy of curriculum planning as pottery making captures her approach to connecting big ideas with standards. She knows the state standards, textbooks, and tests students will encounter quite well. As a scholar, writer, teacher, and member of a diverse community, she is passionately interested in learning to look at the world from viewpoints of other people and building bridges across differences.

I asked her where this passion and insight came from. She explained that it probably came from numerous experiences.

My parents were really open, and just embracing the world. And I think that's where it comes from. They wanted to be with another culture, I mean they made sure that they moved to areas where they were basically maybe the only White people in the area. . . . They really liked the neighborhood, they liked the people there. And there weren't that many White families, and that made them very happy, they really loved being with other cultures. . . . And it was just this huge support group, everybody helping, they were just these young kids moving into the same place, and they just seemed really to appreciate, once again, being with another cultural group. (February 24, 2003)

Growing up in racially diverse neighborhoods, she developed comfort and identification with diverse contexts. In high school and college, "I was always hanging out with different groups, and just learning, learning their language and just listening to them, going to their homes, meeting their families. . . . You could start a conversation with somebody or a friendship with somebody that just changes your whole point of view" (February 24, 2003). While some people would find this threatening, Christi found it interesting and normal. So she took her life experience and beliefs about people, her passion about writing, and the state's curriculum standards, and she worked it all together, leading with central ideas she believes are worthwhile.

Christi developed and taught a complex unit that connected immigration, from adolescent points of view, with reading and writing standards. Since California is experiencing large waves of immigration, Christi was concerned that her students develop empathy rather than hostility toward newcomers. She described the characteristics of the unit:

> This unit touches on a myriad of themes: respect for other cultures, understanding of our multicultural region, historical perspectives of our immigrant nation, family bonds, identity and culture and the American high school experience. I see the entire unit as a vehicle to assist students in gaining a better grasp of our immigrant nation, to search for connection and commonalities among immigrants, and to forge a sense of what makes cultures unique. (December 13, 2003)

At the same time, "it also remains firmly anchored in the required California ELA [English Language Arts] 9th–10th grade standards" (December 13, 2003). As an English teacher, the standards she was to address focused largely on developing students' reading comprehension of grade-level text and their skill in producing writing in various genres, using English language conventions of writing appropriately.

The learning outcomes Christi developed for the unit appear in Figure 3.2. Students completed assignments that connect directly with the learning outcomes. There were three major writing assignments: a narrative from the point of view of a fictitious immigrant, a fictitious diary the immigrant might write about school for 4 days, and a poem of 12 lines or more in which the fictitious immigrant expresses feelings. Christi mapped these against the state standards, and posted the mapping on a Web site that she created for this unit. The unit also included a research assignment, in which students were to write a short research paper about a West Coast immigrant group to provide background for the other three writing assignments. A culminating assignment—a Web page students were to create—synthesized their work in the above assignments. The next chapter will continue describing this unit and its assignments in relationship to how Christi monitored students' learning.

Figure 3.2. West Coast Immigration Learning Outcomes

Students will:

- Write up research material that includes evidence in support of a thesis.

- Read and interpret historically and culturally significant works of literature that reflect the West Coast immigrant experience and enhance their studies of history and social science.

- Analyze the positions that are presented to formulate a picture of the immigrant experience.

- Synthesize the content of the works into various creative writings.

- Connect the works they read to their own writing to demonstrate comprehension.

- Extend ideas presented in primary and secondary sources through original analysis, evaluation, and elaboration.

- Compare works that express a universal theme and provide evidence to support ideas expressed in the works.

- Write biographical narratives.

- Relate a sequence of events and communicate the significance of the events to their audience.

- Locate scenes and incidents in specific places.

- Describe sensory details: the sights, sounds, and the smells of scenes and the specific actions and feelings of the character.

- Demonstrate an understanding of proper English usage and control of grammar, paragraph and sentence structure, diction, and syntax.

- Employ appropriate technology to organize and record information.

IDEOLOGY AND CONTENT STANDARDS

As noted earlier, content standards are generally promulgated as consensus documents that represent agreement over what is most worth teaching and knowing within a discipline. However, presenting them this way may well hide ideological selections of knowledge that they embody and how particular conceptions about knowledge grow out of particular social locations. Asking epistemological questions concerning what counts as knowledge, according to what criteria, and who gets to decide, is very complex.

Danziger's (1990) view of knowledge as a "collective enterprise" is useful here. He described knowledge production as "governed by definite

rules that are reflected in the form of the product. The knowledge product . . . always takes the form of an ordered array of some kind. The nature
of such an array depends on the ordering principles that are incorporated
in the constituting practices" (p. 195). Investigating any body of knowledge involves uncovering the principles that order it, and the "human
action and social relations" in which it was constructed—the communities, vested interests, and purposes in which the ordering principles make
sense (p. 195). To those who inhabit the social location from which any
set of standards comes, their deeply embedded assumptions may not be
apparent. But to the extent that they drive what is taught in classrooms,
they have power to teach students particular ways of interpreting the
world.

It is important for teachers to look critically at content standards as
a guard against teaching an ideology one does not intend. Critiquing content standards does not necessarily mean not using them, but rather using
them reflectively. Figure 3.3 shows three sets of questions that can guide
analysis of content standards. A colleague and I have used them to analyze California's history–social science, and reading–language arts frameworks and standards (Sleeter & Stillman, 2005). These are similar to the
kinds of questions that can guide textbook analysis, but they begin by
identifying how standards conceptualize the nature of knowledge within
a discipline itself.

Figure 3.3. Questions for Standards Analysis

Below are three sets of questions that can guide analysis of a standards document. Using
these questions is probably most productive when done in conjunction with reading a
body of knowledge from a historically underrepresented point of view.

1. What is the main organizational structure of the discipline as it is reflected in the
   standards document? What does this organizational structure suggest about how the
   discipline, and knowledge in this discipline, is conceptualized? What does it suggest
   about how learning is conceptualized? Are there alternative ways of conceptualizing
   this discipline? If so, how does the conceptualization in this set of standards compare
   with alternatives?

2. What key themes do the standards embody? What main concepts repeat themselves
   throughout the document? What concepts that are relevant to the discipline from a
   multicultural perspective are absent or appear only in the background?

3. What is indicated by a count of words, items, or sociocultural group membership?
   For example, what is indicated by counting the demographic characteristics of people
   named for study in social studies? The demographics of authors of recommended
   children's literature? The references to English-language learners throughout a
   language arts document?

At first, teachers may find these questions too broad to use as an analytic tool. I suggest analyzing standards in conjunction with reading a body of knowledge from a historically underrepresented point of view, as discussed in Chapter 5. Recall from Chapter 2 that teachers were best able to identify and reflect on their own ideology when it was juxtaposed against alternative ideologies. Similarly, teachers are most likely to identify underlying assumptions of standards documents when these are juxtaposed against alternatives such as those reflected in ethnic studies, women's studies, disability studies, postcolonial studies, or gay/lesbian studies.

I will illustrate using the questions in Figure 3.1 with a brief look at the *History–Social Science Framework and Standards for California Public Schools* (California Department of Education, 2001).

1. *What is the main organizational structure of the discipline as it is reflected in the standards document?* These standards conceptualize history and social science largely as a story that students should learn. There are alternative ways of structuring a social studies or history curriculum: a story is one of several possibilities. Brophy and VanSledright (1997) argued that social studies should be constructed as a process of reflective inquiry. Wineburg (2001) suggested teaching students to think like historians. By that, he meant teaching students to analyze the past like historians do, that is, to analyze historical texts as artifacts of human production in specific contexts. So, if a teacher constructs a history and social studies curriculum according to the standards, it will most likely reflect a story more than it reflects a process of learning to think historically, unless a teacher intentionally plans for something different. If history is constructed as a story, however, one can then ask, Whose story does it tell? This leads to the next question.

2. *What key themes do the standards embody?* The writers of California's standards decided to construct the story mainly as an immigrant story, with a story line that runs geographically from east to west. This structure fits a story of European immigration; it does not fit history as indigenous people tell it or as Mexicans or Asians tell it. So, if teachers follow the standards in California, students will experience the disappearance of indigenous people, who appear on the East Coast of the United States in the elementary curriculum, then gradually disappear as the story line moves westward. Also, stressing voluntary immigration downplays the violence and involuntary nature of slavery. (By contrast, one of my faculty colleagues has taught a U.S. history course from a Mexican perspective, starting not with the East Coast of the United States, but rather with Aztlán, and moving south to north rather than east to west.)

3. What is indicated by a count of words, items, or sociocultural group membership? When I counted representation of people named for study in the history–social science framework, I found that, of the 96 Americans who were named for study, 82 percent were male and 18 percent were female. They were 77 percent White, 18 percent African American, 4 percent Native American, 1 percent Latino, and 0 percent Asian American. Of the 95 people outside the United States named for study, they were 86 percent male and 14 percent female. Sixty percent were European, 5 percent were African, 2 percent were Latin American, 14 percent were Asian, 4 percent were Russian, 1 percent were Caribbean, and 14 percent were Middle Eastern (mainly Biblical figures). This further suggests that the story the standards tell is one that centers largely around European American men. Again, one could construct the curriculum differently, but would need to plan for that to happen.

Now consider how this narrative structure and point of view teaches an ideology teachers may not intend.[1] In spring 2003, while watching TV coverage of the U.S. invasion of Iraq, I happened to be examining this framework and standards document, and was struck by some additional parallels between its basic assumptions and those being used to justify the war. It struck me that, by planning curriculum around the content standards, one could end up teaching an ideology that supports U.S. imperialism, without realizing one was doing so. Most U.S. citizens deny strongly that the United States is an imperial power, even though the United States was born of British imperialism and acquired its territory through imperialism. Imperialist nations generally teach their own version of the colonization process, while at the same time actively discounting or eradicating alternative versions and denying their imperialist history.

California's content standards obscure the negative impacts of European and U.S. imperialism mainly by glossing over the process of conquest, while presenting imperialism through maps, time lines, and stories of adventure. For example, in third, fourth, fifth and eighth grades, U.S. acquisition of California from Mexico, the westward movement of Whites, and the policy of Manifest Destiny are presented largely as map study and as exciting stories of adventure. Similarly, European exploration and colonization are presented mainly as map study and adventures of explorers. The term *colonist* in the standards refers simply to some people of European descent who lived in the Northeast between the 1600s and 1700s. The standards mention expansionist wars such as the Spanish-American War, but not in terms of the United States acquiring other people's land (such as Puerto Rico). Thus, when studying U.S. and European expansionism, the standards do not mention the brutality of conquest, ethical questions about appropriating the land of other people or using power to gain wealth, or substantive study of colonization from points of view of colonized peoples.

While denying that the United States is or has been an imperial power, the standards guide students in learning to divide the world into a we-they binary, empathize with "we," and see U.S. institutions as innately superior. From sixth grade on, the standards embody three overlapping binaries:

1. *Western versus non-Western.* Sixth and seventh graders study various civilizations of the past, categorized as Western and non-Western. They are to learn that the United States grew from Western civilizations (a theme that is repeated in 10th and 12th grades). They are to identify how the ancient Greeks, Romans, and Hebrews influenced values and institutions of the West, providing a basis for Enlightenment philosophy and English parliamentary systems. Non-Western ancient civilizations (e.g., Mesopotamia, Egypt, India, China, Japan, north Africa), while studied, remain disconnected from "our" culture, values, and institutions.

2. *Judeo-Christian versus other religious traditions.* Standards for sixth and seventh grades specify studying world religions, giving most attention to the history of Christianity. Students also study a little about values and beliefs of Buddhism, Confucianism, Judaism, and civilizations of Islam, but Judeo-Christian stories predominate.

3. *Democratic political systems and free-market economies versus totalitarian systems.* Students compare democratic–free-market systems with totalitarianism systems mainly at the high school level. In 12th grade, they compare and contrast various forms of government, particularly dictatorships versus democracies. Communist systems receive considerable attention, emphasizing their poor human rights records, their restrictions on individual liberty, and their general failure.

The standards fold diverse people of the United States into this Western, Judeo-Christian "we" mainly by recommending celebration of cultural contributions of diverse groups, using the cultural difference ideology. Cultural celebration is a comfortable theme that can be layered onto U.S. expansion and conquest without disrupting it. The standards have difficulty incorporating people the United States had previously colonized, so they simply ignore colonized peoples outside of California such as Puerto Ricans and Hawaiians. The standards treat Mexicans mainly within the immigrant paradigm. They treat American Indians implicitly more as "they" than "we," mainly by persistently locating indigenous people in the past.

The standards paint the political and economic systems of the United States in positive terms, and nondemocratic as well as noncapitalistic systems in negative terms. The terms *free, choice, rational,* and *liberty* are linked repeatedly with both capitalism and representative democracy. From first through twelfth grade, students are to learn how free-market economies take their direction from individual choices of consumers, as representative democracies obtain power from the consent of citizens. In seventh grade, for example, they are to learn that capitalism grew out of the Enlightenment: As Europeans developed rational thinking, they also developed capitalist market economies based on private ownership and free choice. (The standards don't point out that corporate boards of directors are not popularly elected, and boards routinely dismiss substantive shareholder participation.) Secondary-level students are to study an amalgamation of totalitarian governments, communist regimes, and socialist economies specifically to emphasize their severe shortcomings. For example, students are to examine the former Soviet Union and China as communist countries that tried unsuccessfully to modernize by imposing collectivism and communist ideology. Further, by conflating political and economic systems, students can learn not to notice economic conquest of nations by absorbing their economies into largely U.S. controlled transnational corporations.

While the curriculum acknowledges that U.S. political and economic systems are imperfect, it claims they are the best humankind has developed. Therefore, the United States has a responsibility to take our systems to other countries, since ours are superior. Claims that the United States is "liberating" other countries when it invades them and then rebuilds them according to a U.S. image, resonate with the deep structure of ideology embedded in the standards. Designed to promote national loyalty, these standards are constructed around a story of "us" as the virtuous people, which makes it difficult to examine injustice squarely, particularly from points of view of colonized peoples.

If a teacher is aware of the underlying ideology, he or she can construct curriculum differently. For example, Chapters 5 and 6 feature Angela, who became concerned about the sharp contrast of the ideology of the history–social science standards and her textbook with that in writings of indigenous scholars, and on that basis developed a short unit in which students confront different historical experiences.

Content standards are not ideologically neutral; they confer power on knowledge systems that derive from someone's point of view. Although I illustrated with history–social science, one can analyze other disciplines for what points of view they embody, and whose knowledge they authorize, blunt, or exclude. For example, in an analysis of proposed national arts standards, Anderson (1996) argued that dividing the arts into four disciplines—"art, music, dance, and theater—and dividing visual art into the DBAE [disciplinary-based art education] ordered disciplines of production, criticism, art history, and aesthetics is quintessentially Western in conception and structure" (p. 58). He went on to point out that in many non-Western cultures, the arts are not constructed around Western disciplines, but are integrated, and do not lend themselves to discipline-based study.

Because of the nonneutrality of standards, I find it useful to distinguish between *standards-driven* curriculum planning and *standards-conscious* curriculum planning. Standards-driven planning starts with the standards and draws big ideas directly from them. The standards become the main source of the curriculum. In standards-conscious planning, the standards are a tool, but not the starting point, and do not define the central organizing ideas and ideology of one's curriculum. Rather, the teacher first selects big ideas from a range of other sources, including transformative knowledge, student interests, and teacher interests. Then the teacher maps curriculum against the standards. Teacher vignettes in this book reflect standards-conscious backward planning around big ideas.

POSSIBILITIES AND CHALLENGES

Quantities of curriculum standards push teachers toward content coverage, a problem that recurs throughout this book. As noted earlier, Kauffman and colleagues (2002) discovered that new teachers saw standards as long lists of concepts and skills to cover and found themselves running frantically from one topic to the next. Elementary teachers, particularly, can find themselves with different standards documents for each subject area, organized differently and with little connection to each other.

Although the English Language Arts standards Christi was expected to follow are voluminous, she was able to "chunk" them into broad skills she could teach meaningfully, such as narrative writing. Once she viewed them as chunks, she could then figure out how to link them with big ideas she wanted to teach. Christi's complex unit spanned 3 weeks time. As a seventh-year teacher, she did not start by planning and teaching something so complex. She explained to me that although she was teaching this unit for the first time, it built on smaller pieces she had designed and taught before.

I've actually been collecting over the last 7 years, because, you know, I've always wanted to do something like this, but it's big, and it's intense, and I wasn't really sure, you know, if I was ready for it before. But now, it's like, I tried it a little bit 2 years ago, little baby steps, and it worked out great! (February 24, 2004)

Over time, she learned how to incorporate multiple standards into a complex project and developed a sense of which standards are most important. Further, she had the support of her building administrators and several teaching colleagues, who did not expect her to march through the standards and textbook.

Other experienced teachers also told me they generally started small and needed time to get to know the basic curriculum for their grade level and subject area. Juanita, a fifth-year teacher who is featured in Chapter 7, spent her first two years becoming familiar with the curriculum for second grade.

[When I started] I did not know the standards that well. I just kind of knew they were out there, somewhere. And we had to implement them, so how? But, with the years of experience I have had, [now] I know my standards. . . . The standards have just guided me, let's put it that way. I don't see them as my core belief, like I believe this is what kids need to know. No, this is what they could *possibly* know by the end of the year. (February 10, 2004)

As a fifth-year teacher, she had developed a sense of which ideas and skills are "enduring," and which are not. She could play with curriculum and still teach skills her students would be expected to know. Also, she had her principal's support for experimenting.

Teachers who were newer to the teaching profession approached standards-conscious curriculum planning with more trepidation and took on smaller chunks. Some said that they were afraid to stray away from the standards and textbooks because they might be fired. I didn't know whether they actually would be fired, but I do know that teachers in schools with low test scores were under tremendous pressure to raise scores. If their principals equated standards and texts with curriculum, and teaching with covering facts and skills, teachers felt boxed into following what they were told to do.

Being in the process of learning to teach, newer teachers tended to trust at least some of the standards and texts, sometimes over their own judgment. For example, Cheryl was a fourth-year teacher, but in her second year of teaching second grade when I visited her classroom (Cheryl is featured in more detail in Chapter 8). She loved children's literature and enjoyed experimenting with ways of extending from and building on main ideas in her school's adopted reading–language arts text. In the context of reading a story by Gary Soto, for example, she expanded by teaching about his background and reading more of his stories. But having been credentialed in a one-year program in which literacy methods coursework prepares for grade levels spanning K through 8, the specific knowledge she brought about teaching reading to second graders was not yet very deep. She said that when she first started to teach, "I knew what the standards were, I was really hitting them, but I was probably jumping around too much, going from here to there" (February 13, 2003). She explained that the scripted second-grade reading curriculum her school was now using was more systematic than what she knew how to organize herself, and it covered what the students would be tested on, so following it made more sense to her than planning new units on her own.

Scripted curriculum packages in fact structure curriculum quite extensively, leaving only small spaces for a teacher's own judgment about what to teach. In addition, the standards and texts structure multicultural content around topics (e.g., Chinese New Year) that might not be those that would emerge from transformative intellectual knowledge. Thus standards documents represent compromises over what is most worth knowing, victories for some, and silencing of others. Teachers cannot fix this problem, but can learn to engage with it.

It takes development of a sense of perspective for learning to identify central ideas, then planning meaningful curriculum around them. Christi explained that it took her several years to work up to her West Coast immigration unit, and Juanita commented that she needed the first 2 years to become familiar with content normally taught at the second grade level. Beginning teachers find identification of big ideas difficult, even if they know their subject matter well, because they are new to teaching at specific grade levels. Nonetheless, the process of thinking through curriculum in relationship to big ideas, rather than as lists of content to cover, is valuable and ultimately leads to well-planned and meaningful curriculum.

It is important for school leaders to recognize the value of designing curriculum around big ideas. As administrators worry about how to bring up test scores, many are increasingly directing teachers to deliver to students long lists of isolated bits of information and skills. Over the short run, such a process of teaching to tests might bring up scores, but over the long run, it does not necessarily engage students intellectually. Since curriculum and assessment are directly linked, the next chapter examines assessment, first in relationship to standardized testing, then in relationship to classroom-based assessment. There, we consider how Christi used qualitative measures of assessment to guide teaching and learning.

NOTE

1. A slightly modified version of this next section appeared in Sleeter (2004), *Rethinking Schools, 19*(1): 26–29. I am grateful to Bill Bigelow for his suggestions on that article, some of which are reflected here.

Chapter 4

Democratized Assessment

In a way, I feel like I'm teaching to the test, I have to. I think, OK, I've seen this on the test, so I'm going to focus on it, so that's my key standard. 'Cause the tests are becoming more standards based. Not to say that's good or bad.
(Juanita, elementary teacher, February 10, 2004)

For me, I hate the tests in the first place, I'll put that on the record anywhere. 'Cause these tests don't show any kind of validity in what [students] are learning, at all, to me.
(Mona, elementary teacher, April 22, 2004)

Assessment tends to drive curriculum. Teachers across the nation feel caught between a test-driven conception of assessment and more authentic forms. Even though Juanita, above, bases many of her curriculum decisions on what engages her students and what will prepare them for college (as will be discussed in Chapter 7), she also keeps an eye on tests they will take and, at times, feels like she ends up teaching to tests. Mona (also featured in Chapter 7) is very concerned about discrepancies between capabilities and knowledge her students display in class and those captured on standardized tests. The feelings of these teachers reflect concerns of others who care deeply about student learning and work hard to teach well, but remain skeptical about test-driven school reform.

Assessment is part of a larger set of questions relating to curriculum. Assessment generally asks how well students learned the curriculum. But what is assessment to be used for, to whom is it accountable, and how does it shape curriculum? As Apple (1977) argued, "while evaluation is considered to be 'merely' a technical problem by many educators, it is just as clearly an ethical concern" (p. 486). Many are concerned that the "reform by testing" context is narrowing curriculum to what is on state tests, particularly in low-achieving schools.

Classroom-based, democratized assessment, on the other hand, should help guide instruction by giving both teachers and students feedback on learning, and should allow students to show what they know and can do. It should also prompt evaluation of the curriculum itself, as teachers try to make sense of how students perceive and experience it. Failure of students to learn or participate may say more about students' resistance to the curriculum (or to the teacher) than about their ability to learn. This chapter continues the "backwards" planning approach from Chapter 3, linking assessment with curriculum organized for student engagement with big ideas. However, since classrooms are situated within standards-based assessment systems that increasingly drive curriculum and instruction at the classroom level, we begin with this larger context.

REFORM-BY-TESTING AND CURRICULUM

The logic behind standards-based reform-by-testing is that if states set clear, high standards, align curriculum to them, teach to them, test student mastery of them, and attach consequences to test results (such as whether a student receives a diploma or whether a school receives good or bad publicity), then teaching and learning will improve (Kornhaber, 2004). This logic comes from the social efficiency perspective about the purpose of schooling: to prepare young people for the needs of society, particularly employment in an expanding capitalist economy. Schools are conceptualized as factories producing workers; curriculum and systems of measuring achievement derive largely from needs of prospective employers (Shepard, 2000).

No Child Left Behind legislation, embedded within this logic, is receiving mixed reviews. While some find standardized testing to be a very useful lever to improve teaching and learning, especially for students from historically underserved communities (e.g., see "Don't turn back the clock," 2003; Hunt, 2003), others find it punishes those very same students (e.g., see Orfield & Kornhaber, 2001). Nationally, there is tremendous controversy over whether standards-based reform by testing promotes or undermines equity. I suspect that some of this controversy results from how assessment is actually used in particular schools, school districts, and states. As Hood (1998) pointed out, the issue is not so much what kind of assessment is used, but "whether inferences and decisions made from test scores are appropriate for different groups" (p. 189).

The extent to which achievement testing can serve as a tool to close teaching and learning gaps probably depends on the extent to which school leaders directly confront the deficiency paradigm. Facing achievement gaps squarely requires interpretation of why they exist. As Gay (2000) argued, there is a real danger in "merely belaboring the disproportionately poor academic performance of certain students of color, or blaming their families and social-class backgrounds" (p. xiii) without seriously reworking the ideology through which academic performance is interpreted and addressed. I have seen panicked schools adopt incredibly simplistic practices in attempts to raise the achievement of students from low-income communities, communities of color, and Spanish-speaking communities. Some of these include trying to treat children as if they were all identical, turning curriculum into test preparation, or threatening untenured teachers with dismissal if they don't bring up test scores. In some schools, teachers are being helped to identify individual students for intense instruction based on the likelihood that their scores will rise enough to make the school or subgroup reach its target. Students who are too far behind are not selected for the same intense help if the effort is deemed unlikely to make the school reach its target.[1]

In 1999 California had established an accountability system similar to No Child Left Behind's system, and now uses both systems to set targets for schools and subgroups within schools.[2] Five of the eight teachers featured in this book teach in our local county where, although there is considerable discussion about the achievement gap problem, it is not clear to what extent test data are helping to close achievement gaps. Test data are reported by school; it is relatively easy to find out whether subgroup targets have been met for individual schools. However, using publicly reported data, it is not as easy to discern average scores of various subgroups, or to compare achievement of various subgroups (for instance, Latinos versus Whites) across schools or school districts. The county Office of Education has focused heavily on raising achievement in the lowest achieving schools, reporting some success in doing so (Friedrich, 2004). But browsing through information made public on the Internet, I had difficulty determining if there was a general trend in closing achievement gaps among racial, ethnic, language, or social-class groups between, rather than within, county schools. Although considerable data are available, analyses of such trends are scarce. Teachers know whether their own school's scores are improving or not, but I have heard informally that they lack a sense of how well achievement gaps are being addressed or how test data are being used to address them. None of the data I gathered from teachers for this book included any discussion of how testing was being used to monitor and address achievement gaps.

Below I briefly review controversy over reform by testing in relationship to comments teachers made in Multicultural Curriculum Design. In fall 2001 testing was not a major topic of discussion since schools were only beginning to feel its full force. But by fall 2003 teachers had a lot to say, mainly expressing frustration. Those who see standards-based reform-by-testing as a tool for promoting equity emphasize its use to monitor the effectiveness of efforts to improve teaching and learning. For example, Reyes, Scribner, and Scribner (1999) found that four high-performing Hispanic schools in Texas used assessment for advocacy rather than simply to assign grades or describe achievement levels. There, norm-referenced testing was used regularly to monitor progress. Testing itself, however, was not dwelt upon. Instead, the schools used additional assessment processes to improve instruction on a daily basis, making considerable use of authentic assessment, as will be discussed later in this chapter. The schools also regularly assessed students' proficiency in both English and Spanish; teachers understood that bilingual children may know more in one language than they can demonstrate in another.

Many reports show measured achievement in specific school districts and states to be improving, and gaps among subgroups closing (Fuller & Johnson, 2001; Haycock, 2001; Palmaffy, 1998; Roderick, Jacob, & Bryk, 2002; Skrla, Scheurich, Johnson, & Koschoreck, 2001). For example, the Education Trust (2003) pointed out that the achievement gap between White students and African American and Latino students narrowed on the National Assessment of Education progress during the 1970s and 1980s, then remained constant. The report went on to cite high-minority, low-income schools in which there has been a significant recent closing of the achievement gap as well as outstanding academic performance on standardized tests. Engelhard Elementary School in Louisville, Kentucky, and Hambrick Middle School in Aldine, Texas, are two such schools. Advocates of reform by testing argue that schools can no longer simply ignore low expectations and underachievement of students from historically oppressed communities, and that testing serves as a tool for addressing this problem. Further, advocates sometimes point out that since tests are used in colleges and elsewhere, everyone needs to learn to take them effectively (C. D. Lee, 1998).

Those who question the use of tests as a tool for promoting equity express concerns about three main areas: (1) the track record of standardized testing in communities of color, (2) curricular consequences of testing, and (3) inequitable student and community consequences. In regard to the first concern, there are equity-related historic reasons to distrust reform by testing. Kornhaber (2004) explained that "historically . . . over-reliance on testing for making decisions about students has not produced sustained efforts to improve educational equity in the United States" (p. 99). Critics point to the history of connections between intelligence testing and the eugenics movement, and the uses of testing to track students of color into lower tracks, classify them as retarded or in need of special education, and block entry into higher education (C. D. Lee, 1998). Townsend

(2002) characterized this history as "testing while Black." Wiley and Wright (2004) argued that the "scientific testing" movement was biased:

> The rise of the modern educational technologist-oriented curriculum making and the rise of the scientific educational testing movement coincided with the period of Americanization and widespread xenophobia toward non-English-speaking immigrants and lynchings of African Americans and discrimination against other racial minority groups. . . . Thus, the so-called scientific testing movement of the early 20th century was intertwined with racism and linguicism at a time when the push for expanded uses of restrictive English-literacy requirements coincided with the period of record immigration. (pp. 158–159)

Leaders of the standards movement insist that today's tests are different since they set uniform standards for everyone and most are criterion-referenced rather than norm-referenced. However, most standards-based tests still retain characteristics that cause concern:

> [They] rely heavily on multiple-choice questions, language skills, problem solving undertaken by individuals in isolation, and time limits and content coverage designed to maximize the spread of scores. . . . Not surprisingly, therefore, on a range of assessments clear differences remain in average scores across economic, racial, and ethnic groups. These score differences continue to affect access to higher level learning opportunities for students. (Kornhaber, 2004. p. 93)

Further, they generate revenue to test developers, confer political gain on politicians who support them, and confer advantages disproportionately to students from upper socioeconomic communities (Grant, 2004). Many teachers in historically underserved communities have pointed out that "results of standardized achievement tests contradicted their first-hand classroom observations and assessments of students of color [which] revealed higher levels of student performance on targeted learning objectives" (Hood, 1998, p. 189). This was Mona's concern at the opening of this chapter.

Some of the teachers in Multicultural Curriculum Design were well aware of this history and wary because of it. An elementary bilingual teacher said,

> We're asked to do this standardized testing, which is racist, it's based on a system of racism. It's normed to certain language groups, and it's basically biased against a whole group of other language learners. And we're asked to use it and advocate for a system we don't believe in. (October 19, 2001)

In regard to the second area of concern, critics of reform by testing emphasize the impact of testing on curriculum. Assessment controls what gets taught; the press to standardize curriculum reduces the possibility of creating curriculum that is culturally relevant to one's own students, and substantially narrows how teachers think about learning or what they see as the purpose of schooling. Many reports document the narrowing of curriculum in which teaching to the test (and teaching how to take tests) substitutes for deeper intellectual inquiry, and subjects and concepts that are not tested are simply dropped (Hillocks, 2002; Jones, Jones, & Hargrove, 2003; Kohn, 2002; Lipman, 2004; McNeil & Valenzuela, 2001; Meier, 2002; Stecher, 2001).

Teachers I worked with expressed variations of this concern more than any other. They emphasized reduced space for creative lessons and increased anxiety about making sure they teach what is on the test. For example, one commented, "Because my school is so small our principal has asked that we share teaching art, science, and social studies. The anxiety that teachers feel to meet standards restricts their sense of creating toward 'inclusion' curriculum" (Mona, October 13, 2003). Others talked about their concern for making sure they hit what children will be tested over as they choose what to spend time teaching and what to skip. For example, one teacher commented, "But still then we have these standards over here for science and social studies. I try and hit the bigger ones, you know. I mean, you can't hit everything, but at least the ones they're going to be tested on. You more or less try to hit that" (Cheryl, February 5, 2004).

Teachers were also concerned about narrowing the vision of what schools are for. For example, one teacher said, "I see this emphasis on testing as a political issue because when one is frantically trying to 'get all the skills,' there is little time or energy left over for examining the content of what is supposed to be taught, and thus the imposed curriculum remains in place" (Kathy, October 13, 2003). Lost is consideration of schools as public spaces where young people might learn to engage with different perspectives, empathize with others, or engage in social problem solving. Lost, too, are discussions about what it means to learn, how to cultivate inquiry and love of learning, or how to encourage the development of artistic or ethical sensibilities.

Further, narrowing of curriculum and pressure to teach to the tests occurs disproportionately in schools serving low-income students and students of color (Kornhaber, 2004; Lipman, 2004; Madaus & Clarke, 2001; McNeil & Valenzuela, 2001). Although tests presume to measure general achievement and learning, critics point out that scores on high-stakes content tests do not necessarily correlate with other established measures of student learning, such as the NAEP, SAT, and advanced placement testing (Amrein & Berliner, 2002; Linn, Baker, & Betebenner, 2002; Shepard, 2000). One of the teachers pointed out that fixation on content standards and tests drew teachers' attention away from what students know and can do, giving the illusion of addressing a problem without actually addressing it.

Finally, in regard to the third area of concern, critics point to consequences on students and communities. It is not clear, for example, what will happen to students who do not pass tests required for graduation. Use of exit exams for graduation tends to reduce graduation rates and increase dropout rates for students of color, language-minority students, and students from poverty communities (Haney, 2000; Madaus & Clarke, 2001; Natriello & Pallas, 2001; Ruiz de Velasco, 2005). Starting with the class of 2006, California students will have to pass an exit exam to graduate. On the exit exam given to sophomores in 2004, only 42 percent of our local county's students classified as not yet fluent in English passed the English section (Friedrich, 2004). In 2 years, what will become of those who have not yet passed? Traditional tests also fail to capture what students with disabilities can do. School administrators are reporting concern that minimum competency graduation exams, especially if imposed without additional resources, will lead students with disabilities to leave school without graduating (Manset-Williamson & Washburn, 2002).

In many communities, testing serves as a substitute for investing resources to reduce class sizes, develop good school libraries, and help teachers plan and teach rich and engaging curricula (Orfield & Kornhaber, 2001; Lipman, 2004); testing is cheaper and seems easier than funding and developing schools as rich intellectual spaces. J. Lee (in press) argues that we should be paying at least as much attention to between-school gaps as within-school gaps, because between-school achievement gaps correlate with and contribute to racial segregation. As long as attention is directed toward achievement gaps within schools, gaps across schools and school districts that overlap with segregated housing are not addressed. Publication of test results in newspapers not only damages teacher morale in low-achieving schools, but is also widely used by realtors to steer home-buyers into some neighborhoods and away from others, increasing residential segregation. For example, in a recent newspaper article, Ginsburg (2004) reported, "Fewer family home buyers are seeking public schools in urban centers like San Francisco and Oakland, where test scores are dismal, where per capita spending is among the nation's worst, where residency does not guarantee acceptance in the nearest school and where homeowners with a choice pick private education." Ultimately, as public schools fail to meet targets, there is growing concern that the system of public education will be replaced by a privatized system in which profit and the market replace the public good as fundamental goals and values (e.g., Apple, 2001; Bracey, 2003; Valenzuela, 2005).

These issues were of great concern to the teachers in Multicultural Curriculum Design, and teachers felt powerless to address them. Nevertheless, although teachers are affected by the context in which they work, teachers' work takes place mainly in their own classrooms, where they do have some power and can implement culturally relevant assessment.

CLASSROOM-BASED ASSESSMENT

Assessment is a useful part of curriculum planning and instruction when used as a guide to improve student learning. *Performance assessment* is particularly useful in this regard. Performance assessment refers to assessing student learning through a variety of means including "things like classroom observation, projects, portfolios, performance exams, and essays" (Neill et al., 1995, p. 1). Performance assessment follows a different logic from standardized testing. According to the logic of performance assessment, educators identify what high-quality work looks like, articulate criteria and standards that can be used to judge it, use those criteria to guide student learning and give ongoing feedback on student work, and evaluate students' finished work according to how close it comes to high-quality work in the discipline (Kornhaber, 2004). Bottom-up planning, in which teachers and even students can participate in the process of constructing assessment systems, is what it means to democratize assessment. This section is entitled "Classroom-Based Assessment" mainly because it focuses on what teachers can do, even within a reform-by-testing context. Classroom-based assessment follows a different logic that could conceivably be used as the driving logic of larger assessment systems.[3]

It is probably possible to make locally developed or locally selected assessment systems culturally relevant for specific students more than statewide systems. All forms of assessment, including testing and classroom-based assessment, should be culturally relevant. Gay (2000) defined culturally responsive or *culturally relevant teaching* as "using the cultural knowledge, prior experiences, frames of reference, and performance styles of ethnically diverse students to make learning encounters more relevant to and effective for them. It teaches to and through the strengths of these students" (p. 29). Based on a review of research on connections between achievement, pedagogy, and student culture, she concluded that when instructional processes are consistent with the cultural orientations, experiences, and learning styles of marginalized African, Latino, Native, and Asian American students, their school achievement improves significantly. This success is most evident in learning "spaces" where culturally relevant content, teacher attitudes and expectations, and instructional actions converge. (p. 181)

It is important to stress that culturally relevant pedagogy and assessment are shaped around the actual lived cultures of one's own students rather than general descriptions of particular groups, an idea elaborated on in Chapter 7.[4]

Culturally relevant assessment involves using tasks or test items and evaluation criteria that relate to the experiences, point of view, and language of the students whose learning is being assessed. As Hood (1998) put it, culturally relevant assessments, like culturally relevant curriculum and pedagogy, "are grounded in the cultural contexts of examinees of color" (p. 188). Mahari (1998) described it as "alternative paths that permit elbow room for varied cultural and participatory styles as well as more mediums and strategies for representing knowledge" (p. 7). Advocates of culturally relevant assessment for students from historically marginalized communities do not see simply replacing traditional tests with performance assessment as the solution, but rather using both (e.g., Hood, 1998; C. D. Lee, 1998).

There are several questions that teachers can use to examine classroom-based assessment for cultural relevance. First, to what extent do assessment items or tasks tap into the knowledge students actually have, or relate to what they know? This does not mean that assessment should cover only what students know, but rather that it should avoid items or tasks that are not central to what is being assessed and require knowledge that students are not familiar with. For example, assessing urban students' math skills with story problems about agriculture turns the assessment into one of agricultural knowledge as well as math. Second, to what extent do the assessment processes facilitate students showing what they know and can do? For example, a social studies assessment that uses essay writing may not allow students who write poorly to show what they know about social studies, whereas one that uses projects or oral performance would. Assessments in English do not allow second-language learners who learned content or skills in another language to show what they know.

Building on these two questions, a teacher might ask, to what extent do assessment results guide ongoing instruction? If assessment is used to help guide instruction, constructing it as a tool to help the teacher become more familiar with what students know makes assessment not only fair to students but also instructionally useful to the teacher. Planning assessment along with a unit's big ideas helps teachers visualize what they actually want students to learn, what sort of evidence of student learning they should look for, what kinds of assignments would provide that evidence, and how to use assessment as a "feedback loop" for continuous modification of curriculum and instruction. In the Multicultural Curriculum Design course, planning assessment begins with identifying the big idea that is central to the unit teachers are designing (using in particular Questions 6 and 9 in Figure 3.1). Wiggins and McTighe (1998) recommended writing out descriptions of what it looks like when students understand the central idea or concept, then identifying the forms of evidence that would demonstrate their understanding.

Having done this in fall 2003, I then asked: "Against what criteria will one judge such evidence? What are the kinds of things to look for?" (Wiggins & McTighe, p. 68). Teachers always use criteria when making judgments about students' learning, but often do not make their criteria explicit. Not only does articulating one's criteria make explicit what one is looking for, but it also offers an opportunity to reflect on the extent to which those criteria are fair and culturally relevant, and the extent to which they relate to other criteria against which teachers and students are being held accountable. Further, reflecting on criteria for evaluating learning is an important way of broadening what counts as learning. If standardized testing tends to narrow what counts as learning to what is on tests, here is where teachers can specify valuing dimensions of learning not in tests, such as empathy, perspective taking, or democratic competence. In the vignette below, Christi used what she referred to as knowledge of the subject and "heart knowledge," or empathy.

To think through assessment criteria, I asked the teachers to take a sample of student work, a sample assignment, or a learning outcome, and describe the criteria they would use when deciding how well students are learning. Then we went on to consider *standards*. Standards identify degrees of understanding. At the very least, teachers make judgments regarding whether students "get" a concept sufficiently to pass or move on. What is the difference between having understood a concept well enough, and *not* well enough? What does this look like? (Teachers often recognize these questions about standards and criteria as questions their students ask.) Wiggins and McTighe (1998) suggested a progression of standards ranging from novice to expert, so that both teachers and students can visualize degrees of understanding. If teachers are to communicate externally what their standards are, reflecting on the meaning of high standards in relationship to a given major concept, skill, or idea is essential. Even though external audiences (such as parents and policy makers) currently are tuned in mainly to test scores, test scores do not describe what standards actually mean. Clear explanations by teachers, using language everyday people can understand, can serve as a tool for making public what operational standards are actually being used in the classroom.

After teachers have thought through and written down answers to these questions, I then have them create rubrics. A *rubric* specifies criteria teachers will use for evaluation and standards that clarify at least two levels: good enough, and *not* good enough. Making visible criteria and standards for evaluation helps students know what a teacher expects. I recently heard a ninth grader explain to her peers that she finds rubrics helpful for this reason. Evaluating student projects with rubrics is not the only form of classroom-based assessment; for example, quizzes can be useful. But even quizzes implicitly embody at least one criterion against which students are being evaluated, and at least two standards—passing and *not* passing.

We also discuss the difference between evaluating students' work at the end of the unit, term, or semester (*summative assessment*), and using assessment as an ongoing tool to give students feedback and to fine-tune instruction along the way (*formative assessment*). After giving teachers time and help developing a rubric and thinking through how and when they might use it, I then have them share their thinking with each other to get feedback on whether it makes sense and seems fair and useful.

Throughout the semester, the teachers in Multicultural Curriculum Design had been experiencing this evaluation system, since I use rubrics to assess all of their assignments, periodically draw teachers' attention to them to show what I am looking for, and occasionally alter rubrics based on teachers' input. For example, Table 4.1 shows a rubric for evaluating a paper that I have teachers write, in which they investigate transformative intellectual knowledge (described in Chapter 5). As the table illustrates, I evaluate this paper on the basis of three criteria: work with historically subjugated knowledge, reflective analysis, and clarity of presentation. The description of the standard "Exemplary" clarifies what I am looking for in strong papers. I return papers at the "Emerging" level for continued work; "Developing" level papers are acceptable. The descriptions within the rubric are fairly compact, and I spend quite a bit of time clarifying them and giving examples. Sometimes I ask teachers to self-evaluate drafts of their own work, or to evaluate each other's work, using rubrics like this. When students can use (and even create) criteria and standards to self-evaluate, assessment becomes a tool for self-empowerment.

We spent one class session on criteria, standards, and rubrics in relationship to units the teachers were developing. This work turned out to be more difficult than I had anticipated. An experienced teacher who was

Table 4.1. Rubric for Evaluating Paper Investigating Transformative
Intellectual Knowledge

Standard	Work with Historically Subjugated Knowledge	Reflective Analysis	Clarity of Presentation
Exemplary	You read and synthesize a focused body of substantive intellectual scholarship of at least one historically underrepresented group, and your paper accurately represents "insider" perspectives of that group based on your reading.	You accurately identify main ideas in the perspective from which authors you read work, and how those ideas can inform curriculum you plan to teach in your unit.	Paper is focused; ideas are well explained for a reader; paper is organized and free of distracting errors. You provide enough information, examples, and details that a reader can follow, and you use complete citations.
Developing	You read and synthesize intellectual work of at least one noted author of a historically underrepresented group, whose work relates to your unit.	You accurately identify main ideas in the work you read, and make some tentative connections to curriculum.	Ideas are fairly well explained and organized around a general focus. Paper may have some distracting errors, lack complete citations, or lack detail.
Emerging	You read material that relates to your unit and to historically underrepresented groups, but your paper doesn't clearly develop an "insider perspective," or lacks depth of content.	You identify information or implications for teaching based on your reading, but your paper doesn't develop a clear connection between your curriculum unit and main ideas in the work you read.	Information is missing, making it hard for a reader to follow. Paper has distracting errors, and may lack a clear focus or organization.

used to writing and using rubrics quickly wrote a clear and useful one. Some of the experienced teachers, such as Christi, realized that they were not yet clear about the assignments they would use in their unit, so they began working on a specific assignment in conjunction with a rubric. Several beginning teachers were still trying to clarify what they wanted students to learn, as opposed to what sorts of activities they would have students do. For example, one filled in rubric boxes with lists of elements that should be in a poster she wanted students to create, but had difficulty explaining how the poster was to reflect learning, and what criteria she might use to determine whether students were learning. By the end of

the semester, Christi's unit had a clear assessment plan. Since her learning outcomes and unit rationale were discussed in Chapter 3, her assessment plan is described below in order to show what classroom-based
assessment for multicultural curriculum can look like.

Christi: Knowledge of the Subject and Heart Knowledge

Christi's unit on West Coast Immigration contained a well-defined plan
for assessing student learning. She posted her entire unit on the Internet
so that it would be available to students. There she described the overall
rationale for the unit, listed the learning outcomes (described in Chapter
3) and content standards to which they related, listed and described the
various assignments students would be doing along with evaluation rubrics for each assignment, and posted notes for each day, including hand-
outs, homework, and readings that would be used in class.

As described earlier, the unit developed students' writing skills as well
as their knowledge of and empathy toward teenage immigrants to the West
Coast. Explaining her basic approach to assessment, Christi said that she
steers clear of testing when teaching writing.

> It doesn't make any sense with this unit to test them, you know.
> Basically, it's just looking at their writing, seeing how are they
> progressing. Looking at their ideas. Are they developing in their
> knowledge of the subject, and also their heart knowledge? Do they
> have insights? (February 24, 2004)

In other words, reasonable evidence of student learning would be writing, as well as insights students articulate in class discussion.

Students completed four projects that combined these general areas
of knowledge and skill: a narrative writing assignment, a diary, a poem,
and a Web page. All four assignments used students' research on West
Coast immigrants and writing skills they developed through the unit.
Working in small groups, students chose an ethnic background of an immigrant to research and write about, so students had some choice in what
they would be assessed over.

Each project included scaffolding and guidelines to help students construct quality work, examples of the form of writing that was asked for,
and an evaluation rubric. The narrative writing assignment, for example,
focused on writing how and why things happen, with plenty of vivid detail. On the Web site for the unit, Christi specified that "the [narrative]
writer uses rich concrete and sensory details that are relevant and combines them to develop a story line that is easy and interesting for the reader

to follow." To help students prepare to write a narrative about an immigrant, she had them begin to do research on their group's immigrant, and read (or view videos) and discuss narratives written from the point of view of an immigrant.

For example, one day the class read "On the Other Side of the War" by Elizabeth Gordon (1990), who was born in Vietnam to a Vietnamese mother and a European American father, then grew up in Tennessee after the Vietnam War. Christi led a discussion about the story that focused on both the author's experiences and biracial identity, as well as how she constructed the narrative and used figurative language. Some of the White students were puzzled by Gordon's struggles around a biracial identity: one asked why schools have students check a box indicating race, and another commented that one's race shouldn't matter.

The discussion of short stories was rather subdued in contrast to students' engagement with video. The Gordon story, for example, was followed by a 15-minute video clip from the film *Lakota Woman* (Pierson, Schellenberg, Runningfox, Cardinal, Bedard, and Brave Bird, 1994). It focused on Mary Crow Dog's experiences in a mission school, particularly the school's efforts to strip Indian youth of their identities, and various ways the youth resisted. The students seemed more engrossed in the video than they had been earlier when reading the Gordon story. I noticed that some rearranged their chairs so they could see it clearly, and a few sat on the floor in front of the TV. Even though the lights were turned down, no one appeared to be asleep. Later Christi commented that narrative stories, and particularly film, drew in students who were struggling with concepts like racism. Speaking about one of the White male students, she remarked, "I don't know, it seems like it engages them, it pulls them in, even if they don't want to be pulled in. And he doesn't want to be pulled in, and it's still, it sort of grabs him once in a while" (February 24, 2004).

To help students visualize how to write a narrative, Christi created a mock-up that illustrated a structure that students could follow. For the mock-up, she took an immigrant story from the book they were reading and "did these little chunks, so they get to read her narrative from the story that I created, as a guide for their own immigrant narratives" (February 24, 2004). Students also analyzed samples of writing to identify mood and tone, point of view, and sensory detail and imagery; and they practiced expanding their own use of detail words in descriptions.

To guide and assess students' written narratives, Christi constructed and used the rubric shown in Table 4.2. It specifies four criteria in two general areas: writing skill, and insight informed by content knowledge about the life of an immigrant. Christi used four qualitative levels (standards), numbered from 4 (high) to 1 (low). Point values could be assigned

Table 4.2. Christi's Rubric for Immigrant Narrative

Criteria

Points	Organization	Content knowledge	Concrete sensory details	Grammar and spelling
4	Student crafts information in a smooth logical sequence of events about the immigrant's growing-up years that engages the reader.	Student demonstrates a full knowledge of the content and presents the life of the immigrant in an insightful and reflective manner.	Student integrates rich concrete sensory details to create a vivid impression of the growing-up experiences of the immigrant.	Student exhibits a command of grammar and spelling.
3	Student effectively presents information in a logical sequence of events of the immigrant's growing-up years that the reader can clearly follow.	Student effectively demonstrates knowledge of the content that establishes some insight and reflection into the life of the immigrant.	Student effectively includes concrete sensory details that illustrate the growing-up experiences of the immigrant.	Student exhibits consistent control of grammar and spelling.
2	Student presents information about the immigrant's growing-up years in a way that is sometimes difficult to follow.	Student demonstrates some knowledge of content that shows little evidence of insight and reflection into the life of the immigrant.	Student introduces some concrete sensory details but in general is vague about growing-up experiences of the immigrant.	Student demonstrates some control of grammar and spelling.
1	Student presents information about the immigrant's growing-up years in a way that is consistently difficult to follow.	Student does not demonstrate a grasp of information and shows no insight or reflection into the life of the immigrant.	Student demonstrates a lack of concrete sensory details about the growing up experiences of the immigrant.	Student demonstrates no control of grammar or spelling.

Total ____

to students' writing. But the sum total of points is far less important than the guidance the rubric gives for what good narrative writing looks like. (It is significant that Christi is herself a narrative writer working on a novel.) This rubric not only reflects writing skills listed in the state's content standards, it also reflects central skills and concerns that narrative writers work with.

Christi's unit was not oriented directly toward teaching to the state's mandated tests. However, as an English teacher, she has to deal with tests her students are required to take:

> The struggle has been the standardized tests and the skills we're supposed to teach, the way we're supposed to teach them, the materials we get, stink. It turns the kids off instantly. They're gone, they're not getting it. . . . My struggle is always, OK, they want the kids to get used to the way the questions are, actually, the way the test looks. (February 24, 2004)

Thus, she was trying to figure out how to incorporate minitests into meaningful context so that the tests would not take over, but students would become familiar with their format.

POSSIBILITIES AND CHALLENGES

Assessment can be empowering when used as a tool for students to show what they know and can do, and for teachers and students to articulate clearly what they are working toward, judge progress and give feedback using understandable yardsticks, and gauge the rigor and integrity of the curriculum in meaningful terms. This is what Wiggins and McTighe (1998) intended when writing *Understanding by Design*. I found it more difficult than I had anticipated, however, to help teachers develop skill in designing and using classroom-based assessment meaningfully, in an intense context of reform by testing.

That context definitely hindered teachers from wanting to develop classroom-based plans for assessment. By academic year 2003–04, teachers in California were required to give so many tests, particularly at the elementary and middle school levels, that initially many viewed more assessment as overkill. For example, when Cheryl, a second-grade teacher, described her school's fairly scripted reading–language arts program, she listed a variety of tests she was required to give routinely to monitor student learning, exclaiming, "I give a whole lot of testing!" (February 5, 2004). Terri, a middle school teacher, described a new testing package her school would be adopting that would give each teacher a profile of each students' performance on specific areas of the state's testing program, so teachers could focus on remediating weaknesses: "So there's a lot more time and focus being given to what skills they're getting and what they're not, based on a test. One test, one day. And it all takes time, it takes time away from other things" (January 20, 2004). It appeared to me that imposed testing systems were substituting for teachers learning to use assessment as a tool in relationship to their own curriculum and students.

Further, teachers worried about the state-mandated tests that would be given in April. This was particularly true of beginning teachers. For example, Angela, a second-year elementary teacher, designed and taught a marvelous 3-day lesson that engaged students with Wampanoag and colonist points of view in the 1600s (Chapter 6). After she finished teaching it, I asked how she planned to continue to develop its ideas. She replied:

> The tests, the big tests, the state tests, they're all coming up in three months, and there's so much to teach, and, now this week everybody's way ahead of me because I took a week to kind of stop and really, really thoroughly investigate the Native Americans, what problems they might have had with the colonists, and all of this. And I think that's really important, but I also think it's really difficult to fit in those things when there's so much to be taught. (January 28, 2004)

The more tests teachers were to give, and the more pressure exerted on them to bring up test scores, the more resentful many felt because they could see their own curriculum being narrowed, and time for engaging activities being reduced.

At the same time, the newer teachers seemed baffled when I asked them to describe criteria against which they judged student learning, and standards they used to figure out degrees of understanding or learning. Their schools were teaching them how to anticipate and give tests, but appeared not to be developing their skill in thinking systematically for themselves about evaluation of student learning, an irony given the standards movement's emphasis on improving learning

An alternative to imposing tests on schools is to help teachers expect more from their students, and articulate and plan for high standards of learning based around curriculum teachers participate in developing. This is what I find intriguing about Nebraska's response to No Child Left Behind. As administrators and teachers in one of the larger districts in Nebraska have explained to me, teachers are involved in helping create their district's assessment system, and in the process are learning to use assessment more effectively and link curriculum and assessment in instructional meaningful ways. Performance assessments that use multiple sources of information and that involve teachers in thinking through assessment criteria and standards have the potential not only to improve teaching but also to empower teachers. However, doing so requires "profound alterations in teacher and student behaviors, substantial professional development, changes in school culture and in the organization of time in schools, and public support. These cannot be mandated, but they can be supported" (Neill & Gayler, 2001, p. 123).

NOTES

1. Gillborn and Youdell (2002) documented this system of educational triage being used in their study of schooling in Britain.

2. The Public School Accountability Act of 1999, passed by the California state legislature, directed the Superintendent of Public Instruction, with approval of the State Board of Education, to develop an Academic Performance Index (API) to measure performance of schools, based on students' academic performance, and gauge academic improvement by all ethnic and socioeconomic subgroups that constitute at least 15 percent of a school's population and at least 30 students. School performance measurements use a combination of state-written content tests and a norm-referenced test, given to all students in grades 2–11. Each school was given a baseline level based on test data in 1999, and for each subsequent year the performance target has been raised. Under this accountability system, beginning in 2000 the API has been used to measure school progress, rank all public schools, designate high-achieving schools, and invite underperforming schools to apply for grant money to fund school improvement programs. Since it forced schools to pay attention to low achievement of historically underserved students, this system led to concern about the achievement gap before this was being discussed on a large scale in many other parts of the nation.

3. I am currently helping an elementary school develop a qualitative performance assessment system they will use alongside the mandated testing system to evaluate learning, plan curriculum, and communicate with external audiences regarding the various subject areas as well as outcomes of the school as a whole.

4. For additional discussions of culturally relevant pedagogy, see Au & Carole, 1997; Franklin, 1992; Howard, 2003a; Irvine & Armento, 2001; Jordan, 1992; King, Hollins, & Hayman, 1997; Ladson-Billings, 1994; Roth & Damico, 1999.

Chapter 5

Transformative Intellectual Knowledge and Curriculum

I thought, what do I really want them to know about Mexico? And felt like the conquest was the really important part of history that they needed to understand, in order to understand modern-day Mexico and Mexican culture, and what the problems are. So I spend a lot of time with reading, writing, and discussion about how the social class system was set up via the conquest, and what are the repercussions of that.

(Gina, middle school dance teacher, December 8, 2001)

The conflict between what agriculture has become in this country and what it can be is at the heart of why I think that it is important to teach this unit, particularly in an area like ours where so many of my students' parents work in agriculture, yet so few can be farmers. . . . In the late 1950s, my uncle decided that he could no longer make a living from farming [the] land, and no one has tried to make a living from it since. In my own reading [of accounts by migrants from the Dust Bowl and other farmers], I've come across several accounts of this love for the land and the pain people feel when they can no longer earn their living by farming, particularly when they lose their land to debt.

(Kathy, first-grade bilingual teacher, December 15, 2003)

These two teachers have visions for who their students can become and what the world might become, based on a historical analysis of how it came to be as it is. Gina situates Mexican dance in a history of conquest and social-class relations, viewing dance as a cultural form that can ground her students and give them power. Kathy situates her students' families within competing paradigms of agriculture and the relationship between humans and the land. Gina's and Kathy's visions derive in part from their own life experience and deep familiarity with their students' communities. They also developed their visions from their study of historical, personal, and theoretical accounts by historically marginalized communities.

For years I have guided teachers and teacher education students in re-working curriculum from multicultural perspectives. However, I became increasingly frustrated when repeatedly I saw them create curriculum that reflected only superficial knowledge about historically marginalized groups, often incorporating stereotypes the teacher was not aware of. This chapter discusses a process I have used to help teachers strengthen their knowledge base in relationship to big ideas in their curriculum. If a teacher figures out the main concepts to teach, he or she can then think through what knowledge to use to develop these concepts. A packed curriculum seems to lack space for adding. But as teachers identify what is and is not essential, they can then identify content to take out, add, or rework to develop central concepts more deeply. After explaining what transformative intellectual knowledge is, this chapter will discuss it in relationship to current textbooks, then describe a process for investigating and working with it.

WHAT IS TRANSFORMATIVE INTELLECTUAL KNOWLEDGE?

The term *transformative intellectual knowledge* captures the "concepts, paradigms, and themes" that emerged through burgeoning critical traditions of scholarship in such areas as ethnic studies, women's studies, and disability studies (Banks, 1993, p. 9). Although the word itself is a mouthful, it contains three main ideas: (1) It serves as an umbrella term for bodies of knowledge that have been historically marginalized or subjugated, such as Chicano studies, gay/lesbian studies, women's studies, or ethnic studies. (2) It draws attention to understandings that challenge many mainstream assumptions, and that reenvision the world in ways that would benefit historically oppressed communities and support justice. (3) It highlights the work of intellectuals, such as historians, philosophers, or literary theorists, who have training in basing conclusions on evidence and in judging evidence on which knowledge claims rest. It goes beyond personal opinion or personal experiences.

Historically, knowledge systems as well as everyday knowledge have been subjugated as peoples have been subjugated. Defining peoples and knowledge as "backward," "uneducated," or "nonscientific" historically served as a rationale for exerting power over them and claiming access to their resources. For historically oppressed communities, unearthing subjugated knowledge is part of the process of political liberation, "a painstaking rediscovery of struggles together with the rude memory of their conflicts" (Foucault, 2000, p. 83). For example, writing about disability studies, Garland-Thomson (2002) explained that "disability—like gender—is a concept that pervades all aspects of culture: its structuring institutions, social identities, cultural practices, political dispositions, historical communities, and the shared experience of embodiment" (p. 4). People with disabilities have been studied for years, but relatively little study has been done from a historical consciousness of people with disabilities. Titchkoski (2000) explains, "What Disability Studies offers the academy is a disciplined way to study and confirm normate culture, and puts forward the possibility that the values and epistemological assumptions of 'normalcy' can be inserted into the world in a new way" (p. 219).

From perspectives of intellectuals from historically marginalized communities, knowledge is always situated in the context in which people create it, constructed, at least to some extent, in the service of knowledge creators' communities. Traditional mainstream academic disciplinary knowledge—the foundation of most school knowledge—has been largely rooted in experiences, concerns, points of view, and ways of knowing that emerged in Europe and among European Americans, particularly economically privileged men. While it has value, it also functions to explain the social order more than to question it. For example, mainstream economic theorists focus more on how supply, demand, and markets work than on how to equalize the distribution of resources.

Banks (1993) distinguished among five types of knowledge that can be used for curriculum construction: personal/cultural knowledge, popular knowledge, mainstream academic knowledge, transformative academic knowledge, and school knowledge. He defined *transformative knowledge* as including the

> concepts, paradigms, themes, and explanations that challenge mainstream academic knowledge and that expand the historical and literary canon. . . . Transformative and mainstream academic knowledge is based on different epistemological assumptions about the nature of knowledge, about the influence of human interests and values on knowledge construction, and about the purpose of knowledge. (p. 9)

Transformative knowledge, grounded in the realities of subjugation and visions of justice, offers "an alternative narration of the arrangement of social space" (Gallegos, 1998, p. 236); it "suggests re-imagining established knowledge and the order of things" (Garland-Thomson, 2002, p. 3). As such, it provides conceptual tools for addressing conditions that have historically oppressed and excluded peoples and communities. Transformative knowledge "is undergirded by critical consciousness . . . that unmasks unequal relations of power and issues of domination and subordination, based on assumptions about 'race,' 'gender,' and class relations . . . it is knowledge that acknowledges the wisdom of 'the people'" (J. M. Anderson, 2002).

LIMITS OF THE ADDITIVE APPROACH TO CURRICULUM

Multicultural curriculum should be strongly informed by transformative intellectual knowledge, but very often it is not. Much that passes as multicultural curriculum is actually mainstream knowledge with bits of "diversity" added in. Most textbooks are good examples of additive rather than transformed curriculum.

Textbooks

Reduction of school knowledge to what is measurable and defined by the state frames teaching as "something like an academic version of the postal service, delivering other people's mail," in which the teacher's role is simply to see that it "was delivered, opened, read, then learned" (Pinar, 2004, p. 210). It disconnects knowledge from values so that teaching becomes "telling students what they have to know," rather than developing their skills and insights. Such a view assumes that textbook knowledge reflects reality—it is simply unbiased truth, or at least worth taking as truth, which is how students generally think of textbooks.

Because of their power to define what gets taught, textbooks have been socially contested for decades. Through the 1970s and early 1980s, textbook publishers in the United States addressed many concerns regarding omissions and stereotypes that had been raised by communities of color and women. Then, with a few exceptions, efforts gradually subsided. One has only to thumb through a text today to see people of different ethnic backgrounds and both sexes. Teachers often assume that publishers have "taken care of" most forms of bias, so I regularly have students/teachers analyze textbooks, then compile their analyses in order to uncover patterns. Readers can do the same.

An easy way to start is to count representation of people in pictures, people named for study, or main characters in stories, by race and sex.[1] It is instructive then to compile analyses of several texts to uncover broad and recurring patterns that students experience across subject areas and grade levels. Although some individual textbooks are quite good, collectively texts produce patterns that teachers should be aware of. In fall 2003 teachers analyzed eleven texts taken largely from their own classrooms, then compiled their analyses.[2]

The teachers reported first on racial/ethnic representation. They found that Whites occupied more space and received more attention than any other racial/ethnic group. A teacher remarked, "Whites are shown as the educators, leaders, policy makers, those in authority. The heroes!" African Americans were, on the average, the next most represented group.

Teachers didn't see a consistent pattern in their representation; depictions ranged from famous authors to athletes to a "deviant" in a sociology text. Native Americans and Latinos followed, each group receiving roughly the same amount of space. Native Americans tended to appear as historical figures in some texts and not at all in others. Latinos were represented mainly as farmworkers, gang members, or a single mother on welfare, although prominent people such as Cesar Chavez also appeared. Asian Americans appeared here and there, mainly in pictures.

Published analyses of texts report similar patterns (Byrne, 2001; Clawson, 2002; Feiner & Morgan, 1987; Foster, 1999; Gordy & Pritchard, 1995; Loewen, 1995; Marquez, 1994; Powell & Garcia, 1988; Reyhner, 1986; Romanowski, 1996; Sleeter & Grant, 1991). Whites receive the most attention and appear in the widest variety of roles, dominating story lines and lists of accomplishments. African Americans, the next most represented racial group, appear in a more limited range of roles and usually receive only a sketchy account historically. Asian Americans and Latinos appear mainly as figures on the landscape with virtually no history or contemporary ethnic experience. Native Americans appear mainly in the past, but also occasionally in contemporary stories in reading books. Arab Americans are not only generally absent (Jacobs, 1981), but also generally ignored in textbook analyses. Texts say very little about contemporary race relations or racial issues, usually sanitizing greatly what they mention.

The teachers reported on gender representation next. Males outnumbered females in 10 of the 11 texts, to widely varying degrees. Teachers found males to be represented as leaders, heroes, and adventurers more than females; females occupied traditional roles more than the teachers had expected. In two elementary texts that included several animal stories, the animals were gender stereotyped. Published analyses of gender bias in texts concur (Feiner & Morgan, 1987; Foley & Boulware, 1996; Humphreys, 1997; Jones, Kitetu, & Sunderland, 1997; Koza, 1994; Potter & Rosser, 1992; Powell & Garcia, 1988; Sleeter & Grant, 1991). Most texts have successfully eliminated most sexist language. However, males are represented more than females, generally. Females appear in both traditional and nontraditional roles, although some texts develop nontraditional roles much more than others. Topics in texts, particularly in social studies, derive from male more than female experiences, and issues of sexism both today and historically are virtually ignored. In texts in which females have a major presence, females of color tend to be stereotyped (Marquez, 1994).

Gay and lesbian people were completely invisible in the texts the teachers analyzed. Although a few people in the texts were gay, they were not identified as such. Gay and lesbian people, usually ignored in textbook analyses, are virtually invisible in textbooks (Hogben & Waterman, 1997). Many texts use gender-neutral language to refer to marriage partners, but in the wake of passage of numerous state propositions in 2004 that define marriage as only between a man and a woman, some publishers are changing gender-neutral language to heterosexual language (e.g., from "marriage partners" to "husband and wife").

The teachers' report on social class revealed the "classlessness" with which texts are usually written. As one teacher put it, "The whole book was undefined, but looked middle class." That was generally the case: all but two teachers reported 80–100 percent of the people in their texts to be middle class, and the other two found the upper class to outnumber everyone else. Lower-class people were either absent or underrepresented, and appeared mainly as people of color (e.g., slaves). Relatively few published analyses have examined social class in texts, and have done so mainly in social studies (Anyon, 1979; Clawson, 2002; Feiner & Morgan, 1987; Loewen, 1995; Sleeter & Grant, 1991). In general, texts suggest that the United States is not stratified by class, that almost everyone is middle class, and that people have not struggled over distribution of wealth. Further, texts often link poverty with people of color, particularly in illustrations. Ideologically, perspectives of the dominant class tend to predominate, but are presented as if they were everyone's perspective.

The teachers found people with disabilities to be depicted in about half of the texts they analyzed. These depictions were mostly pictures with little or no discussion. Disability is addressed in only a few textbook analyses (Sleeter & Grant, 1991; Taub & Fanflik, 2000), which have found people with disabilities very underrepresented, and information about disability scarce.

In short, even when textbooks look multicultural on the surface (e.g., having added people of color to lists of famous people to study, or stories by authors of color to reading texts), most present a sanitized view of the world that suggests everyone is fairly content. The issues that do not show up in major texts (such as why millions of U.S. citizens continue to live in poverty, or what happened to indigenous people who used to have sovereignty in the Americas) present very loud silences to those who are aware of them. Textbooks can serve as useful resources in multicultural curricula, if their use is informed by transformative knowledge.

Most textbooks reflect an additive approach to multicultural curriculum: The "look" of the curriculum is changed, but not the substance. A *contributions approach* adds content largely limited to holidays and heroes, and an *additive approach* adds content, concepts, and themes to otherwise unreconstructed lessons, units, and courses of study (Banks, 1999). Contributions and additive curricula that teach about "others" very often take a form that Derman-Sparks (1989) referred to as the "tourist curriculum" in which "children 'visit' nonwhite cultures and then 'go home' to the daily classroom, which reflects the dominant culture" (p. 7). A few elements of living culture through which people interpret and negotiate daily life are taken out of context and simplified, translated for students, and frozen in time and space; multicultural curriculum as food or songs is an example.

Heroes, Heroines, and Group Characteristics

When teachers try to create multicultural curriculum without having extended their own knowledge about at least one or two historically marginalized groups, they usually end up with additive curriculum. A common pattern is adding in heroes or heroines, cultural artifacts, or surveys of group characteristics (such as studying what the Japanese are like). Writing about art, Nochlin (1971) traced layers behind the curriculum question, Why are there no great women artists? in order to probe limitations of an additive approach. Often the first reaction is "to dig up examples of worthy or insufficiently appreciated women artists throughout history" (p. 480). I often see teachers digging up and adding in heroes and heroines, such as great women artists, African American scientists, or Latino political leaders. While this is a start, it only gets one so far. Loutzenheiser and MacIntosh (2004), for example, asked what lessons accomplish "that take as their only gay and lesbian content the highlighting of the sexualities of those who have been identified as non-heterosexual (e.g., Oscar Wilde, Virginia Woolf, James Baldwin)." Adding famous people may offer role models, but it does so without questioning "the story's larger themes of freedom, equality, and opportunity" (Zimmerman, 2002, p. 4).

In art, as Nochlin (1971) pointed out, even after adding in women artists, it became apparent that great men artists still outnumber great women artists. In response to limitations of adding famous women, the next question was directed at "male" standards of greatness. This question assumed such a thing as "male art" and "female art," and that women are underrepresented because the kinds of art women do are not valued. While asking what kinds of art women make and why they are devalued opens up useful inquiry, the question also assumes a dichotomy between what men produce and what women produce.

The "group characteristics" additive approach asks, What are "they" like? It responds with a description presumed to be true, then generalized to people presumed to belong to the group. In so doing, this additive approach generally creates stereotypes (e.g., characteristics of women's art, beliefs of Asians), characteristics "taken to be essential—to which the historical and cultural diversity of phenomena can be reduced"(Cacoullos,

2001). The complexity of any given group is oversimplified or washed away, and presumed boundaries around groups go unquestioned. Cruz-Jansen (2001), for example, asked how we can think about Black Latinos, if Black and Latino are taken as two distinct groups.

Focusing on group characteristics also ignores issues of power and powerlessness, dominance and exclusion. As Nochlin pointed out, assuming that there is male art and female art is a "misconception of what art is," and trivializes what is worth fighting for. "If women have, in fact, achieved the same status as men in the arts, then the status quo is fine as it is" (pp. 482–483). Commonly, teachers lack the knowledge base to get beyond contributions and additive approaches without first doing some serious investigation.

COUNTERNARRATIVES AND TRANSFORMATIVE INTELLECTUAL KNOWLEDGE

According to Banks (1999), a *transformative approach* to curriculum design "changes the canon, paradigms, and basic assumptions of the curriculum and enables students to view concepts, issues, themes, and problems from different perspectives and points of view" (p. 31). A *social action* approach extends the transformative approach by connecting knowledge to action, engaging students in action projects that address issues they have studied. Both make substantive use of the counterideologies in transformative intellectual knowledge. As Banks (2004b) argued, "The knowledge that emanates from marginalized epistemological communities often contests existing political, economic, and educational practices and calls for fundamental change and reform. It often reveals the inconsistency between the democratic ideals within a society and its social arrangements and educational practices" (p. 237). The term *counternarrative* draws attention to such knowledge by offering not only facts and important people who are marginalized in traditional academic knowledge but also historical accounts and interpretations of facts that differ from and often run counter to those of the mainstream.

The Mohawk Education Project, for example, was undertaken to improve education for Mohawk Indian students using culturally relevant curriculum. Agbo (2001) explained that "in contrast to the stupendous and complex educational content that reduces the Mohawk student to conditions of abstraction and anonymity, we embarked on a cultural model viewed as the repository of cherished knowledge that places culture as the nexus in the education of the Mohawk child" (p. 33). Using participatory research, a team of teachers, community members, and university researchers gathered information from a wide variety of sources to figure out what should be taught and how, then constructed an ethnic-content, bicultural curriculum based on Mohawk knowledge. Twenty general themes (or big ideas), derived from Mohawk culture spiraled through it.

Clan system	Food
Ceremonies	Clothing
Thanksgiving	Traditional homes
Iroquois Confederacy	Survival skills
Cycle of life and the	Storytelling and drama
traditional circle	Native games and sports
Roles of the family	Communication and
Spiritual cleansing	transportation
and healing	Art forms and media
Medicines	Environmental awareness
Study of Akwesasne	Systems of government (from Agbor,
Songs and dances	2001)

Non-Mohawk teachers needed to work with the Mohawk community in order to learn to teach this curriculum around these themes. The project was also used to construct standards for American Indian education, specifying what an academically rich, culturally centered curriculum would look like.

There is evidence that curriculum organized through a transformative or social action approach makes a stronger impact on students than when organized through an additive or contributions approach. Studies of the development of children's racial attitudes have found that curricula that simply label groups or group members (e.g., pointing out the race, ethnicity, or gender of historical figures) draw students' attention to group markers and differences, inviting stereotyping (Bigler, 1995; Bigler, Brown, & Markell, 2001). Curricula that provide limited counterstereotypic information about members of marginalized groups have little effect in countering stereotypes children are exposed to outside school (Bigler, 1999).

In contrast to additive tinkering with curriculum, providing information about racism (possibly along with successful challenges to racism) appears to have a measurably positive impact on racial attitudes of both children of color and White children toward fairness and toward people of color (Milligan & Bigler, in press). This is probably because such curricula provide information about why some groups seem to fare better than others, as well as examples of steps taken toward building fairness. It is quite possible that studying people from dominant sociocultural backgrounds who have worked for justice, along with studying why others perpetrated injustice, may help build social justice–oriented identities among dominant group members.

It often requires some depth of study of historically marginalized knowledge to identify key concepts in that body of knowledge that do not immediately fit into traditional curriculum. For example, an important theme in women's studies is "motherwork"—the work of reproduction and nurturance that women do in the home (Grumet & Stone, 2000). Since school curricula generally assume a division between "public" and "private" domains of knowledge, insights about "building capacity in the areas of communal and family living" disappear from curriculum as one goes up the grades and may not seem to fit anywhere except in home economics (Crocco, 2001). Taking knowledge of women seriously means questioning dualisms that divide feminine from masculine, and home from public. The task is not simply one of adding women into the curriculum, but also figuring out domains of women's knowledge that have been excluded and how those domains relate to exclusion of women from broader social participation, becoming familiar with that knowledge, and then figuring out how to use it. As this example suggests, transformative intellectual knowledge might lead to a reconceptualization of the central ideas themselves.

INVESTIGATING TRANSFORMATIVE INTELLECTUAL KNOWLEDGE

For teachers, the process of retrieving subjugated knowledge and then transforming curriculum is complex because it involves not only new learning but also coming to grips with a different (and possibly very unfamiliar) ideology. Therefore, I require teachers to complete a research paper in which they investigate a body of transformative, historically subjugated knowledge in relationship to the big idea of a unit they plan to teach. The purpose of doing the research is to acquire background knowledge as well as a sense of perspective about the unit's big idea from scholarship in ethnic, women's, gay/lesbian, or other critical studies. Doing this research substantially improves the quality of curriculum teachers develop. (See Figure 5.1 for my instructions for this research paper.)

For the heart of the paper, the teacher selects a sociocultural group whose experiences, perspectives, and/or intellectual work relates to the big idea for her or his curriculum, but is marginalized in it. Then the teacher reads material by scholars of that group, in some depth. I encourage teachers to read from one group's writings rather than several groups because doing so helps the teacher explore a point of view that tends to be shared

Figure 5.1. Guide for Research Into Transformative Intellectual Knowledge

1. Discuss briefly how, and from whose perspective, the big idea for curriculum you are designing is presented in school generally (e.g., in textbooks or curriculum guides). Whose knowledge is best represented? What broader ideology is reflected?

2. Select a sociocultural group whose experiences, perspectives, and/or intellectual work relates to the big idea but is marginalized in curriculum. By reading books and journal articles, investigate how selections of work written by scholars who are members of that group address it. For this paper, read work written for adults rather than work written for children.

3. Write no more than eight pages discussing the main ideas, perspective, and ideology from this body of work that could inform curriculum content.

4. Discuss your main goals for teaching the unit's central idea in light of what you read.

by group members; otherwise, the teachers may gather facts without also seeing another point of view.

I encourage teachers to consider who their students are when deciding whose knowledge to read. While curriculum need not always reflect the demographics of one's students, curriculum does interact with students' identities. Perry, Steele, and Hilliard (2003), for example, pointed out the devastating impact on African American youth of society's imagery of African Americans as intellectually inferior, and the potential power of counternarratives to challenge that negative imagery.

I also guide teachers in selecting and reading work written for adults, as often teachers select children's books without considering the fact that they do not capture the intellectual depth of work written for adults. Relying on children's books as the primary source of knowledge would be like relying on Cliffs Notes for background to teach Shakespeare. One of the biggest challenges some teachers encounter when doing this research is realizing that I am asking them to broaden their own education before they try to broaden that of their students. Fifth-grade teacher Bob Peterson (2002) tells his prospective student teachers:

> The first thing . . . is to really educate yourself. I tell all of my student teachers if they want to be a student teacher in my classroom, they need to read Howard Zinn's *A People's History of the United States*. Sometimes I also suggest Ronald Takaki's *A Different Mirror*. Teachers should read these books because they need to ground themselves in the history and worldview of those who have been left out of history. This need doesn't just apply to history, it applies to literature, to geography, science, current events, and language.

Often teachers need guidance locating material. I suggest using a library's databases and doing keyword searches, using as a keyword the big idea for the curriculum, plus terms such as African American, Latino, Hispanic, Asian American, Native American, American Indian, other names of specific ethnic groups, indigenous, ethnic, multicultural, women, disability, lesbian. Teachers may need to try various terms and databases before they locate a useful body of work to read. For example, I was recently asked what an algebra teacher would read. Using the ERIC database, and entering the keywords "algebra" plus African American, then Latino, then Hispanic, then American Indian, I located nine journal articles.[3] Using the World Cat database to access books, and entering the same keywords, I located seven books.[4] The articles and books addressed topics such as relationships between math and language, relationships between students' life experiences and algebraic thinking, and algebra as a political tool. These two searches unearthed not only potential material to read, but also names of authors writing about math and communities of color. One can then find out if the identified authors have written anything else. For example, Hankes coauthored a book published by the National Council of Teachers of Mathematics, entitled *Perspectives on Indigenous People of North America* (Hankes & Fast, 2002). When I searched her name to see what else she had written, I discovered the book *Native American Pedagogy and Cognitive-Based Mathematics Instruction* (Hankes, 1998). While not everything would necessarily be relevant, some sources would be relevant. Thus, even with a topic that seems as removed from transformative intellectual knowledge as algebra, some digging in the library using this search process retrieved material.

The next step is to start reading the material to find out what the authors are writing about, and then figure out what implications the general topics have for the curriculum. For example, Banks (2003) suggested key concepts that emerge in ethnic studies scholarship; these key concepts, shown in Figure 5.2, can ground a multiethnic curriculum.

Typically teachers also need guidance deciding whose voice is "authentic," and how would one know. Banks's (1998) typology distinguishing whether an author is a member of the community written about and how the author's work is regarded by the community is very helpful. According to Banks, *external outsiders* to historically oppressed communities have generated much of what is written and taught in schools. An external outsider "is socialized within a community different from the one in which she is doing research," and "has a partial understanding of and little appreciation for the values, perspectives, and knowledge of the community she is studying, and consequently often misunderstands and misinterprets

Figure 5.2. Key Concepts for Teaching a Multiethnic Curriculum

Culture, ethnicity, and related concepts	Culture
	Ethnic group
	Ethnic minority group
	Stages of ethnicity
	Cultural assimilation
	Acculturation
	Community culture
Socialization and related concepts	Socialization
	Prejudice
	Discrimination
	Race
	Racism
	Ethnocentrism
	Values
Intercultural communication and related concepts	Communication
	Intercultural communication
	Perception
	Historical bias
Power and related concepts	Power
	Social protest and resistance
The movement of ethnic groups	Migration
	Immigration

Note. From Banks (2003), p. 59. Reprinted with the permission of the author.

the behaviors within the studied community" (p. 8). Members of the dominant society have tended to believe that, with training, anyone can come to valid and objective conclusions about any community. Because external outsiders to historically subordinate communities dominate what gets published, these are the authors teachers often select without guidance. But authors who are members of the group about which they write are more likely to offer a valid insider perspective. An *indigenous insider* "endorses the unique values, perspectives, behaviors, beliefs, and knowledge of her indigenous community and culture and is perceived by people within the community as a legitimate community member who can speak with authority about it" (pp. 7–8). The point of view of an indigenous insider differs from that of an *indigenous outsider*, a member of a marginalized group who has become assimilated into the dominant society. To members of dominant groups, indigenous outsiders often "make sense" because their ideology resonates with that of the dominant society, while indigenous insiders can sound threatening. An *external insider* is not a member of the group she or he is writing about; "however, because of experiences, the individual rejects many of the values, beliefs, and knowledge claims within her indigenous community and endorses those of the studied community. The external insider is viewed by the new community as an 'adopted' insider" (p. 8).

I encourage teachers to read widely. Teachers should not simply judge some authors as "valid" and others as "invalid," but rather place what any author says within an examination of where that author is "coming from" and whom that author works with. I also use Collins's (1998, pp. 198–199) criteria for evaluating social theory as a guide. First, does it "speak the truth to people about the reality of their lives"? This question echoes Banks's concern about situating work within the scholar's relationship to the community about which he or she writes. Second, what is its "stance toward freedom—its vision of emancipation as well as the pragmatic strategies it suggests"? Would the actions a book or an article authorizes lead to a more just world, or would they replace one hierarchy with another? And third, "does this critical social theory move people toward struggle"? Is it grounded in a compelling moral authority that asks not only whether the facts are accurate, but also whether the principles on which they rest are ethical?

Thirty-seven of the 39 educators in both classes of Multicultural Curriculum Design completed this research paper; their experiences illustrate struggles and insights teachers have when locating and working with transformative knowledge. Thirteen of the teachers had difficulty grasping the use of historically subjugated knowledge to inform curriculum content. Seven of them used it minimally in their research papers, for different reasons. For example, despite my requirement that teachers read adult-level work, two elementary teachers used children's literature for at least half of their source material for Native Americans. I was not sure whether they simply ran out of time or, because indigenous peoples are often taught through the lens of children's literature, did not understand conceptual differences between children's literature and adult-level scholarship. Three teachers focused on teaching strategies rather than content (for example, implications of research on Asian American families for how to teach Asian American children). Five teachers developed substantive papers, but did not use this material to inform curriculum they developed; for example, one wrote a very interesting paper about feminist perspectives of technology but did not realize that it was supposed to inform the content of her unit.

The rest of the teachers (26) made constructive use of their research as they planned curriculum. For example, a middle school literature teacher who planned to teach the idea that any piece of literature reflects the point of view of its writer, investigated the concept of viewpoint in authorship through writings by Chicano literary figures. Some teachers started with very little knowledge about how their unit's main idea might be developed in scholarship of a historically subordinate group, and used this paper as an exploration. For example, a former high school math teacher, who had struggled to teach decontextualized math to urban African American students, had not seen how he might contextualize it until reading works of African American mathematicians (such as Robert Moses). A middle school social studies teacher who was exploring how to teach about religion used this opportunity to read about Islam and the diversity of nations and ethnicities within the Arab world.

Eight teachers significantly rethought their main idea based on their research. For example, a Chicana kindergarten bilingual teacher started with the main idea of grandparents, but after doing research to explore how grandparents, and older people generally, are viewed cross-culturally by African Americans and Native Americans, she shifted her main idea to "elders." This shift allowed her to examine how elders are valued in many cultural communities, but often devalued by the dominant U.S. society, reflected in connotations of the term *elderly*.

The rest of this section considers how two teachers approached the research and worked with it. Gina had learned to investigate and work with transformative intellectual knowledge years ago, and illustrates ongoing learning. Angela, a beginning teacher, was new to transformative intellectual knowledge.

Gina: Contextualizing Dance in History and Culture

Gina was in her 16th year of teaching when I visited her classroom. Now primarily a middle school dance teacher, over the years she had taught grades ranging from primary to high school, and at the secondary level she had also taught Spanish. As a student in my Multicultural Curriculum Design course, she brought a very clear understanding of transformative intellectual knowledge.

When meeting Gina for the first time, people often assume that she is Mexican. She speaks Spanish fluently, teaches Mexican dance, and performs in a Mexican dance company; she has long dark hair and dark eyes; and her last name is Rodriguez. However, ethnically she is Portuguese; over time, she intentionally developed an extensive knowledge base about Mexican culture and history.

Gina majored in Spanish in college and took her first teaching job as a high school Spanish teacher. As a Spanish major, she had acquired academic knowledge about Mexican culture. In her first teaching assignment, she found herself teaching Spanish in a predominantly White context "to kids who hadn't ever seen a brown person before." This was not what she wanted to continue doing, so she moved to southern California, near the Mexican border, where she was hired as an elementary bilingual teacher. She described that experience:

> Ninety-nine point nine percent of my kids were Mexican, there was maybe one White kid in the whole school. And so I had to learn about my students. I already knew Spanish, you know, I got my BA in Spanish, and I had spent time in Mexico, I already knew the academic knowledge. But the insider's knowledge, I had to get that, just from experience. (January 22, 2004)

Gina recognized that her academic knowledge had value, but was not the same as the everyday knowledge and viewpoints shared by indigenous insiders. She could also see from the way her school implemented Cinco de Mayo celebrations (the only time of the year when Mexican culture was acknowledged) that having a little bit of knowledge can be damaging. "They dressed [the kids] in the Mexican flag and I was just really embarrassed, the teachers thought they were doing this service for students, you know, this cultural example. And I had been to Mexico, I've seen groups there, so I knew this wasn't right" (January 22, 2004). Gina was also puzzled by the fact that while many people in the community crossed the border regularly to take advantage of cultural resources on both sides, teachers rarely did the same.

Gina then began to study dance in various universities in Mexico. Although she had studied dance, she had not studied Mexican dance. Her first class was every weekend with a professor in Mexicali, just over the border. She explained, "Once I started studying with that professor, I realized that I've got to, he kind of showed me how to investigate and how to pursue it" (January 22, 2004). He used ethnographic methods to learn about the people and context of dances he studied, and taught Gina to do the same. "His work felt just as revolutionary as it was artistic" (Rodriguez, 2002, p. 4).

He launched Gina on an ongoing learning path. "So then I would go to different places in Mexico in the summers and enroll as a Mexican, and it was great because it was really cheap. I would just enroll and take their dance classes" (January 22, 2004). The dance classes involved serious and in-depth study that included the historical context of each dance and an investigation into the cultural context using ethnographic research. The classes strove for authenticity, including how to make authentic costumes. Gina explained, "The more I learned, the more I realized how little I knew about the multitude of dances that have various significances for over 50 different ethnic groups in Mexico" (Rodriguez, 2002, p. 5). Gina learned a good deal of the tremendous ethnic, linguistic, and regional variation of Mexico, as well as political relationships that are legacies of European conquest. Over a period of time, as she studied in different regions of Mexico, she developed considerable depth and breadth of knowledge.

Gina is part of a local community of dance scholars who regularly travel to Mexico to study dance. Like Gina, other members of the dance company Esperanza del Valle have been studying dance in Mexico for many years. In 1997 they received funding for a United States-Mexico collaborative project, which enabled the company to engage in primary research in Mexico. Janet Rachel Johns, founder and artistic director of the company, became particularly interested in helping preserve ancient indigenous *danzas* in the Huasteca area of Mexico. She explained, "Indigenous peoples of the world have had to struggle to 'rescue' and preserve their cultural traditions and art forms in spite of conquest, colonialism, and the threat of eradication of language and culture" (Johns, 2003, p. 26). The dances themselves have religious and cultural significance that is quite different from Western dances, and although many survived the religious conquest of the Catholic church, "today they confront political, economic, social, and religious pressures that threaten their existence. . . . [In many ways, indigenous dances were a] means of identity, resistance, and power" (p. 104). Engaging in the work of learning them, collaborating with communities to preserve them, and bringing them and their historical significance to California was transformative work on a variety of levels.

For her paper in Multicultural Curriculum Design, Gina researched Maya political issues today, using work by Maya and Zapatista authors such as the edited book *First World, Ha, Ha, Ha!* (Katzenberger, 1995). This research helped her develop her unit's main idea, which involved analyzing contemporary issues in Mexico in relationship to their historic roots in conquest. For Gina, this research assignment linked with the kind of learning she had been doing for years, and she used it as an opportunity to deepen a segment of her dance curriculum.

Gina's extensive ongoing study of dance is the basis for her curriculum. She has her middle school students for one period each day for 9 weeks. In that time period, she teaches several dances, as well as the historical and cultural context of each. She explained that even though most of her students are Mexican or Mexican American, [students] come with, you know, just Mexico as this one place. And so through dance I can really show that because each dance shows a different kind of music, a different region, a different culture, a different ethnic group, I can really use dance as a vehicle for demonstrating that diversity. And then of course I bring in the history too, so they have a deeper understanding, not just about dance. (January 22, 2004)

She connects the political contexts of culture in Mexico with local politics in an effort to help students see that they have power to advocate for themselves. She also uses her work as a vehicle to attempt to transform students' feelings about themselves. She constantly combats the various ways Mexican-descent students absorbed deficit imagery of themselves in the United States. For example, she pointed out that recently she had heard students using the term *Oaxaca* as an insult. "The reason why that is, is because there's a high percentage of Indians in Oaxaca, and they're this latest immigration group" (January 22, 2004). She also recognized that, "the racism is against themselves": whether her students were from Oaxaca or not, their insults were directed toward manifestations of indigenous blood and culture. When I was visiting her class, she directly addressed this issue by teaching the students about Oaxaca, as well as about racism against indigenous people in the context of a history of conquest.

"But you know, that's not in the standards," she commented (January 22, 2004). Gina said that the arts standards are broad enough that she is able to teach dance as serious study of Mexican culture and history. Also, the fact that the arts are not part of the state's testing regime has had the contradictory effect of pushing arts out of some schools while creating relatively unregulated space for transformative work in others.

Gina mentioned that she is sometimes criticized for teaching just one culture. She counters that is it far better to go deeply into one group than superficially into many. She has seen other arts teachers who throw into lessons a little bit about Black culture and Mexican culture, without a very good grasp on either of them, and end up with a very superficial curriculum. Besides, as she found in her study of Mexico, what seems to be one culture may be very diverse, once a teacher begins to go deeply into it.

Angela: Looking Into Indigenous Knowledge

Angela was a second-year elementary teacher when she enrolled in Multicultural Curriculum Design and when I subsequently visited her classroom. Of Italian American descent, she had moved to California from the

East Coast. One of her student teaching experiences was in London, where she taught students who were Pakistani and Afghani. In the process, she learned a little bit about Islam and Arabic culture, and became interested in learning more. This experience also provided a springboard from which she began to critique the mainstream curriculum. She commented, "When I came home, I taught this fifth grade about the cultures I learned over there, and they had no idea what Arabic was, what Muslim, what Mohammed, nothing" (January 28, 2004). These experiences prompted her initial interest in learning to develop and teach multicultural curriculum.

In Multicultural Curriculum Design, Angela decided to focus on social studies and was especially interested in reexamining the story of how the United States was founded. After analyzing her textbook, she realized that "the history text teaches the story of American history as 'We the People' as a succession" story that is "never rethought after colonization." She noted that students generally believe that "the United States was settled in the year 1620, because that is how American history is taught" (December 12, 2003). She had some awareness that this point of view ignored the indigenous people who were already in North America, and the impact of colonization on them. But she did not have much knowledge beyond this awareness.

She decided to use the assigned research paper as a learning tool. Initially she wasn't sure where to start, except with the question, What are Native American perspectives on colonialism? I suggested that she narrow her question down to a specific time period, place, and tribe or nation. She decided to focus on the Iroquois during the 1600s. For general background, she read *Lies My Teacher Told Me* (Loewen, 1995) and *Rethinking Columbus* (Bigelow & Peterson, 1998). She also read work by Laduke (1999), Churchill (2002), Lepore (1999), and Sale (1991). Her research ended up focusing on the Haudenosaunee (Iroquois), Wampanoag, and Pequot during the late 1600s.

As she read, she saw clearly a different story from the one in the school's history textbook. She was shocked, for example, to learn that the Puritans, rather than being gentle people as portrayed in the textbook, tried to kill off the Wampanoag people. At one point, she commented in class, "topics just kept spinning off each other and it was hard to stop, or to figure out what to actually use" (December 8, 2003). As she came to recognize a very different ideology in Indian writings than what she had learned in school and what the textbook taught, she struggled with how to rethink her curriculum. How she resolved that problem is examined in Chapter 6.

Over a 4-month period, Angela plunged into a body of transformative intellectual knowledge and read deeply enough to recognize that it told a different story. To design and teach two 45-minute lessons that focused directly on the Haudenosaunee, Wampanoag, and Pequot during the late 1600s, she recognized that she needed to learn a good deal more specifics, in addition to making sure that she understood the overall viewpoint correctly. For example, it was not enough to know that the Haudenosaunee had a well-developed democratic governmental and legal system; she also had to be able to describe some of its features accurately in order to teach about it. She commented on the amount of time it took to do background research for two lessons:

> Just when I was planning this lesson I went and spent another few hours finding those words and finding all the Native American names. . . . I spent time on Native American Web sites. And researching this is something I'm kind of interested in. I mean, I've looked up some different Native American beliefs and traditions just for my own personal knowledge. (January 28, 2004)

By working through the research paper outlined in Figure 5.1, Angela had learned a process for accessing and working with transformative intellectual knowledge, through which she began to relearn U.S. history from indigenous perspectives. At the time of this writing, her main sources were books and the Internet; she did not know any Haudenosaunee people. With time and continued interest, it is possible that, like Gina, she might find ways of connecting with living communities and continuing her learning. Doing so, however, would be on top of the work teachers already do. She recognized that, since American Indians gradually fade from social studies curricula that are based on the story of Europeans and European Americans, she could stop the learning she had begun and be in full compliance with state requirements. But she felt that the issues she was learning about were too important to drop.

> We need to teach diversity, because of everything that's going on in the world. If we make it like a natural process, then people won't grow up to have prejudice and hate. That's why I think it's important to teach it. (January 28, 2004)

POSSIBILITIES AND CHALLENGES

Gina and Angela illustrate teachers researching bodies of transformative intellectual knowledge deeply enough to rethink and design curriculum in meaningful ways. Later chapters will show how they used this knowledge in their teaching. Generally, however, one does not find teachers working with transformative knowledge in depth for reasons that are both institutional and personal.

Content standards, texts, and tests structure what teachers are supposed to teach. Even if a teacher has interest and time to do the kind of reading and research explored in this chapter, the teacher may find little room for curriculum modification. As a second-year teacher, Angela was overwhelmed with preparing lessons addressing the standards in all content areas. The short unit she developed based on her research took time away from the curriculum as defined in the standards, and she was feeling behind when she finished teaching it. She commented, "I'm really struggling with science, because they kind of just gave us these huge binders of things to teach, from cells and atoms and nucleus and the periodic table, things I need to study at home before I can teach it to fifth grade. And there's a new state-mandated fifth-grade science test this year" (January 28, 2004). As noted earlier, experienced teachers were better able than beginning teachers to judge which standards they should emphasize and which they could skip or de-emphasize, and were able to be more creative with curriculum as a result.

Working with transformative intellectual knowledge depends on teacher interest. My Multicultural Curriculum Design course attracts a self-selected group of very diverse teachers who are interested in and receptive to doing the research to go beyond the superficial multicultural content. They have been quick to point out, however, that most of their colleagues do not see value in doing so. Mona, for example, an elementary teacher who had been working with new teachers for years, had a good idea how teachers throughout her district saw curriculum. She explained that she may be the only teacher her students ever have who teaches science from a multicultural perspective:

> So at least they're getting some kind of knowledge, when the facts are presented later when they get to high school or middle school, they've got this background. I'm providing a foundation for that. And it's good to provide a different viewpoint, 'cause I don't know if they'll ever get this again, from another teacher. (April 22, 2004)

Generally, teachers are not required to develop depth of familiarity with transformative intellectual knowledge at any point in their education or teaching career. If they are not personally interested, they see no incentive; not only does it involve extra work, but many are threatened by its ideology, and all are held accountable for following the texts and teaching what will be tested.

How teachers who are interested actually approach transformative intellectual knowledge depends on the filters they bring. There is no unified body of such knowledge, since it originates within very diverse communities. Does one start, for example, with women, African Americans, or the working class? To African American working class women, this question makes no sense. But White women may not ask the question. For example, one teacher who had taken a women's studies course investigated how women were subjugated in the eighteenth century. When she submitted her research paper (the first time), it included only readings by and about White women, and in so doing, made inaccurate generalizations about women as a whole. I required her to read some specific works by women historians of color and then revise the paper, which she did.

One needs to start somewhere, and starting with any group moves toward considerable complexity if one continues to learn, as Gina's experience illustrates. One can know a good deal about the group studied but be ignorant about others. Attempts to lump diverse groups together under a conceptualization that was developed with reference to one community can marginalize others. Consider, for example, a teacher who has extensive background knowledge about gay history and contemporary life, and attempts to extend insights from that knowledge to constructing culturally relevant curriculum for Southeast Asian students. Some insights deriving from a general sensitivity to difference transfer up to a point. But sensitivity would not substitute for knowledge from Asian studies. This implies that teachers who are interested in learning and working with transformative intellectual knowledge should be willing to engage in ongoing learning and allow assumptions and ignorance to be challenged.

How teachers think about the nature of knowledge itself is another factor affecting what teachers do with it. As Powell's (1996) comparison of two teachers (described in Chapter 2) showed, teachers who strongly value traditional academic knowledge may well struggle to see the relevance of transformative intellectual knowledge, particularly at the K–12 levels where everyone is supposed to learn the "basics."

Teachers who confront these personal issues may be able to grow beyond them. The reason I structure my research assignment around a concept the teacher plans to teach is so that what the teacher reads and learns has relevance to the teacher's work. The teacher must then decide what to do with it, but cannot deny that such knowledge exists or that it is accessible. The institutionalization of knowledge cannot be confronted directly on an individual level, however. This book shows what teachers are able to do within constraints placed upon them, but that does not make the constraints themselves any less real.

NOTES

1. A more complex textbook analysis instrument appears in Grant and Sleeter (2003).

2. The discussion that follows focuses on U.S. texts (elementary through college levels), but parallel research has been reported around the world, including Australia (Leonard, 2002), Britain (Osler, 1994; Walford, 1983), Canada (Hayibor & Peterat, 1995; Tupper, 2002), China (Chow, 1987; D. Wang, 2002), Congo (Mbandaka, 1995), Iran (Shorish, 1988), Russia (Wertsch, 1999), and Taiwan (Su, 1997/98).

3. Brenner, 1998; Mestre & Gerace, 1986; Moses & Cobb, 2001a; Ortiz-Franco, 1990; Owens & Waxman, 1994; Peritt, 1997; Schaufele & Srivastava, 1995; Singh & Granville, 1999; Valadez, 2002.

4. Cooney & Hirsch, 1990; Denbo & Beaulieu, 2002; Hankes & Fast, 2002; Johnson, Maddux, & Liu, 1997; Levine, 1995; Russell, 1998; Segarra & Dobles, 1999.

Chapter 6

Students as Curriculum

I just think that as teachers, we've kind of gone along with what we've been handed to teach, we forget about the other important things that will connect the child to the learning.

(Bilingual elementary teacher, March 10, 2002)

Talk to the students as much as possible, I mean, there's a rich resource right in your own classroom. Sometimes it's hard in here because it's like, rush in, rush out. . . . But I try to grab 'em every once in a while, when I can, and talk about things, you know? What are their perspectives about school as being taught, so as often as possible, you know, having discussions, hearing their input. A lot of times what I see happen is, you don't get those really good insights from the students who may feel like their ideas aren't popular, but they're important ideas. But they don't want to share because it's not mainstream.

(Christi, high school teacher, February 24, 2004)

Teachers never construct curriculum entirely for generic students. Teaching involves people, and one of the biggest challenges for a teacher is connecting subject matter with students. The standards movement tends to construct students as receivers of knowledge defined elsewhere, rather than as sources of knowledge. A multicultural curriculum, in contrast, conceptualizes students and their communities as sources and producers of knowledge, in their own right, as well as a foundation on which to build new academic knowledge.

Students learn a tremendous amount about others, themselves in relationship to others, and social systems by observing the world around them. Certainly mass media function as a powerful curriculum affecting how young people view themselves and their own communities, as well as sociocultural groups they are not members of and may have no direct contact with (Cortés, 2000; Jhally, 1995). In school, young people also learn about others in ways that school might not intend by observing who does what or who is treated in what way. For example, if young people see mainly White students in upper track classes and mainly students of color in lower track classes, they develop ideas about who is smart and who is not. If they see mainly students from affluent backgrounds getting the most privileges and teacher attention while students from low-income backgrounds are generally ignored, they develop an understanding of who "belongs" in school and who does not.

This chapter focuses on students as part of curriculum. It discusses planning curriculum to connect students' community-based knowledge with academic knowledge and to enable students to learn from each other.

KNOWLEDGE STUDENTS BRING TO SCHOOL

Curriculum should build on what students have learned out of school. Vygotsky (1930) explained:

> That children's learning begins long before they attend school is the starting point of this discussion. Any learning a child encounters in school always has a previous history. For example, children begin to study arithmetic in school, but long beforehand they have had some experience with quantity—they have had to deal with operations of division, addition, subtraction, and determination of size.

The banking model, which much of the standards movement implicitly supports, treats students as empty vessels into which knowledge is poured for retrieval later. State standards, textbooks, and standardized tests, by their nature, define curriculum apart from students and local contexts. Arguing against the banking model, Freire (1998) emphasized repeatedly that "to teach is not to transfer the comprehension of the object to a student but to instigate the student, who is a knowing subject, to become capable of comprehending and of communicating what has been comprehended" (p. 106). Rather than one of pouring knowledge into presumed empty heads, the role of the teacher is "one of inciting the student to produce his or her own comprehension of the object" (p. 106). In order to do this, the teacher must view students and the knowledge they bring as part of curriculum.

It is the teacher's responsibility to find out, become familiar with, and respect knowledge students bring to school, and to organize curriculum and learning activities in such a way that students are able to activate and use that knowledge. Contrasting the predominantly White school he attended as a child with the Black Baptist Church he attended at the same time, Murrell (2002), who is African American, pointed out that even though the school had more material resources, the Church had more intellectually meaningful resources. For him, it was "more real," by which he meant "in the world—a glimpse of the panorama of human conditions such as it was in Milwaukee in the 1950s and 1960s . . . more real in that it was the context of Black doings" (p. 5). By grounding its teaching in African American community life, the Church offered a more powerful intellectual context than the school. But the school could have done the same.

Often stereotypes about students' lives outside school substitute for knowledge of their lives. For example, Noguera (2003) described meeting with a group of urban high school teachers who believed that a school improvement project wouldn't work because "the families of their students simply did not value education" (p. 47). But when he asked if they had spoken with parents, he discovered that most had not done so and knew very little about students' lives; few even knew precisely where their students lived. Further, he found that they lacked strategies for learning from the community and weren't sure what to do with what they might learn.

Even teachers from students' same ethnic background can make unwarranted assumptions about what students know. For example, Cheryl, a second-grade teacher, mentioned in a class discussion that the fact that Bob Moses (Moses & Cobb, 2001b) used subways to teach abstract algebra concepts to urban students should not be taken to mean that African American students at large will profit from a subway analogy. She pointed out that although she is African American, she had never ridden a subway until the previous week when visiting Washington, D.C. Further, the African American community in central California is different from that in Washington, D.C. She explained, "I thought I was really more connected to my own group before my trip. . . . I teach to other students who are African Americans, and I'm thinking, well I've had the same experiences as them. But they come from different places, so perhaps that's not the case at all" (October 19, 2001). She emphasized that teachers need to be careful about making assumptions, and should take the time to get to know their students, students' communities, and their actual lived experiences.

Murrell (2001) developed the idea of *community teacher* to characterize teachers who learn to construct meaningful learning environments for students from historically oppressed communities. He described the community teacher as someone who "is aware of and, when necessary, actively researches the knowledge traditions of the cultures represented among the children, families, and communities he or she serves," and then "enacts those knowledge traditions as a means of making meaningful connections for or with the children and their families" (p. 4). A community teacher learns to "forge strong connections with children in diverse community settings as they elicit development and achievement in real practice" (p. 52). The most effective teachers continually work to get to know their students, both in and out of school, in order to build new learning on what they actually know or find interesting. Gutiérrez (2000a, 2000b), for example, found that effective math teachers of Black and Latino students seek out resources that relate to students' interests and connect to challenging mathematics concepts. They get to know their students well enough to know how to relate new ideas to students' lives and personal interests.

Learning About and From Students' Communities

Teachers can use many tools to learn about and from their students' communities. Elsewhere, I have published mini-investigations that I've had teachers use over the years (Sleeter, 2001). For example, teachers can walk through students' neighborhoods, noting what students see everyday that can be connected with curriculum concepts. If one is preparing math lessons, what kind of quantitative reasoning might students do as they shop with their parents in local stores? If one is preparing science lessons, what kinds of plants, minerals, birds, or animals are students likely to be familiar with? Even better, take a neighborhood walk with some students and encourage them to act as tour guides; they will give a students'-eye-view of the community, and talk about not only what is there, but what interests them, what they notice, what kinds of connections they make, or what they wonder about.

Adults in the community are often receptive to talking with teachers about the community's culture, assets, and upcoming events that teachers might attend. A teacher can invite two or three adults who live in the neighborhood to talk about the community; often the school secretary or custodian turn out to be excellent interviewees. When conducting these interviews, teachers and preservice students have found the following questions (Sleeter, 2001) useful:

1. What are the main assets of this community?
2. What are people in this community especially good at?
3. Describe how you would like this community to be 10 years from now.
4. What does this community have going for it that will help reach that goal?
5. What are the main barriers to reaching that goal? What is the community doing to address those barriers?
6. What needs does the community have?
7. As a teacher, how can I best serve this community?

I have found interviews such as this to challenge deficit views some teachers have, and to open up conversations that suggest links between curriculum and the community.

Teachers can also interview their students, or have students interview parents or grandparents. After teachers have identified a tentative big idea for unit construction, I ask them to have open-ended conversations with several students in order to find out whether they are interested in that idea, what they already know about it (or think they know), where they learned what they know, and what they would like to know.[1] Almost every teacher who has done this has discovered some surprises. For example, a middle school teacher planning a unit on religion found that about half of her students had many questions (more than she had anticipated), but a few wanted to learn "nothing," which also surprised her. Students' questions gave her ideas to work with; those that wanted to learn "nothing" intrigued her to find out more about their thinking. An elementary teacher realized that his students knew less about the history and geography of the local area, but more about their parents' jobs, than he had anticipated. This interview helped him to see how to build on what the children knew about their parents' work to teach about the local region. Several teachers have been surprised to learn that their students believe there are few or no Native Americans today; typically students have far more stereotyped perspectives about Native Americans than teachers realize.

In most cases, such discoveries have helped teachers identify student-oriented meaningful questions with which to begin. One of the teachers in Multicultural Curriculum Design observed that students learned more and worked harder when she connected concepts—even those as boring as grammar—with what interested them:

> When students were engaged by what they were studying, it was much easier for them to learn it or develop the skills it was intended to offer them (not to mention that I had a much happier classroom). What really fascinated me though was the fact that when the students prepared some homework related to something they found interesting . . . they would regularly make every effort to present a result that was flawless not only in content but in vocabulary, grammar, syntax, and structure as well. In such cases, when students did make some errors in these subjects, they were equally interested in learning what the correct syntax or grammar was, in order to correct them. (International secondary teacher, November 10, 2003)

The concept of community funds of knowledge links community context and curriculum (Moll & Gonzalez, 2004). Classrooms in which students, teacher, and subject matter are rooted in a similar cultural context are likely to activate knowledge students bring, regardless of whether the teacher specifically plans for this or not. But classrooms in which students' cultural context is different from that of the teacher and/or subject matter do not necessarily activate students' prior knowledge. When students' prior knowledge is not activated, and teachers are unfamiliar with their lives outside the classroom, they may assume students know far less than they actually do, an assumption that feeds the deficit ideology.

Households and communities, including those in impoverished neighborhoods, have organized funds of knowledge that people use in everyday life; and as children grow up, they become familiar with this knowledge through interaction with adults. Moll and Gonzalez (2004) taught teachers to listen and observe, then helped them plan household visits with families of a few of their students, in order to gain insights about household knowledge that could be activated in the classroom. As suggested above, teachers can learn to do this by becoming careful listeners and learners, meeting parents or other community members on their own "turf," then using what they learn in order to build meaningful classroom instruction.

Activating knowledge students bring to the classroom is the basis for the five standards for effective pedagogy developed by the Center for Research on Education, Diversity and Excellence (CREDE):

1. Teachers and students work together in group activities, jointly creating an idea or a product.
2. Language and literacy skills and strategies are developed in all subject areas across the curriculum.
3. Teachers connect lessons to students' lives, including their experiences at home, in the community, and at school.
4. Teachers engage students with challenging lessons that maintain high standards for student performance, and in doing so, they design activities to advance students' understanding to more complex levels.
5. Teachers emphasize teacher-student dialogue over lectures, especially academic, goal-directed, small-group conversations. (From *Five Standards* by the Center for Research on Education, Diversity & Excellence, 2002)

These standards are based on research in classrooms of teachers who are effective with children from minority backgrounds, low-income communities, or who are learning English as a second language. They serve as principles for effective curriculum and instruction for all students, including those of diverse cultural backgrounds, social-class backgrounds, and primary-language backgrounds.

When teachers are designing multicultural curriculum, therefore, I require that they write out a description of what their students already know related to their unit's big idea and describe how they found out. Below, Kathy shows how she linked students' family knowledge with math, as part of an interdisciplinary thematic unit in first grade. We will first look at the context of the broader unit, then more specifically at how she worked with math concepts.

Kathy: Anchoring Curriculum in Community Knowledge

Kathy had taught for over 20 years as a bilingual teacher, mainly at the first-grade level. She had been teaching in her current school for 15 years when she enrolled in Multicultural Curriculum Design. In her school, 98.5 percent of the students were Latino; all of Kathy's students were of Mexican descent, many having recently emigrated from Mexico. In accordance with the bilingual program that students' parents had requested, Kathy taught most of the day in Spanish to give students full access to grade-level curriculum.

Kathy was born in Mexico of White parents who had been working there for the American Friends Service Committee, and learned Spanish as her first language. When she was a toddler, her family returned to Ohio where she lived until she finished college. Then she returned to Mexico for 3½ years and became fluent in Spanish. As a teacher, she lived close to the school in which she taught. She was involved with and identified strongly with the students and their community; she welcomed parents to volunteer in her classroom as they were able to do so. Having lived in the school's community for 17 years, she maintained contact with many of her former students and their parents. Her master's thesis was based on interviews with parents of some of her former students, to explore how they support their children's academic success at home.

Kathy regards teaching as a political and ethical act and stated "If I refuse to take a position on something I consider to be harmful to children, I am contributing to that harm" (November 24, 2003). Her vision for students' learning is ambitious. She wrote, for example, "I want to make them hungry for books. I don't want them to think of reading as using the . . . text and workbooks. I want them to be able to apply their abilities to analyze, to question, to figure out meanings in text, . . . to be able to draw parallels between nature and their lives, and between one book and another" (November 10, 2003). In her master's thesis Kathy explained that the parents strongly desire for their children to have a better future and that they see school as an important vehicle toward this end. Kathy could not imagine teaching in a way that did not ground curriculum in students' family knowledge because it made learning relevant, engaging, and real.

Class meetings were a regular feature in her classroom. They provided a space in which student concerns led the agenda, and students took charge of problem solving. Kathy explained that she held class meetings often, although not everyday. "We always have a time for compliments first and then problems. And I figure if kids learn to resolve problems at this level, they're a lot more likely to resolve them later. And I've been amazed at their problem-solving abilities and their compassion" (March 23, 2004). She went on to describe interpersonal problems that students worked out with her guidance in class meetings. Kathy used class meeting space as a template for student-centered teaching during the rest of the day, and as a venue to get to know her students' interests and concerns.

For Multicultural Curriculum Design, Kathy extended an interdisciplinary thematic unit she had taught previously on Monterey County agriculture. She linked the unit to both reading–language arts and math standards for first grade, the "Farm Fresh" unit of her English Language Development text, and the first-grade life science curriculum. She credited her principal for giving her freedom to construct curriculum, as long as it met key state standards.

Kathy explained that she chose to develop this unit because "agriculture directly affects the lives of my students. Out of my 20 students, most have at least one parent who is employed in agriculture or an agriculture-related industry such as vegetable packing. The parents' income and work schedules are determined by the crops and the large companies which grow them" (December 15, 2003). She wanted the children to learn more about their parents' work, not in order to become agricultural workers themselves, but to respect the work their parents do. She explained that some of her students "have only a very vague idea of the role their parents play in agriculture" (December 15, 2003). She knew their parents personally and emphasized that "most of the parents don't want their kids to grow up to be farm workers, . . . that's why they want their children to get more education" (March 23, 2004).

Because she herself had grown up on a farm, she believed that everyone should know where food comes from and situate that knowledge within a vision of environmentally sustainable farms that ordinary people can afford to own. She was deeply concerned about "the conflict between what agriculture has become in this country and what it can be," a topic she explored in her paper looking into transformative intellectual knowledge. Increasingly, large corporations control agriculture and thereby also dominate "land use, water use and availability, pesticide use, and economic and political power." Kathy was concerned that "so many of my students' parents work in agriculture, yet so few can be farmers" (December 15, 2003). Her students who had emigrated from Mexico had memories of small, rural, family-owned farms, but were now surrounded by corporate farming. So, through this unit, in addition to teaching reading, writing, math, social studies, and science, Kathy also taught critical analysis of the political context in which students' families live and work, and a vision anchored in memories and possibilities.

Using various books, guest speakers, and pictures, Kathy explored with students the differences between large-scale corporate farms and small family farms. For example, she invited a parent with experience working in agriculture locally as well as in Mexico to come to class to describe the nature of work in both places. Using slides she had taken in rural Mexico, Kathy had students compare the small farm system there with the local agribusiness farms. Students planted seeds in order to observe how plants grow, and examined which foods are grown locally. They also learned plant vocabulary and developed a fruit and vegetable alphabet book. In addition, they studied the history and struggles of the United Farm Workers, particularly the work of local organizers.

Although people often say that first grade is too young to study political issues, Kathy explained that children regularly hear adults discuss political issues at home and want to know more, as reflected in questions they would ask during class meetings:

> They're not [too young]. In fact, last fall when on the ballot there was the tax to keep Natividad Medical Center [county hospital] open, one of my children brought that up in class and we talked about it. . . . This one little girl said, "Yeah, everybody has to go vote or they're going to close the hospital, and there won't be any place left to go." We talked about that. She's heard her parents and aunts and uncles discussing it. The war in Iraq—a year ago one of the kids brought in a picture of the soldiers from Salinas that had appeared in the paper, soldiers from Salinas that were serving in Iraq. And so we talked about it. (March 23, 2004)

Since most of the children's parents worked in agriculture, and since Kathy believed firmly that agribusiness is not the only (or best) way to construct farming systems, she wanted students to explore not only the science of plant growth, but also the economic and political systems surrounding that. Ironically, a popular local field trip for elementary schools is a visit to a farm, but the farm that students visit is set up like a small traditional family farm, not like the large commercial farms that prevail locally. Rarely do teachers point out to students that they are visiting a romanticized image that has been replaced by large-scale commercial agriculture.

I visited Kathy's class while she was teaching the math portion of the unit. It included several math concepts that are in the first-grade curriculum standards: numbers to 100, the concept of more than/less than, units and tens, and graphing. For example, the first-grade math content standards specify that "students can organize, represent, and compare categorical data on simple graphs and charts," and the science standards require that students learn to "record observations on a bar graph." Kathy's approach to teaching these concepts echoed Vygotsky's premise that school learning needs to build on children's previous history with reasoning.

The class constructed a bar graph using 3 × 3 in. cards on which each student indicated the crop with which their parents worked. Across the bottom of the graph were cards with the names and drawings of vegetables and other options. Students placed their cards above the vegetable work site that fit where their parents worked; when placed vertically, these cards became bars. Each of the following work sites had the following number of cards placed vertically when the bar graph was complete: *Apio* (celery): 1; *Flores* (flowers): 1; *La lechuga* (lettuce): 4; *La alcachofa* (artichoke): 2; *La coliflor* (cauliflower): 1; *Las uvas* (grapes): 3; *Las fresas* (strawberries): 5; *El brocoli* (brocoli): 2; *Empaque* (packing): 5; *En casa* (at home): 7; *Otros trabajos* (other work): 9.

The next day Kathy first engaged students orally, as a whole group, in quantitative reasoning from the graph; then she had them pair up to work through questions that asked them to make numerical sense of data on the graph: *¿Cuántas personas trabajan en la lechuga?* (How many people work in lettuce?) *¿Trabaja más gente en la casa o en un empaque?* (Do more people work at home or in packing?) Students appeared to find the worksheet challenging for several reasons. It stretched their reading skills—some of them hadn't known the names of some vegetables (such as *alcachofa*/artichoke); drawing conclusions from a bar graph was new to them; and the concept of more than/less than was difficult. Kathy explained later that first graders always struggle with this concept, but eventually get it. As she helped students use the bar graph of parents' work to reason through that concept, she tried to get them to think in terms of not just isolated numbers, but also their sense of what the numbers mean, such as how many students are in the class, and how many of their parents do what kind of work. When a child would write down a wrong answer, Kathy would restate the question and send the child back to the graph to try again. Linking the abstract concept to what they saw around them helped students "get it."

As students finished the worksheet, they moved to tables to cut out pictures of vegetables that would become part of a large picture graph. The purpose of the picture graph was to represent how many thousands of acres are planted in each of the most prevalent crops in the county. Kathy wanted the students to have a quantitative idea about the crops. She had located data on the Internet that detailed the acreage of crops. To help students visualize an acre, she took them out to the playground, which was a little smaller than an acre but gave them a rough idea. She cut out "fields" from brown butcher paper, using the scale of 1/8 sq. in. = 1 acre. The children drew and cut specified numbers of vegetables and fruits, cutting out one picture for each 1,000 acres that had been planted.

The day they constructed the picture graph, Kathy (with my help) laid out the "fields" to form a large quilt on the floor, each labeled with a crop name. Children glued crops on the fields. Then long black strips of paper were glued between the fields to make roads. The children found gluing large items unwieldy, so Kathy and I finished this part while the children completed a poetry assignment from earlier in the day, then read self-selected books. As we finished the roads, Kathy gave yellow chalk to a couple of students to make lines down the roads, and several students cut out cars to glue on the roads.

After the children were dismissed for the day and the glue had dried, we hung the picture graph in the hall. Kathy used it later in the week to have students figure out and discuss the relative acreage of various crops, again working with the concept of more than/less than. As she explained,

> They can see that there are only a few acres of carrots relatively speaking planted in Monterey County. There are more strawberries and artichokes than there are carrots and asparagus. There's a lot of broccoli, there's a lot of two different kinds of lettuce, head lettuce and leaf lettuce. So they can see relative amounts. (March 23, 2004)

In this way, Kathy had developed math concepts around what was familiar to the children. They found interpreting the bar graph to be difficult, but liked doing this in pairs, and found it easier to understand when asked to think in terms of what they were familiar with. They also thought the graphs were fun. As Kathy commented, "They like working in partners and small groups, they like, I mean from the time I came in this morning they said, OK, when are we gonna do the roads?" (March 23, 2004).

Kathy saw the curriculum standards as a guide, not as the curriculum itself: "I certainly look at them and think, OK, have I covered this, how am I thinking about covering it. Some of the standards seem much more important than others, so I try to make sure I cover those" (March 23, 2004). She showed me a xeroxed copy of first-grade content standards on which she had made notes regarding how this unit addressed various standards. But, rather than starting curriculum planning with the textbook or the standards, she started by identifying a rich theme that was significant to the lives of the children and their families in which subject matter content could be anchored. When I asked how her students were doing on the district's tests, Kathy explained that the first graders do not participate in the mandated testing program, but were doing well on benchmark math assessments.

CURRICULUM AS A COMPLICATED CONVERSATION ACROSS DIVERSE PERSPECTIVES

In a complex world, learning to engage across diverse points of view and experiences is not only important, but might be ultimately essential to our survival. How might the United States work out solutions to conflicts with nations that hold very different values and perspectives from those that dominate in the United States, without resorting to military conflict or cultural imposition? How might we address more local problems such as how to ensure everyone access to decent health care? Like others who view schools as sites for learning to participate in democracy, I see classrooms as public places where young people can learn to engage diverse perspectives and use that engagement for mutually beneficial creative problem solving.

Transformative intellectual knowledge makes explicit the viewpoint and social location from which it comes, and makes visible the viewpoints in the mainstream curriculum. Students also bring diverse experiences and perspectives that can become part of the curriculum. Even in classrooms that appear homogeneous, students bring different viewpoints. As Pinar (2004) argues, curriculum is never simply about disciplinary knowledge; rather, it involves people who bring their identities, interests, and perspectives. Curriculum that prepares young people for democratic participation can be thought of as "an extraordinarily complicated conversation" (p. 186).

Perspective Taking

Many teachers encourage students to share with each other their home culture, family histories, and outside interests, as ways of getting to know diverse people. This kind of sharing can build a foundation on which to dig into deeper issues. For example, Terri is a middle school teacher who taught a 2-hour language arts–social studies block for students for whom English is a second language during fall 2003. (She is featured in Chapter 9.) In her class were 13 different languages; half of the students had emigrated from countries around the world (such as Greece, Brazil, Taiwan, Bulgaria) and half were Mexican Americans who were behind in reading and language arts skills in both English and Spanish. Terri regularly constructed ways for students to share their backgrounds in the context of academic work. For example, after the students had studied an English translation of a poem by Pablo Neruda in language arts, Terri had them write a memorial about something in their own lives, using vocabulary and spelling words such as *memorial* and *historical* that appeared in the textbook. Students wrote about topics that ranged from a pet dying, to a relative killed in a drive-by shooting, to a national hero killed in a war. When it was time to share, most volunteered to read orally, and they listened with interest to each other's memorials. I also noticed a Bulgarian girl showing an Indonesian girl how to read Bulgarian words in a document she brought to share; Terri said that this interest in language "pops up quite a lot" (September 5, 2003).

From this kind of sharing, students can then learn to hear and engage with diverse viewpoints and perspectives. Teaching diverse perspectives does not mean preaching a particular perspective or getting into arguments about whose opinion is right. Rather, it involves helping students learn to identify and understand experiences, evidence, or values behind various viewpoints or ideologies. They may be those of sociocultural groups whose viewpoints students do not understand; they may be those of other class members. Students need not necessarily agree with other viewpoints, but should come to understand how they could make sense from the point of view of those who hold them, and learn to work through solutions to problems or conflicts on the basis of that understanding. *Empathy* has been conceptualized as being able to discriminate emotion in other people, being able to take the role and perspective of another, and being able to modulate one's own emotional expression as a result (Feshbach, 1975). Students can learn to empathize with others through work in perspective taking and attention to emotion, that is integrated into curriculum (Feshbach & Feshbach, 1987).

Athanases (1996) described how a teacher integrated a gay-themed lesson into a 10th-grade multicultural literature curriculum, helping the students grapple constructively with viewpoints new to some of them. She used much discussion and writing around why-questions, insisting that students back up what they say with evidence that included text materials and personal interaction with gay and lesbian people. This lesson was not an isolated one-shot exposure to diverse perspectives. Rather, over the year, she structured considerable practice examining controversial issues from diverse points of view through literature. Her students learned to discuss openly and respectfully, asking for evidence and reasoning behind viewpoints they did not agree with rather than becoming angry, defensive, or dismissive. Similarly, Fine, Weis, and Powell (1997) analyzed a World Literature classroom in which students and adults learned to speak openly and honestly about difficult issues related to race, racism, and power. The teachers worked hard to create safe spaces in which differences could be not only acknowledged, but openly interrogated. Although on some days classroom life was uninspiring, and on other days it was very difficult, "these classrooms, teachers, and students are mostly magic—the magic of imagining and creating a world that does not yet exist, a world in which difference is lifted and complicated" (p. 275).

Teachers Explore Multiple Perspectives

In Multicultural Curriculum Design, I use a mixture of structured and unstructured activities to engage with multiple perspectives. Some activities involve discussion of controversial issues in which class members disagree, and some involve personal stories that draw out different experiences. In fall 2003 we used an activity developed by Judith Flores (2003), one of my previous students, to connect examination of power and privilege with one's own life in a way that includes experiences of students from relatively privileged backgrounds. The week prior to this activity, students are asked to select one or two objects that have personal significance because they reflect membership in a sociocultural group (e.g., racial or ethnic, gender, sexual orientation, language) and a struggle for rights and/or identity related to membership in that group. The objects should allow them to share personal information about how they have claimed identity, space, and rights in society and/or in a specific community. The more thoughtfully students select struggles over identity and rights to discuss, the more meaningful their interaction will be.

The evening we did this activity, the teachers shared a great deal that enabled personal and intellectual connections. For example, several women of Italian descent discussed the importance of family, which both grounded their identity and had bound them to the kitchen while their children were growing up. An Italian American woman moved the group emotionally with her story of not being allowed to attend college when she was younger, despite her strong intellect. Two biracial students described their quest to claim an ethnic identity, given that they do not fit into an ethnic box, and they knew fairly little about parts of their ancestry. Several Catholic students brought rosaries and discussed both the spiritual grounding as well as limitations they had experienced through the Catholic Church. The activity provided space for students to connect abstract ideas about power, privilege, identity, and ideology with personal experiences. Subsequently, many made conceptual connections they had struggled with earlier. For example, several White teachers who had struggled to understand Macedo's (1994) analysis of ideology and power in education began to verbalize what he was getting at after listening to experiences of some of their colleagues of color. Mexican American and Italian American women discovered similarities in their family and school experiences that sometimes positioned them as outsiders in an Anglo-dominant society, and as subordinate in patriarchal families.

I structure activities that engage teachers in comparing how diverse sources view a specific issue in order to unpack the basis on which different points of view might make sense. For example, in one activity I had pairs review several Web sites that discussed Mount Shasta through viewpoints ranging from indigenous religion, to environmentalism, to commercial recreation. For each Web site, teachers were to figure out whose point of view is represented; who sponsored the Web site; what the Web site authors take to be a problem or an issue and what they want readers to do; and how the site's perspective is similar to or different from those of the other Web sites. After discussing the diverse perspectives in the Web sites, we discussed how teachers could help their own students identify and explore multiple viewpoints using a similar process.

A more elaborate structured activity that gets at diverse experiences and perspectives involves creating a multimedia, hyperlinked collection of stories around a theme. In fall 2001 we selected the theme "health issues in diverse communities." We brainstormed diverse communities for which health issues could be investigated, and each teacher selected one. They were to locate an insider perspective about a health issue, either through a personal interview or through reading, and bring what they found to the next class session. They chose issues such as hepatitis in the Chinese community, high blood pressure among African American women, Hmong perspectives about spirituality and health, and access to health care systems among Native Americans, Mexican Americans, and Greeks. The next class session was held in the computer lab, where each teacher created a small Hyperstudio stack displaying his or her information in text and pictures. Then I copied all 18 stacks, burned them onto a CD-ROM, and gave small groups a complete set. Working in groups, the teachers were to figure out issues and viewpoints emerging from the collection of stacks, group them, and create new Hyperstudio cards on which they discussed key questions and perspectives, and used buttons or hyperlinks to connect stacks. One group, for example, connected stacks that discussed health and religion from perspectives of Muslims, the Hmong community, Christian Scientists, Seventh-Day Adventists, and Jehovah's Witnesses.

At the next class session the teachers presented their work and discussed how they connected the various stacks conceptually, which led to a good discussion about perspective. For example, in the process of trying to investigate Muslim women's perspectives about postpartum depression, one teacher had had to confront her own assumptions about how she judges the credibility of knowledge. She realized that she tended to take the word of a doctor at face value rather than asking whose viewpoint it represents, and in the process never did access perspectives of Muslim women. A Chinese American teacher, who had investigated hepatitis within the Chinese community, realized that one can be an insider to a group, yet an outsider to knowledge about an issue. When she began the research, she positioned herself as an insider to the Chinese community but outsider to hepatitis sufferers. As she worked, she realized that hepatitis had run in her own family, and she began to reflect on what it means to be an insider or an outsider to specific communities.

As a teacher, I routinely find myself investing a tremendous amount of time and energy laying groundwork for complicated conversations in ways that engage teachers' experiences, viewpoints, and identities. Throughout this book, particularly in Chapter 2, I have discussed various activities designed to do so. Conflicts surface, some small and others major. But I have found it possible to build a living multicultural learning community through alternating between discussions based on sharing what is relatively "safe" with discussions and activities that draw out difficult issues and engage teachers in grappling with conflicts among their perspectives.

The last class session in fall 2003 illustrates the power of building complicated conversations over time. Following a potluck dinner, teachers were free to leave. Rather than leaving, however, they stayed on for another hour and a half, chatting in small groups. None of the groups was racially or ethnically homogenous. And while many of the conversations were entirely social, some teachers continued to discuss ideas and issues we had been working with over the semester. An African teacher pulled me aside to tell me about the course's impact on her. In my journal later that evening I wrote down what she shared:

> She said that when she first came here, she had a lot of biases, but she kept them under control because she needed to. But what she has learned is that our differences are very interesting, and she appreciates the program for giving her that. . . . She said that as she grew up, she grew to hate French people. But now, she hates [that

her country had] been colonized and hates abuse of power, but there are things about French people that she also realizes that she likes. She wants to go back to fight for education rights of her own people, but can do that and also find differences interesting, at the same time. (December 15, 2003)

That evening (as has been the case many other times), I saw a very diverse group that had at times battled about issues and wrestled over differences, coming together as a community. Some of their fears had given way to respect; and some of their hatred of people had been replaced by determination to fight against unjust systems. As a group, we had developed a basis for hearing and working through some (but certainly not all) of our differences. I thought to myself, this is what a living democracy should look like!

Angela, one of the teachers in that class, had tried to figure out how to help her fifth-grade students see U.S. history through opposing points of view, given her research into Iroquois perspectives about colonization (described in Chapter 5). The next section examines what she decided to do.

Angela: Teaching Multiple Perspectives

Angela taught fifth grade in a low-income school with a very diverse student population. Her class was about half Latino, a third African American, and the rest Vietnamese and Anglo. Standard 5.3 for California's fifth-grade social studies curriculum states: "Students describe the cooperation and conflict that existed among the American Indians and between the Indian nations and the new settlers." As noted earlier, her textbook represented a largely European American point of view, not an indigenous point of view. Since perspectives of indigenous people were radically different from those of the colonists, she wondered which she should teach and how she could engage students in debating diverse perspectives without losing control of the class.

Angela brought to teaching an interest in group activities and hands-on learning, but had not been successful using these with this class. She commented, "When given manipulatives in math, they were thrown sometimes. In language arts we worked in writing workshop groups, and more times than not there were disagreements and fights. The science experiments resulted in many referrals and suspensions" (November 3, 2003). Her new-teacher mentor told her that "this kind of population needs seat work and a definite routine everyday. . . . As a result, I backed off on these activities and have a 'whole class' teaching method instead of learning centers" (November 3, 2003). She believed that education should empower students rather than silencing them, but wasn't sure how to construct this. "My dilemma here is, how to have a classroom where students speak out, learn in different ways, and in group settings, without having troublesome discipline problems" (November 3, 2003). How could she engage students in debating conflicting viewpoints without having it turn into a free-for-all?

Angela used the suggestion of a colleague to organize a short unit around a trial. The unit included three 45-minute lessons. The fictitious trial focused on the Wampanoag nation's frustrations with colonists who were misusing natural resources, and particularly overkilling the deer population. The trial followed the process of the Haudenosaunee Great Law of Peace and Good Mind for building consensus about solutions to community problems. The first day of the unit was spent giving background information about the Wampanoag, the Haudenosaunee Great Law, locations of tribes on the East Coast, and basic structure of a trial. The second day involved a simulation of the ecology of the deer population without, and then with, active hunters; Angela linked this lesson with ecology in the science curriculum. (In the gym, students were somewhat rowdy; in the recitation session in her classroom afterward, they were fidgety.)

On the third day, students acted out the Wampanoag tribe bringing the European colonists to trial for misusing natural resources. Angela had given each student a role card that included a name, designation as Wampanoag or colonist, and specific role in the trial. Students got out their cards, and Angela explained who would be sitting where: defendants at one table, plaintiffs at another, jury at yet another table, and judges at a circular table in front. She reviewed terms, and explained that the Wampanoag are the plaintiffs because the deer that they depend on are missing. She also explained that the five judges include two colonists, two Wampanoag, and one from another tribe to act as a tie-breaker if needed. When students had moved into their places, she passed out worksheets appropriate to each role. For example, plaintiffs received questions such as "Why do you think the defendants are guilty? How did they hurt you? Explain your answer." Witnesses received questions such as, "Are you a witness for the defendant or plaintiff? What will you say to help the plaintiff or the defendant?" For the most part, students looked attentive and interested as Angela ran through this orientation.

Then the role play started. First, the Wampanoag witnesses testified, one by one, after being sworn in by the bailiff, with Angela acting as the questioner. Students mostly stuck to lines on their role cards, but a few knew their parts and extemporized. After witnesses for both sides had testified, other witnesses contradicted some of the testimony. For example, a witness for the colonists said that she saw a Wampanoag woman with food; a witness for the Wampanoag said he saw a colonist kill two small female deer, which were supposed to be off limits to hunters. Students looked very attentive as they listened. Then Angela took the jurors out of the room where they had 2 minutes to render a verdict. While they were deliberating, she had the rest of the students finish their worksheet. The jury returned and found the colonists guilty.

Then the judges deliberated about a sentence. While they were out of the room, Angela asked the students in the room what they thought about the verdict. After a small amount of silliness, students brainstormed several ideas, such as suggesting that the colonists could learn from the Indians what grows. The judges returned and sentenced the colonists to share all of the deer with the Native Americans for 2 years. Angela then led a whole-class discussion about whether students thought the verdict and sentence were fair. She also had students review a chart, constructed the previous day, about fluctuations in the deer population and the influence of hunters, asking whether the deer population might replenish in 2 years and whether the Native Americans would teach the colonists how to hunt deer without killing them off.

Students participated with thought and enthusiasm throughout the role play. (A parent who happened to be visiting class commented that he wished he had brought a video camera that day.) Angela had packed a lot into three 45-minute lessons, including background information about the Wampanoag, Pequot, and Haudenosaunee nations and legal system, colonists who arrived in Massachusetts and why they came, the ecology of deer populations, and court systems. She explained:

> Two weeks ago, I said, what do you know about the courtroom, and they just said, Judge Judy—they had no idea what a jury was, a plaintiff, a defendant, a bailiff, nothing. So . . . we did all of these lessons on the judicial system first. So, I think I spent a lot of time on that when I could have spent a little more time on the background of the Wampanoag and the Pequots. . . . They do have a deeper knowledge of some of the tribes in that area that aren't in their social studies book, which is good. (January 28, 2004)

Angela and I both viewed this unit as a viable way of having students explore two contrasting perspectives, then add their own perspectives into a problem-solving discussion.

Further, the unit helped Angela to see a connection between planning, student engagement, and classroom behavior. During the trial, students were much more engaged than usual, participating in ways that showed they were thinking about the conflict between colonists and Wampanoag, and engaging in far less off-task, fidgety behavior than usual. As we discussed this lesson, Angela realized that because the trial was carefully structured so each student had a role, and it was interesting, off-task classroom behavior was minimal, and their thinking was better than usual. Discipline problems are at least partly a consequence of pedagogy, rather than a characteristic of students themselves. And students can learn to examine, debate, and think through multiple perspectives when curriculum is well planned.

POSSIBILITIES AND CHALLENGES

Getting to know students and their communities can be threatening. Teachers need to have a secure sense of their own identity, so as not to feel threatened when students or parents say what they honestly think. Christi described some of her Latino students writing sugar-coated essays about school because they had learned which viewpoints teachers found acceptable and which they did not. In private conversations, she asked the students if they were writing the truth as they experienced it.

> And once they knew I was committed to hearing what they really had to say, and I wasn't going to get down on them, I wasn't going to grade them down, then they really started opening up. But it requires, with some students, that I actually sit down and talk about things with them. "That's OK, if that's how you feel, you know, just go ahead and write that down." And, after that, then I started getting these really amazing stories. (February 24, 2004)

Teachers featured in this book were determined to open up space for students in their curriculum, but most also experienced the standards pressing against such spaces, particularly in schools with low test scores. For example, although Angela and I both felt her short unit was worth teaching, she also worried that she was behind in covering the required content.

Ironically, the more standardized we make curriculum to improve students' achievement, the more we cut ourselves off from students' cultural, experiential, and personal resources on which learning should be built. In a study of a highly experienced elementary teacher's use of a scripted reading package, Meyer (2002) observed:

> In case you haven't noticed it, I have mentioned only superficial descriptions of Karen's children, beyond their behavior. That is because, during the teaching of phonics, issues of difference are erased and ignored by the phonics program. This is a program that the publishers' consultants, when they visit

the district, tell teachers "is good for all children." The quest for homogene-
ity of curriculum and the systematic dismissal of children's and teachers'
identities may seem efficient to the delivering of curriculum. (p. 91)

But, as Meyer went on to show, this quest for standardization and homo-
geneity makes culturally relevant teaching impossible, reducing what
teachers learn of students to their behavioral responses to packaged
curriculum.

And as the teachers in this book have shown, there is a lot more to
schooling than getting the one right answer. We need to get schools "right"
for students just as much as need to get students "right" for school.

NOTE

1. Many teachers construct KWL charts (*Know*, *Want* to learn, *Learned*) with
their class in order to access student knowledge. But individual interviews with a
few often reveal more depth in how students think and why, which is why I recommend doing interviews.

Chapter 7

Intellectual Challenge of Curriculum

I've seen the achievement of kids, post 227 [state proposition that considerably restricted bilingual education] plummet. ELD [English Language Development] actually lowers expectations. . . . The sad part is that so many people think that the standards will cure things, and they totally disregard the kids and the communities the kids are from.
(Gina, middle school teacher, January 22, 2004)

I want them [my second graders] to be exposed to publishing. Publishing is my main goal, and it's our main goal in this classroom. . . . I thought, what skill is mostly needed in middle school or in high school? Talking to teachers who are in those grade levels, they said, oh, word processing. . . . We start playing with the computer, and playing games, then we go to Microsoft Word. Then we use the Internet, then we use scanning, then we download, we do research.
(Juanita, second-grade bilingual teacher, February 10, 2004)

A multicultural curriculum should be planned and taught to high academic expectations; not doing so is inequitable. Teacher expectations are critical. Whether or not one's students are currently achieving well, the question to ask when planning curriculum is what one believes they are capable of, with teacher support. Too often, when I suggest that curriculum should aim toward building access to college, someone will say, "But not everyone will go to college. Aren't we doing students a disservice by suggesting that college is the only worthwhile goal?" The "not everyones" the questioner refers to usually come from poverty-level homes. Often questioners interpret high expectations as meaning preaching college rather than strengthening the curriculum's academic challenge and student academic support, or delivering a traditional college preparatory curriculum rather than one that is responsive to one's students. This chapter considers curriculum planning from the vantage point of intellectual challenge, start-

126

ing with an examination of teacher expectations, then moving to various tools for curriculum design.

EXPECTATIONS

The importance of teacher expectations for curriculum planning cannot be overstated. Researchers consistently find expectations of many teachers to vary according to students' race and class background. Teachers commonly see students who are White and Asian as more teachable than students who are Black and Latino, and students of middle- or upper-class backgrounds as more teachable than those from lower-class backgrounds. Commonly, low expectations are justified on the basis of family background, particularly teachers' beliefs about the extent to which parents value education (Baron, Tom, & Cooper, 1985; Codjoe, 2001; Cooper & Moore, 1995; Hauser-Cram, Sirin, & Stipek, 2003; Pang & Sablan, 1998; Tettegah, 1996; Warren, 2002).

Teachers generally describe students' present academic performance accurately. The problem is in projecting potential for the future. Based on a comprehensive review of research on teacher expectations of African American and White students, Ferguson (2003) maintained that, while teachers' perceptions of students based on past and present academic performance may accurately capture present performance, teachers underestimate potential by equating future performance with the present. Ferguson went on to connect expectations with teaching: "If they expect that Black children have less potential, teachers probably search with less conviction than they should for ways of helping Black children to improve and miss opportunities to reduce the Black-White test score gap" (p. 494).

What teachers are willing to try in the classroom, relationships teachers build with students, the extent to which teachers encourage students, and the general climate teachers create—all of which affect learning—grow out of expectations (Jussim, Eccles, & Madon, 1996). This is precisely the problem that has led so many African American and Latino school superintendents to endorse the testing movement as a lever for raising expectations of students ("Don't turn back the clock," 2003). Ironically, Lipman's (2004) study of Chicago Public Schools illustrated how some districts have created new forms of tracking (such as specialty schools and separate academic programs) in response to the standards accountability system that disproportionately offer affluent and White students access to an intellectually rich curriculum that is not structured around test preparation, while low-income and working-class students of color get primarily a test prep curriculum.

Research consistently shows that students from communities that have been historically underserved can achieve *when the teachers and school believe they can and take responsibility to make it happen* (e.g., Comer, 1988; Desmond, 1996; Diamond, Randolph, & Spillane, 2004; Foster, 1995; Haberman, 1995; Jackson, Logsdon, & Taylor, 1983; Ladson-Billings, 1994; Meier, 1998; Perry et al., 2003; Reyes et al., 1999). Teachers who take responsibility for student learning recognize challenges students and their families face, but are convinced that those challenges do not prevent learning and that a strong education will serve students. They consistently describe their students in terms of strengths and assets rather than deficits and persistently seek ways to address students' needs. Rather than attributing poor student achievement to lack of parental support, they build relationships with parents as well as they can and seek various ways to ensure that students get academic support, whether parents are able to provide it or not.

What this means for curriculum planning is thinking beyond students' present level of academic performance, and even beyond closing the achievement gap. As Hilliard (Perry et al., 2003) argued, fixation on the achievement gap can limit one's thinking by setting the current average achievement of White native English speakers as the goal for everyone, while in many international comparisons their academic performance is actually mediocre. He explained, "Too often, by using the European [American] students' normative performance as the universal standard, not only do we use a low standard, but we tend to be satisfied with the performance of minority cultural groups when a substantial reduction in this gap occurs" (p. 138). In the area of gender equity and achievement, for example, females not only caught up with males in many domains, but also surpassed them (Bae, Choy, Geddes, Sable, & Snyder, 2000), aiming higher than closing the gap.

Families that have been historically well served by schools expect far more than grade-level proficiency for their own children: They expect and demand complex intellectual work that will prepare their children for top colleges and leadership roles as adults. Students who succeed in college have learned to read complex material critically, think as they read, and make connections across ideas. They have learned to use basic concepts and skills in problem solving that requires higher order thinking. Standards for college preparation can serve as a guide to curriculum planning for all students (Perry et al., 2003). For example, the guide *Standards for Success* (Center for Educational Policy Research, 2003) emphasizes higher order thinking within the disciplines of English, mathematics, natural sciences, social sciences, second language, and the arts. Whether students actually enter college or not, these kinds of complex thinking skills matter for securing a job; those who have not developed them are increasingly condemned to low-skill, low-pay work (Skilton-Sylvester, 2003).

Systemically, expectations can be raised by eliminating lower level courses. Rockville Centre School District in New York, for example, has been "leveling up" over the past 10 years, so that all students are served in heterogeneous upper track classes. Results, as measured on standardized tests such as the Advanced Placement calculus exam and the Regents exam, are showing increases among both traditionally low and high achievers and a marked closing of the racial achievement gap (Burris, Heubert, & Levin, 2004). Other studies have found both high-achieving and low-achieving students more likely to *fail* lower level than upper level courses and do better in upper level courses (Haycock, 2003). This is probably because lower level courses are more boring, upper level courses are more interesting and challenging, and teachers of heterogeneous courses learn to tune into individual students more effectively. This is a research-based insight that can be taken right into the classroom. If teachers plan and teach challenging and interesting curriculum and provide academic support as needed, students will tend to rise to the occasion.

Subsequent sections of this chapter will suggest curriculum planning strategies and frameworks for teaching higher order thinking and demanding intellectual work when students are academically "behind" grade level. First, however, teachers must expect that their students can be high achievers and be willing to work to make it happen. An example is a second-grade teacher who is preparing her low-income, Spanish-speaking students for college.

Juanita: Publishing in Second Grade

Juanita was in her fifth year of teaching when I visited her second-grade classroom. As a teenager, she immigrated to the United States from Guanajuato, Mexico, and came to the university about 6 years later after graduating from a local high school. She had been a student in at least five courses I taught, including two courses in the master's degree program of which Multicultural Curriculum Design was a part, although she had not taken that course. I had been one of her mentors for about 10 years, and in other courses (including mine) she had studied concepts and planning processes similar to those in Multicultural Curriculum Design.

Juanita had been teaching in the same school since earning her credential. At the time I visited her classroom, she had 19 students, all of whom were from Mexican backgrounds. Some were born in Mexico, others in the United States. Juanita further explained, "All of my kids' parents work either in the agricultural fields or in packing companies" (February 10, 2004). Since all had Spanish as their primary language and their parents had requested a bilingual program, Juanita taught in Spanish for at least half of the day.

I was intrigued by Juanita's work because by her fourth year of teaching, her second graders were creating books using the computer. The previous year, the class had produced five books, each of which included papers written by every student. The five books included a biography, an interview, an autobiography, a research paper about a nonfiction topic of student choice, and a fiction story. Students used Microsoft Word, augmenting text with pictures (such as scanned photos or clip art) and other decorative touches (such as Word Art). They also did Internet research. For example, for the biography book each child chose a person to research on the Internet, wrote a page about the person's life, and inserted a downloaded photo of the person. Most of the students chose pop stars, such as Selena, but some chose to write about presidents, sports stars, and inventors. Each book had a table of contents, was bound with a decorated cover, and had a pocket with a library card so children could check them out. Juanita explained that each child checked out each book to take home for a couple of days.

This year, the class was in the process of producing six books, one for each theme of the language arts curriculum. In addition, Juanita would also help all the children compile a personal book based on their own writings, which they were saving on their own disk. She explained one of her goals:

> I want all kids to be exposed to technology. . . . Many of my kids don't have that opportunity. Many of them live in a one-bedroom apartment, with 7, 8 different members, and they don't have a chance to use a computer. That's not to say none of my kids do. But the majority don't. Or don't get a chance to go to the library and use it. So I want them to be exposed to publishing. (February 10, 2004)

Juanita started teaching the children to produce books when she realized that too much of the standard instructional program was boring. "I enjoy teaching but I didn't find it fun. I did not find anything fun about it, it was all about paper and pencil, paper and pencil, and I knew the kids were getting bored. I was getting bored myself, because I'm used to more interactive and engaging activities" (February 10, 2004). She also reflected on her own experience as a learner. She had become "really hooked on computers in high school," partly because they helped her learn English. She stuck with computers through college, and became very skilled at using them. In the university, she also came to see herself as an author. In several of her university courses, books were created with student writings. Juanita said that after graduation when she was cleaning out her materials, she threw away her papers but kept the student-written books. "I would be thinking about college and those years, and I would go pull that book and read it, and I'd think, Oh my god, I remember this class, I remember what book we read" (February 10, 2004).

When she learned to use computers and to produce knowledge and write for an audience that would read what she wrote, she was both engaged and empowered. As a teacher, she realized that she in turn could empower her students in the same way:

> We're expecting students to get power in college. College doesn't—
> college gives you power, but you must bring it with you, from
> when you're little. That's when I realized, wait a minute! . . . I need
> to teach my students to be creative people, responsible citizens,
> independent thinkers, people who speak their minds, all of those
> things. I need to teach my little ones all of that and more. (February
> 10, 2004)

It took some experimentation and persistence to learn to teach her second graders to create documents on computers. She told me that at first the experience was chaotic. Her classroom had a computer station where small groups of students worked while she instructed other small groups in reading, but after a few minutes the students on computers were "all over the place." Only a few were getting their work done; the majority were not. Sometimes teachers give up at this point, but the next year Juanita decided to try systematically teaching computer use from the beginning of the school year.

> And so now we go to the computer lab for 30 minutes, twice a
> week. . . . I train them all, all of them at once, how to use it, play a
> little bit with them, show them some computer games first, we start
> easy, we start playing with the computer, and playing games, then
> we go to Microsoft Word. Then we use the Internet, then we use
> scanning, then we download, we do research. (February 10, 2004)

She kept the computer station in her classroom and developed learning stations for reading–language arts. But she now teaches children how to help each other: "I train kids, like I may teach one child how to do one thing, so if another child comes to the same question, I direct that child to the other student so that I don't have to repeat myself two, three, four, five times." This has helped the children learn independence and peer tutoring and has enabled Juanita to focus on small-group reading instruction without constant interruptions. When I visited her classroom, this process was working very smoothly.

Through her whole curriculum, Juanita explained that she uses the grade-level standards as a guide, but expects and teaches more than they require:

> I expect more than what's in the curriculum. Therefore I give them more. For example, our curriculum expects them to be able to multiply times tables twos, threes, fours, and fives. That's all. When they finish [my] second-grade [class], they know how to multiply times six and all the way up to eleven and twelve. And they have to be able to divide with remainders. Remainders! A remainder is a third-grade curriculum. But I expect them to do it. . . . The standards say for second graders to be able to write a paragraph or two paragraphs. But why not three paragraphs? Or why not four or five at the end of the year? (February 10, 2004)

In order to teach beyond the expected curriculum, Juanita carefully studies the standards and adopted texts, and figures out what is key and what she can skip. A combination of experience, staff development, and cues in the texts has helped her identify which standards to attend to. She also keeps an eye on what demands of college-level work look like. She commented, "If you were to cover every standard, you would be 70 years old by the time you finished with all of them. It's too much, so I pick key standards for math, key standards for language arts." Being selective and knowing where to focus has enabled her to teach more deeply to higher levels than if she tried to cover everything.

Juanita also tries to make the content as multicultural as she can, given limitations of available resources. She explained that the students enjoy learning about other cultures, and they also enjoy Aztec dance when she has taught it; these further stimulate their engagement. Not only are her students intellectually engaged, but their measured skills are improving:

> I've seen students improve in their reading, and I can see from the day they come in. Just to compare, this year out of 19 students I had 14 below benchmark, two above benchmark and the rest of them, average. And right now I have 5 below benchmark, only 5 out of 14. I had 2 kids above benchmark, right now I have 7 above. I'm really pleased with their work, because kids are reading 100 words per minute [in Spanish]. And in English they're reading close

to ninety and a hundred, they're really close to that, in English and Spanish you can see both languages pulling up, and I like that. (February 10, 2004)

Juanita's curriculum packs reading, writing, math, and technology skills around project-based higher order thinking. Further, Juanita has figured out which concepts and skills provide the most powerful basis for further learning, and spends time developing them (mainly in students' primary language) rather than trying to cover everything.

CURRICULUM PLANNING AND INTELLECTUAL CHALLENGE

Curriculum planning for intellectual challenge can be connected with planning around a big idea that has been developed through transformative intellectual knowledge, and in relationship to (and possibly with) one's students. How can curriculum also be planned so that it is intellectually demanding and teaches a variety of academic skills? Too often I have seen teachers plan either intellectually demanding work that slides over skill development, or skill-drill curriculum that is short on higher order thinking.

Bloom's (1956) taxonomy, shown in Table 7.1, is a useful planning tool. Bloom identified six levels of thinking that range from recall and basic understanding to application of ideas, to prediction and synthesis of ideas, to evaluation. The verb lists in Table 7.1 help teachers identify the nature of thinking they are asking students to do. Too often students from historically underserved communities get a curriculum that dwells on lower order thinking, which can become so boring that students simply tune out, thereby not learning even the basics very well.

To use Bloom's taxonomy, I recommend working through four main questions:[1]

1. How does the unit as you have planned it so far, or as you have taught it before, address each of the six levels of Bloom's taxonomy?
2. How do the curriculum standards for the unit you are developing address the levels of Bloom's taxonomy?
3. How does the textbook address the levels of Bloom's taxonomy?
4. Using Bloom's taxonomy as a guide, if your students were to be prepared for college, what should they be learning to do in this unit that isn't listed above?

The questions start with an inventory of the levels of thinking one's current curriculum concentrates on, and levels that might be overlooked. The

Table 7.1. Objective and Verbs Used with the Cognitive Domains in Bloom's Taxonomy. (From Benjamin S. Bloom et al., *Taxonomy of Educational Objectives*. Published by Allyn and Bacon, Boston, MA. Copyright © 1984 by Pearson Education. Adapted by permission of the publisher.)

	Knowledge	Comprehension	Application	Analysis	Synthesis	Evaluation
Educational Objective	Recall information such as dates, events, places. Recall major ideas.	Explain what information means. Interpret information. Translate knowledge into new context. Order, group, infer causes. Predict consequences from information.	Use information, methods, skills, or concepts in new situations to solve problems or answer questions.	Recognize components and patterns. Organize parts. Compare and contrast similarities and differences.	Use old ideas to create new ones. Generalize from given facts. Relate knowledge from several areas. Combine different ideas or concepts.	Discriminate between ideas. Assess value of evidence supporting ideas. Make choices based on reasoned argument. Recognize subjectivity.
Associated Verbs	list, define, tell, describe, identify, show, label, examine, tabulate, quote, name, who, when, where	summarize, describe, interpret, contrast, predict, associate, distinguish, estimate, differentiate, discuss, extend	apply, demonstrate, calculate, complete, illustrate, show, solve, modify, relate, change, classify, experiment, discover	analyze, separate, order, explain, connect, classify, arrange, divide, compare, select, explain, infer	combine, integrate, modify, rearrange, substitute, plan, create, design, invent, compose, formulate, prepare, generalize, rewrite	assess, decide, rank, test, measure, recommend, convince, select, judge, evaluate, discriminate, support, conclude, compare, summarize

first question helps teachers identify levels of thinking they have tended to concentrate on, and others they may have skipped. The second and third questions help to identify thinking most likely to be developed within one's planning and teaching resources.

The fourth question asks the teacher to project beyond the students' current grade level to the kinds of thinking students should be developing in order to succeed at higher levels of schooling. As Juanita mentioned, when teachers have long lists of content to cover, it makes more sense to identify the richest concepts that are foundational to learning and develop those well rather than trying to cover the waterfront (which usually reduces the curriculum to the lower levels of the taxonomy at the expense of higher levels). Here is where guides for college preparation, such as *Standards for Success* (Center for Educational Policy Research, 2003), mentioned earlier, are useful. Using the lens of learning beyond the students' current grade level can help teachers decide what is foundational and what is not—a question that goes back to what is "enduring" and what is not (Chapter 3).

Generally speaking, I suggest that every unit a teacher designs and teaches should work with at least five of the six levels of Bloom's taxonomy. While any given unit might concentrate on some levels more than others, I have found that asking teachers to plan for at least five often results in very interesting curriculum that links ideas and skills, and embeds lower level skill development and content acquisition with higher level thinking. In the next section, Mona's approach to teaching science illustrates connecting a wide range of kinds of thinking.

Mona: Mini University

Mona had been teaching 18 years when she enrolled in Multicultural Curriculum Design and I subsequently visited her classroom. She taught a combined fourth- and fifth-grade class in a very diverse, low-income elementary school in which no racial/ethnic group was in the majority and about one-third of the students were classified as English-language learners. The mixture of her class was reflective of Mona's family. "I'm a multicultural United Nations in itself, you know, my dad's family with eleven kids all going to different cultures, marrying different ethnicities" (April 22, 2004). Ethnically, Mona is mainly Filipina, with an Iroquois-Black grandfather. Through extensive family intermarriage, she grew up seeing multicultural as normal.

She had worked as an instructional aide before earning her teaching certificate. Over her career, she had taught K–7 in several different schools, mostly in another school district. She loves working with low-income students, second-language learners, and children of refugee families. She believes strongly in maintaining high academic expectations and preparing her students to think in terms of college. Her own family history is a testament to education as a powerful tool of social mobility and teacher expectations as central. At the same time, she is critical of test-driven, one-size-fits-all definitions of academics. The observation related here shows how she filters her commitments through her science curriculum.

California's science content standards focus largely on acquisition of facts and basic concepts, with limited hands-on learning. They are written as lists of concepts to "know"; for example, fifth-grade students are to *"know* the Sun, an average star, is the central and largest body in the solar system and is composed primarily of hydrogen and helium" (California Department of Education, 2003, Standard 5.a). Students are also supposed to learn to use the scientific method. Science had just been added to the state's testing battery, so students will be held accountable for learning the prescribed content.

Mona had several concerns about all of this. First, "the unfortunate reality is that many teachers 'skip' teaching science because they concentrate on reading and math and the writing curriculum;" her fourth and fifth graders were about to be tested over material they had not been taught (September 29, 2003). Second, she was concerned that the test itself would be fact-driven, rather than comprehension-driven. Since many of her students were in the process of learning English, while they were capable of learning basic concepts and ideas, they may not know all of the "facts" or know them in English. Third, Mona believed strongly that elementary students need a foundation that connects concepts with what they already know, rather than an accumulation of disconnected facts. In a previous extended experience with DISTAR,[2] she had learned that second-language learners "were just mimicking the words and sentences, and when it came to comprehension they didn't have a clue about vocabulary, let alone story content" (November 3, 2004). She argued that it is easier for teachers to "teach to the test, thus feeding loads of data and information into students," but this is not the same as providing "comprehensible connectors" with students' prior knowledge that will help them understand and remember new knowledge. She was also concerned that teaching factual knowledge for recall would exclude developing critical thinking (September 29, 2003).

Fourth, Mona valued teaching everything, including science, from a multicultural perspective. Doing that helps her connect concepts with her students; it also helps her raise questions or insights that other teachers might not raise. She told a story to illustrate the power of cultural connections to foster reading:

> My grandfather was a Buffalo Soldier. And I had to do a report, and
> there it was, Buffalo Soldiers! I took a book that I checked out, and
> took it home to my dad. My dad has only an eighth-grade education.
> My mother said that was the first time she ever saw him read a book
> in her life. And he read it! And he asked me if he can have it. I
> ordered it from Borders. And my mom said he keeps that book and
> it's the only book he ever read that she ever saw. (April 22, 2004)

Would her father have developed an interest in reading if he had been
given culturally relevant books when he was in school, rather than wait-
ing until he was middle-aged? Her family history taught her that family
knowledge and academic knowledge can be bridged through culturally
diverse stories. As I watched Mona teach about the solar system, I saw her
explore how diverse cultural groups have made sense of the solar system
through creation stories.

I will examine Mona's solar system unit in relationship to culture,
academic expectations, and Bloom's levels of thinking. When I walked into
Mona's classroom, I was struck by its parallels with a college classroom:
Her students work from a syllabus; she has eight Internet-wired computers students use for research; her students write reports as Word documents and give presentations illustrated with Power Point; and she teaches
them how to take notes on minilectures. She emphasizes teaching students to give formal presentations to an audience; one of her fourth graders who at the beginning of the year "wouldn't even talk" had just given
a presentation to the school board. Mona explained, "This is mini university, . . . I tell them, this is stuff like we do in college. And when we get
service learners, student teachers that come to observe me—Wow! . . . It
blows them away that these guys are doing it" (April 22, 2004). By constructing visible parallels between her fourth-fifth classroom and a college
classroom, Mona intentionally tries to demystify college for her students
and help them envision college in their futures.

Mona linked the solar system unit with literature and language arts.
While the big idea was exploring what makes up the solar system, the unit
also explored how different cultural groups, particularly various Native
American tribes, have made sense of creation and the relationship between
humans and the sky. (She described her planning process as taking an idea
and looking at it with a magnifying glass for depth.) At the lower levels of
Bloom's taxonomy, her solar system curriculum was fairly traditional and
tied to the standards; at the upper levels, it was not.

Mona organized students into cooperative groups, with each group
assigned a planet. At the *knowledge and comprehension levels*, students were

to learn basic information about the whole solar system and specialize in one planet. Each group was to locate specific factual information on their planet using various books as well as the Internet. Each student also had a chart on which to organize notes they took on the solar system as a whole. I watched as Mona ran through several planets with the class, working with students' research. For example, she asked the Pluto group to report. A boy stood and read from his group's research; Mona showed the rest of the students where to take notes on the chart. They went through information such as where the planet is located in the solar system, distance from the sun and diameter. She took them planet by planet, starting with facts students had collected, then elaborating and making sure the class was following specific information about each planet.

She interspersed planet facts with thinking questions, such as why it is hot in North America in summer but cold in winter, and what the planets might be made of. For thinking questions she gave small groups a minute or so, then called on students. The thinking questions served as *application level* exercises, in which students were to use concepts they had learned earlier to figure out something about the solar system. For example, she expected students to draw on what they had learned about rocks and states of matter to speculate what planets at various distances from the sun are made of.

By connecting science with literature and math, Mona prompted students to use concepts and factual knowledge in meaningful ways that involved *analysis* and *synthesis*. She had gathered children's books from the library that told stories about the planets from several cultural groups' perspectives. (Working with the school librarian, she had the students do a scavenger hunt in the library for books written by diverse cultural groups about the planets.) For example, students read *Earth Namer* (Bernstein & Kobrin, 1974), a story from Bungee Indian tradition in Canada; *The Lizard and the Sun* (Ada, 1999), a bilingual Mexican American story; and *Ahaiyute and Cloud Eater* (Hulpach & Zwadsky, 1996), a Zuni story. For language arts, students were to write a report discussing, comparing and contrasting three of these (*analysis*). For science, they were to write a fictitious creation story of their planet that used factual knowledge about the planet, as well as literary devices of folktales, fairy tales, prophecy, fables, legends, or folklore in the books students read for their book analysis paper (*synthesis*). They were also supposed to embed their planet within a fictitious solar system and galaxy, using math instruments they were learning as part of their math curriculum (protractor, compass, ruler) to construct a picture. Planet groups would make a presentation to the class about their planet based on their research and writing; each group could determine how to organize its presentation.

After minilecture-discussions on planet facts, planet groups had time to work on their research, their book analysis report, and their presentation. Students were particularly enthusiastic about working on computers. For example, one small group was glued to a Web site called Nine Planets, which they were using for research. A couple of groups were using Kid Pix Slide Show or Power Point to begin to organize presentation of information about their planet, while Mona showed another group how to use Microsoft Word presentation templates as tools for organizing written work. While most of the students were on computers, others were working at desks on their book analysis report.

As students worked in small groups, I saw a good deal of peer helping. Students helped each other locate useful Web sites, figure out how to use Kid Pix or Power Point, and figure out what to write for their book report. While taking notes during Mona's minilecture, students also occasionally helped each other figure out what they should write down, and where. Mona commented, "That's why I like putting them in groups. 'Cause they are learning from the others. And they're helping each other. . . . They all want to be teachers!" (April 22, 2004).

Linking her science and language arts curriculum gave Mona a way to design curriculum that took big ideas into depth, from diverse cultural perspectives, engaging students in learning and thinking across the spectrum of Bloom's taxonomy. Mona mentioned that earlier, when teaching about rocks, she used the same planning strategy: "When we did the rocks, we had [Native American] stories that went with it, about the rocks, and how they picked their territory to live in, the kind of housing they developed according to the environment of the rocks, and the landscaping" (April 22, 2004). In other words, by linking rocks and minerals with Native American stories, the class could explore the relationship between the natural environment and human cultural artifacts such as housing. In this way, she could work with factual material in the science standards, but make that material meaningful by connecting it with concepts familiar to students, and with the reading, writing, research, and presentation skills they were developing in language arts.

BUILDING ENABLING STRATEGIES INTO CURRICULUM

Enabling strategies assist students in learning how to think more complexly than they can do presently by themselves. To enable students to succeed at doing something difficult, the teacher explicitly builds a temporary support system. Modeling, for example, involves not just showing students how to do something, but talking them through one's thinking process.

There is an important ideological issue here that teachers need to confront: how they conceive of the nature of knowledge, and how knowledge and learning relate. Recall from Chapter 2 Powell's (1996) contrast between a teacher who held a disciplinary perspective about knowledge with one who held a developmentalist perspective. That same distinction affects how teachers think about constructing academic challenge of curriculum in relationship to their students.

Teachers who see knowledge as structured hierarchically focus on concepts that build on each other sequentially, believing that students need to learn particular bodies of facts and skills *before* they can go on to more complex ideas. This perspective was taken by the writers of California's content standards.[3] If one applies a hierarchical view of knowledge to second-language learners in an English-only context, one is likely to believe that they need to be taught English before upper level language skills and content, so that they can do the upper level, complex work in English. Similarly, a hierarchical view of knowledge applied to culture suggests that children from nonmainstream cultural backgrounds should learn mainstream culture first, *before* going on to upper level learning.

Teachers who take a hierarchical perspective about disciplinary knowledge, language, and culture tend to drill students who are below grade level on the "basics" as preparation for higher level work at some point in the future (see also Hauser-Cram et al., 2003). The problem with this is that drills on basics become boring, and some students never get to the more interesting, thought-demanding curriculum. Second-language learners are especially vulnerable when teachers retreat to the grade level at which the students can function in English, which may be far below their intellectual capability in their own language. Students of color, particularly African American students, also get locked into lower level, skill-based curriculum for similar reasons.

An alternative perspective about knowledge—what Powell (1996) referred to as a developmentalist perspective—focuses less on the structure of disciplinary knowledge than on the process of knowing. According to this perspective, mastery of particular content is less important than students' ability to work meaningfully with content. Content is still important, but in relationship to student thinking; students making meaning of content trumps students memorizing content as defined by disciplinary experts. Teachers who take this perspective are more likely to individualize instruction and try to connect curriculum with their students. Applied to second-language learners, this perspective values learning English alongside rather than prior to academic skills and content. This is why Juanita and Kathy taught Spanish-dominant students in Spanish—they could get the students farther in language and math when teaching in the students' strongest language. Juanita and Kathy also taught students English, but their math and language learning did not have to wait for their English skills to catch up.

I see this second perspective as much more useful than the first for bridging students' current academic performance with their future potential. But as mentioned earlier, content standards may well present teachers with curriculum based on a particular set of assumptions. To decide what to do in their own classrooms and in the context of what they are presented with, teachers may need to grapple with their beliefs about the nature of disciplinary knowledge in order to identify how those beliefs shape curriculum planning.

Scaffolding

Scaffolding is a very useful enabling strategy to bridge students' current academic performance with potential; it refers to temporary curricular supports for students as they learn to do something new and complex. Scaffolding helps teachers build higher order thinking alongside lower-order concepts and skills. Gibbons (2002), for example, described a cycle to scaffold complex writing on intellectually challenging topics for second-language learners. In Stage 1 (building knowledge of the topic), students learn varied ways of retrieving what they already know, and linking it with new knowledge. Discussions, word walls, KWL (Know, Want to learn, Learned) charts, and pictures are examples of techniques. In Stage 2, the teacher talks through text construction using a model similar to the kind students will write, involving students in writing portions of texts, using retrieved knowledge. (As a university professor, I use this form of scaffolding extensively when helping graduate students write literature reviews.) In Stage 3, the teacher jointly constructs text with students, starting with the student's verbalization of what is to be written, then helping students with sentence construction, wording, and so forth as needed. The teacher may also give students an outline of the text they are to produce, with spaces for them to write, to help students get the idea of a report's construction. In Stage 4, students write independently.

Figure 7.1 illustrates a scaffolding guide for learning to write a paragraph using a topic sentence and supporting sentences. In this example, students are assisted in writing a paragraph that explains how the Mexican Zapotec calendar is similar to or different from their own calendar at home, after reading a paragraph about the Zapotec calendar. Before writing, they brainstorm words that describe both calendars. They

Figure 7.1. Scaffolding Guide for Writing a Paragraph with a Topic Sentence and Support

---

Calendars

1. List words that describe the Zapotec calendar.

2. List words that describe your calendar at home.

3. Complete:

    The Zapotec calendar is _____ from my calendar in_____ ways.

First,

Second,

Third,

---

complete the topic sentence, and then construct three supporting sentences using words they brainstormed. After students get the idea of writing a paragraph, they will not need this kind of assistance.

To determine the kinds of enabling strategies or scaffolds students might need, teachers can start with assessment rubrics (Chapter 4) that describe what learning looks like by the end of a unit. Doing this helps to break down complex work into constituent pieces. Then teachers can identify the pieces for which students might need explicit instruction, modeling, or scaffolding guides to assist them. For example, Christi's rubric for assessing students' narrative about the life of an immigrant (Table 4.2 in Chapter 4) specifies that the narrative should have an organizational structure (such as sequence), use content knowledge about the life of an immigrant insightfully, use rich, concrete sensory detail, and exhibit accurate spelling and grammar. Students who do not write well may need scaffolding (such as an outline) that assists them in organizing paragraphs or papers. After they have constructed a draft that is organized and uses content knowledge, second and third drafts can amplify sensory detail and correct spelling and grammar. The teacher might model adding sensory detail to a draft, for example, then model editing for spelling and grammar.

A note of caution: teachers can overscaffold, reducing complicated thinking to following an outline or putting pieces together in a predetermined way. Skilton-Sylvester (2003), for example, reflected on his experience as a teacher trying to find the space in which students have to struggle intellectually with a complicated problem, while given enough support to enable successful completion but not so much that the problem becomes easy. He commented, "While breaking tasks into subtasks may sometimes be necessary, problems result if students are never pushed to complete whole tasks by themselves" (p. 27). Below, Gina illustrates how she embeds lower level skill development and scaffolding within complex wholes, as she teaches dance and literary analysis.

Gina: Scaffolding Spanish Literature Analysis

Gina, introduced in Chapter 5, teaches middle school dance most of the day, and also one period of Spanish. She is very critical of local educators' low expectations of Latino students. I interviewed her during the second year her school had been designated as a low-performing school. To remedy low achievement, "They want us to hit on what's on the test" (January 22, 2004) and display the standards on the classroom wall; Gina had experienced administrative visits that start by scanning the walls rather than the students and pedagogy. However, she pointed out that the school's test scores have been flat. One major reason she saw was what she referred to as "the ELD [English Language Development] diet." She explained that Proposition 227, by mandating English as the medium of instruction, relegated bilingual and English as a second language classes to remedial status because as soon as students can function in English, they are transitioned into English-only classes. As a result, reflecting a hierarchical conception of knowledge and language, language instruction for students who are not yet fluent in English has become intensely remedial. Students' development in both languages is not being embedded in challenging upper level thinking.

As mentioned earlier, Gina performs in a community dance company and has studied dance in Mexico for several years. Her teaching is guided by a clear sense of what excellent performance looks like, and what key knowledge and skills support that. In addition, her experience studying in Mexican universities has developed her vision of high-level academic learning in Spanish.

In dance classes, Gina integrates performance with academic study of the history and culture of specific dances. "I always tell this to the kids, you can't get up on stage and represent something you know nothing about" (January 22, 2004). During the hour she has the students, she keeps up a fast pace, running her class like a dance studio. I watched her rehearse a new dance with a class, and noted how she taught dance holistically while at the same time teaching specific skills. The dance as a whole used several key skills, including maintaining rhythm, keeping rows straight, and spotting while turning. Gina had students run through a portion of the dance, then stopped briefly to model and practice spotting, then ran the class through the whole again, then stopped briefly to model and practice keeping rows straight. She kept a focus on the complex dance as a whole, stopping to work through specifics as needed, but always connecting them to the larger whole.

She uses a similar approach to teaching language skills in Spanish: embedding specific skills in more complicated intellectual work, and using explicit instruction, scaffolding, or modeling as needed to help students with specific skills that connect to the larger project. Gina explained how a system that is designed to transition students away from Spanish tends to leave them without very good academic language in either Spanish or English:

> Sometimes the kids had Spanish instruction in elementary school, but it stops in third grade. Then they have it, this is the first year, eighth grade, that they're starting to write in Spanish again. Some have had zero, but they've spoken Spanish in their house. So again, it's like bringing that home language to an academic level. And heightening their awareness that they're gonna need it, not only in their personal lives, but to go the university, in high school, et cetera et cetera. That's the idea of the Spanish classes, preparing them for their future. (January 22, 2004)

Students come to Gina's Spanish class generally with Spanish vocabulary and comprehension that is below grade level, but she uses grade-level thinking and materials in her teaching. For example, I watched her guide the students through a literary analysis of the novel *La Ciudad de las Bestias* by Isabel Allende (2002). She wanted students to learn to analyze, compare, and contrast characters, while at the same time developing their skill in comprehending Spanish. For that purpose she had developed a scaffolding guide to help students compare and contrast four characters in terms of their role in the expedition the story was about, their perceptions of indigenous people of the Amazon, who they got along with well and badly, and whether they would be considered friends by the students and why. The guide consisted of a chart with names of four characters across the top, and down the left-hand side questions to ask such as *¿Con quién(es) se lleva bien o mal en el viaje?* (Who does the person get along with well or poorly on the trip?). Students worked first in small groups and then as a whole class to construct a comparative character analysis.

Later on they should be able to develop their own analysis without assistance of a teacher-made chart. Gina said that taking on a novel was a stretch for the students, but it will prepare them for AP coursework in high school and college. They struggle at first, but "eventually they do get it, it comes together" (January 22, 2004).

POSSIBILITIES AND CHALLENGES

Juanita, Mona, and Gina illustrate possibilities of pushing students beyond grade-level curriculum and lower level thinking. Their work illustrates teaching as intellectual apprenticeship; it also highlights the challenge of teaching students from historically underserved communities to become knowledge producers in a standards-testing context that constructs them as remedial learners.

If classrooms were thought of as intellectual spaces, the teacher would be the senior practicing intellectual who is apprenticing young people in a world of complex academic work. Apprenticeship links development of professional identity and social identity, both of which constitute self-images and "a projection of oneself in the future" (Dubar, cited by Cohen-Scali, 2003, p. 239). Professional and social identities are developed in the context of social relationships. Under apprenticeship, the young person is specifically given guidance, assistance, and feedback in learning new tasks, as well as social support in constructing a sense of self within the new role.

The importance of teachers' ongoing intellectual engagement and their work apprenticing students in that engagement struck me as I visited classrooms. Gina apprentices her students into her love of and exacting standards for dance performance and cultural study. Juanita and Mona apprentice them as researchers and writers producing knowledge in a technological environment. Christi, who was teaching her ninth graders to write narrative fiction from the point of view of a fictitious but believable immigrant, was in the process of writing a novel and working with the same problem of telling a story from someone else's point of view. Such teachers build close personal relationships with students and "use their personal relationships to model learning and enhance the teaching-learning process" (Haberman, 1995, p. 58; see also Meier, 2002;

Moses & Cobb, 2001b; Stanton-Salazar, 2004). As Christi put it, "When you feel passionate about something, it's so exciting to engage your students in that kind of activity. . . . Passion is contagious" (February 24, 2004).

However, the structure of knowledge embedded in the standards-textbook-test trilogy tended to frame their own students as knowledge consumers rather than intellectual workers who produce knowledge. In a knowledge consumption and training paradigm, students consume prespecified content and develop practical skills for later use in specific jobs. In an intellectual paradigm, students learn to appropriate the academic tools of disciplines in order to become not only self-directed learners, but also producers of knowledge (Aronowitz, 2000). Teaching for intellectual challenge suggests the latter. However, a combination of low academic expectations, a hierarchical view of disciplinary knowledge, and a crowded curriculum can push teachers of students from historically marginalized communities toward the training–knowledge consumption paradigm, ultimately leaving them behind students from White, affluent communities.

NOTES

1. Cognitive psychologists such as Moore (1982) caution that the hierarchical structure of the cognitive domain as it is represented in Bloom's taxonomy does not actually reflect the nature of the learning process. Although I find this taxonomy a useful device for planning to a range of kinds of thinking, I am aware that there is disagreement about its usefulness.

2. DISTAR stands for Direct Instructional System for Teaching and Remediation. It is a phonics-based program that was created in the 1960s to help children whose reading achievement was lagging. Its value has been widely debated, with some praising its results while others criticize its strong focus on drill and lack of use of higher levels of thinking.

3. In 1985 a math framework was adopted that "in many ways was the antecedent of the 1989 NCTM [National Council for the Teaching of Mathematics] Standards" (Schoenfeld, 2004, p. 269) in its emphasis on thinking and problem solving. Similarly, in 1987 a reading–language arts framework that reflected a constructivist, literature-based approach was adopted. Both were loudly condemned by conservative groups that objected to pedagogical processes such as invented spelling, constructivist learning, writing about personal feelings, or teaching math reasoning over math facts. New curriculum committees were appointed for both areas, headed by advocates of direct instruction. Both rewrote the frameworks and standards around a direct instruction view of teaching and a view of knowledge as something located outside learners, to be learned largely through memorization. In 1997 the California State Board of Education adopted the revised math and reading–language arts curriculum documents. That same year,

the state appointed a science committee to draft science standards. These were written and adopted quickly, with fairly little public debate or input (Schultz, 1998). The resulting science standards, like the second version of the math and reading–language arts standards, are long on facts to memorize, but limit the time to be spent on hands-on discovery learning to no more than 20–25 percent of instructional time (Hake, 2004).

Chapter 8

Curriculum Resources

A problem in today's classrooms in implementing a multicultural curriculum is the textbooks. Teachers today do not have the information and resources that the turbulent sixties provided. You can no longer turn on the television and read in the newspaper, on a daily basis, of the protests, revolts, and uprising against the social and racial injustices. Some school officials, districts, administrators and teachers, in recent years, have failed to adopt and purchase multicultural teaching materials.

(College instructor, November 24, 2003)

I find some of them [students] are so relieved to finally read something they're interested in, like sometimes I'll have novels, cuentos, *traditional stories that we'll read. And they just love those stories, they'll eat them up, they ask me to take home the book.*

(Gina, middle school teacher, January 22, 2004)

Students encounter curriculum through the resources that are used, as well as through personal interactions. What teachers read as background when planning curriculum is not exactly the same as what students encounter in the classroom. A wide range of possible curriculum resources exist, including books of all kinds, community resources, media, popular culture, realia, and Internet resources. Yet textbooks have dominated for decades. As F. Wang (2002) put it, "for most students in the United States textbooks are the primary basis of instruction. Studies on the role of textbooks show that up to 90 percent of classroom time is structured around them, and that the weaker the teacher, the greater the reliance upon the printed pages."

The standards-textbook-test trilogy has elevated the importance of textbooks, with the effect of drawing teachers' attention away from rather than toward the curriculum design elements developed in this book. By aligning curriculum to state content standards and tests, many schools are narrowing curriculum resources to textbooks and commercially produced curriculum packages. The college instructor quoted above pointed out that not only does that institutionalize the ideology in texts, but it also has the side effect of reducing purchases of alternative published resources.

Ironically, some argue that standards-based curriculum, by focusing attention on student learning, should actually *remove* the textbook from the center of curriculum planning (Ruggieri, 2003). Rather than conceptualizing teaching as content coverage and students as empty vessels to fill, standards, by directing us toward learning, should prompt the question: What tools best facilitate learning? Starting there, teachers would then select and use resources and strategies that engage their students actively in meaning making, drawing from the wide range that is available (Ward, 2001).

This chapter explores the wealth of possible resources teachers can use, with some classroom illustrations. It situates resources in a discussion of interaction between student identity and resources, and resource form and thinking. The chapter concludes by examining those possibilities in context of the press toward standardizing curriculum materials, and erosion of state revenues for funding schools.

STUDENT IDENTITY AND CURRICULUM RESOURCES

Every time we construct curriculum, we construct imagined student identities that the curriculum is for and imagined identities of people we expect students to become and to learn about (Britzman, 1995). As public spheres, classrooms and schools are spaces in which young people construct their identities in relationship to what they encounter there. As Wexler (1992) argued, "becoming somebody, the identity project" is central to what happens in school (p. 128). Certainly out of school, young people "are offered, bombarded and seduced by an astonishing variety of minutely nuanced subject positions based on seemingly endless permutations of consumption with gender, race, class, culture" (Lucey & Reay, 2000).

In school, curricular resources, among other things, interact with students' identities. Style (1996) conceptualized curriculum as offering students both a window and a mirror; her window-mirror metaphor is a useful tool for thinking about the interface of curriculum resources and student identity. She wrote, "If the student is understood as occupying a dwelling of self, education needs to enable the student to look through window frames in order to see the realities of others and into mirrors in order to see her/his own reality reflected." This chapter applies the window-mirror metaphor to curriculum materials, although the metaphor also relates to curriculum more broadly construed.

From the student's point of view, both mirrors into his or her own world and windows into someone else's have value, but for different reasons. This can be illustrated through Singer and Smith's (2003) study of how two classes of college students, one predominantly white and the other African American, responded to the book *From the Notebooks of Melanin Sun* (Woodson, 1995). Featuring an African American woman and her adolescent son, the book concerns the mother's attraction to a White woman, and the son's struggle to understand. Students made sense of the book in relationship to their own identities and life experiences. Most of the students identified with the main character because the book is well-written. At the same time, race acted as a mirror for the African American students and a window for the White students: Black students strongly identified with the book's racial issues, while White students had to struggle to make sense of them. Black readers tended to empathize strongly with the son, while White readers tended to relate from a distance. Students with gay family members found affirmation of their experiences, while students without such family members felt a dissonance that can lead to learning. Although students all read the same book, they experienced, interpreted, and learned from it quite differently.

Resources as Mirrors

Students from dominant groups are most likely to experience textbooks as mirrors as they go through school. Recall patterns from textbook analyses, discussed in Chapter 5. Generally speaking, textbooks present realities, points of view, experiences, and people of White Americans more than other racial or ethnic groups; students who are Latino, Asian, or Native American may see little of their own worlds mirrored in textbooks. Although textbooks are more gender balanced than they used to be, males are still more likely to dominate than females, sometimes markedly so. Textbooks represent realities and experiences of middle- and upper-middle-class communities, generally reflecting very little of low-income communities. People who are gay or lesbian and people with disabilities are virtually absent.

Everyone needs to see her or his own reality mirrored in the curriculum. Students who experience curriculum mainly as a window into someone else's world often disengage after a while. Ford and Harris (2000) interviewed 43 gifted African American middle school students to explore this issue. All of the students wanted to learn more about African American people in school, most agreed that this would make school more interesting, and almost half agreed that they got tired of learning about White people all the time. An eighth grader, for instance, stated:

You get tired of learning about the same White people and the same things. We need to broaden our horizons and learn about other people, even other countries. The White people are just trying to advance other White people and leave Blacks behind and ignorant. I feel like being in the class more when I learn about Blacks and my heritage. It gives me encouragement and lets me know that I have rights. It helps to improve my grades. Learning about White people doesn't help me know about myself. . . . I'd like to educate my children about my heritage when I get older. I want to feel good about who I am. Why shouldn't I want to learn more about Black people?

In other words, the African American students became frustrated and disengaged when resources served mainly as a window into the White world rather than as a mirror.

Similarly, girls can tune out of curriculum in which they see few females. Wineburg (2001) reported a study of the ways in which boys and girls picture the past and project themselves into it, given the predominance of men in history texts. Seventy-three fifth graders and 88 eighth graders were asked to draw illustrations of a pilgrim, a western settler, and a hippie. Generally, the boys drew male figures. Although the girls were more likely than the boys to draw female figures, they too drew mainly male figures, suggesting that both sexes had learned to see mainly males in history. Wineburg noted that on national history tests, boys tend to outscore girls, which may be due to girls finding it more difficult to see themselves in history than boys.

Evidence suggests that students learn more when they can see themselves and their communities in classroom resources. After reviewing the research, which is rather sparse, Gay (2000) concluded that it indicates that even curricula with minimal culturally relevant content

> improves student achievement, according to a variety of indicators, across ethnic groups, grade levels, and subject or skill areas. The multiple achievement effects include higher scores on standardized tests, higher grade point averages, improved student self-concepts and self-confidence, and greater varieties and levels of student engagement with subject matter. (p. 146)

For example, research on the Multicultural Literacy Program, which uses multicultural children's literature in the context of a whole language, constructivist approach, found that as teachers learned to incorporate culturally relevant materials into student-responsive instruction, students reported increased enjoyment of reading and writing. Further, they demonstrated growth in various measures of reading and writing skill, such as vocabulary, fluency, and sentence production (Diamond & Moore, 1995).

Sustained exposure to books and other resources in students' primary language also helps students learn (Neuman, 1999; Schon, Hopkins, & Davis, 1982). Research on a bilingual-bicultural program in American Indian communities provides an example (McCarty, 1994; Watahomigie & McCarty, 1994). With assistance from a Title VII grant, over several years teachers in Rough Rock, Arizona, developed a Navajo-centered curriculum designed to help elementary students develop fluency in both English and Navajo (McCarty, 2002). The curriculum served as a mirror reflecting Navajo culture and taught through the Navajo language. On the Comprehensive Test of Basic Skills, students outperformed a local comparison group of Navajo students who were not in the program. According to McCarty, "Students who came to school speaking Navajo, and who had the benefit of cumulative early literacy experiences in Navajo, made the greatest gains on local and national measures of achievement," including developing fluency in English reading (p. 184).

All of this implies a link between curriculum resources as mirror, and student achievement. And this makes sense: All people generally feel more interested when material relates to them, and they are generally "smarter" when they can connect it with what they know already. Although using the same materials with everyone gives an illusion of equity, doing so actually is not equitable because of the diverse identities and experiences students bring.

Resources as Windows

Curriculum resources act as a window when they help students learn about people different from themselves. Although learning about others may not improve achievement scores, learning to respect and empathize with experiences and viewpoints of other people has intrinsic value in a diverse world. Based on a review of numerous research studies, Banks (1991a) concluded that curriculum interventions help students develop more positive attitudes toward people of other races and less sex-role stereotyping, particularly when used with young children. Multicultural and gender-fair materials tend to work better when they are discussed and used, but some studies found that exposure to materials alone affect students' attitudes about others, even when they were not discussed.

For example, Schall and Kauffman (2003) explored use of children's literature with gay/lesbian characters in a fourth- and fifth-grade classroom in Tucson. In the school, children routinely insulted each other using the words *gay* and *fag*. The teacher constructed a thematic unit that explored survival and name-calling; the unit included books with gay/lesbian characters, as well as heterosexual characters. (She was pleasantly surprised at the lack of parent complaints during the unit.) She introduced the books with a discussion about *gay* as an insult based on ignorance. Students were able to select books to read; only five chose not to read books with gay/lesbian characters. As students began to read the books, there was a lot of tension and giggling. However, over time as heterosexual students came to realize that the characters lived normal lives, they began to wonder why anyone should care that a person loves another of the same sex. They "recognized that many times when confronted with situations they didn't understand, they responded in negative ways. They thought that if they were told what was going on and were helped to understand others, they would be more tolerant of each other" (p. 41). The students also found that they could empathize with many situations the characters experienced, such as loss of friendships and family relationships. In other words, once the students got past the idea of gay/lesbian people being strange, they wanted to learn. The books served as helpful windows.

Some of the major publishing houses have collections of multicultural resources, particularly for children's literature and social studies. Teachers sometimes point out that one must ask specifically about these; since school district budgets are usually limited, often teachers are presented only with basic texts. Teachers also need to bring the same critical eye to multicultural collections as to textbooks (Mitchell-Powell, 1995). For example, although many collections of women's history resources feature women from a variety of backgrounds, some continue to overrepresent White women. Children's books with Native American characters vary widely in quality; some are excellent, but some replicate stereotypes (Sanchez, 2001). Collections of multicultural resources often ignore disability issues and people with disabilities; characters with disabilities, when featured, may or may not be authentic. Books with deaf characters may still be written as if the hearing world is the main point of reference (Bailes, 2002). In other words, just as texts need to be examined for who is there and who isn't, and whose ideology predominates, so do multicultural collections. Cheryl's use of her collection of multicultural children's literature is described below.

Cheryl: Multicultural Children's Literature as Window and Mirror

Cheryl is an African American teacher of second grade in a low-income, diverse urban school. I visited during her second year in this school; previously she had taught 2 years in a different district. Her classroom has an ambience that is warm, inviting, and well organized. A visitor is immediately struck by her rich collection of children's literature. Around the room are themed clusters of children's books that coordinate with themes in her reading curriculum. A tall bookcase in one corner is filled with children's literature Cheryl uses to reconfigure themed clusters throughout the year.

Along the front whiteboard, I noticed books about community helpers, which was a current theme in the students' reading text. Some of the book titles included *Police Officer, Pet Shop, A Day with Firefighters, Call Mr. Vasquez, He'll Fix it!* and *A Busy Day at Mr. Kang's Grocery Store*. People shown on the covers mirrored the diversity of children in Cheryl's class. Along another wall was a collection of books on black history, including *Drylongso* (Hamilton, 1997) and *Mary McLeod Bethune* (Greenfield, 1977), and books featuring Latino stories. Some of the Latino stories were in Spanish, such as *Los Tres Pequeños Jabalíes* (Lowell, 1996); others were in English, such as *Abuela's Weave* (Castañeda, 1993). Yet another group of books featured stories by Chinese American authors, which Cheryl had used in conjunction with Chinese New Year.

I asked Cheryl where she obtained her extensive collection. She explained, "The schools really don't provide a whole lot other than what's here" (referring to the reading and math texts). She pointed to the bookcase, saying, "Those books, I got those free because I did that summer school intervention." She had also spent her own money to purchase many of the books.

> There are other ways, the library I guess, but I never go to our school library. I could probably get books there. It takes a little bit of work because you're the one that has to make it line up with the curriculum, you know? You just can't come in and, you know, expect it to be there. (February 5, 2004)

She also mentioned that "probably because I'm African American I'm more sensitive to the importance of having a multicultural education" (February 5, 2004).

Indeed, I had been impressed by her ability to interface multicultural children's literature with whatever she was teaching. As a student in Multicultural Curriculum Design, she had designed a very interesting unit entitled "Recycling with a Global Conscience." Although that unit focused mainly on science and social studies, it included an array of multicultural children's literature that related to recycling.

In her second-grade teaching assignment, Cheryl was expected to follow a scripted reading package, and since this was only her second year teaching in this school and teaching second grade, she saw a benefit in doing so. As an early-career teacher, she felt that the systematic design of the reading–language arts program was better than what she could construct on her own:

If you would have asked me a few years ago, I'd have been totally against it, but actually using this program, I can say it works quite well. It is heavily phonics based, you know, and it gives them every thing that they need, and it's designed to adhere to the standards, so you get standards-based material, that works quite well. Because when you're designing your own thing, I used to just pull out a book and say, OK, I'm gonna hit this one, and this, and this. This program is very systematic. (February 5, 2004)

At the same time, she was also concerned that it left too little time for other things she valued, such as guided reading, extensive writing, and hands-on science.

Given the constraints of the curriculum her school had adopted, Cheryl integrated multicultural children's literature as much as possible. She emphasized that this is something teachers can do, even in a scripted-curriculum environment. The day I visited her classroom, she asked the children what book they would like me to read to them. An African American boy had been wanting to hear the book *Duke Ellington* (Pinkney, 1998), so Cheryl asked if I would read it. As I read, I could tell that some of its vocabulary was over the children's heads, but at the same time, the author played skillfully with language. One passage, for instance, depicted the music as jumping; words on the page jumped and swung with the illustrations. We paused when a girl asked what it meant for words to jump. I moved my body to illustrate, and other students chimed in explanations and examples. I finished reading the book, skipping over some of the longer sentences, but enjoying the book's wordplay. Although Cheryl and I agreed that some of its vocabulary was difficult, the children had nevertheless enjoyed listening to its poetic and figurative language, made even livelier by the vivid illustrations on every page.

Later in the morning, as students finished a workbook assignment, Cheryl encouraged them to select and read a book of their choice. I took note of their generally enthusiastic responses. The following excerpt from my notes captures students selecting books as windows into someone else's life:

One girl (from the Philippines) was reading out loud to herself the English part of a book that is written in English and Spanish. She concentrated on the book very well, tuned out everything else around her. A girl from Mexico took a book about a boy in Cameroon to her desk and seemed pretty absorbed in it. A Black girl picked *Chato's Kitchen* by Soto (1995), and a kid from Mexico picked *Happy Birthday, Martin Luther King* (Marzollo & Pinkney, 1993). . . .

My impression was that the kids liked the books, and that reading them was a treat. There was a lot to pick from. (February 5, 2004)

With a wealth of books to choose from, some children chose books that mirrored their identities while others chose windows into someone else's world.

Although the 3 hours Cheryl spent every day with the reading–language arts package limited the amount of time she had for children's literature, she still found ways to connect it meaningfully to the curriculum. For example, that day in the reading text students were working with the story "Jamaica Louise James." Earlier in the week Cheryl had paired it with a book entitled *Jamaica Tag-Along* (Havill, 1990); both stories featured African American elementary-age girls. The previous month, the textbook had featured a story by Gary Soto. Cheryl connected it with other books by Soto, such as *Too Many Tamales* (1992). She also mentioned that the students from Mexico who speak Spanish were able to interpret Spanish words for other class members, which drew out one of the quiet Spanish-speaking children. Beginning teachers should appreciate that Cheryl had developed her extensive collection and her knowledge of children's literature over several years. She pointed out that the important thing had been recognizing its value, then gradually building a collection and learning to connect the books to themes in the curriculum.

RESOURCE FORM AND STUDENT LEARNING

Dewey (1938) saw textbook-driven teaching as inherently anti-intellectual because it denies the ability of human intelligence to make sense out of lived experience. He argued that teachers should, above all, "know how to utilize the surroundings, physical and social, that exist so as to extract from them all that they have to contribute to building up experiences that are worthwhile" (p. 40). He did not, however, simply celebrate experience for its own sake. Rather, he viewed cognitive interaction with experience as the base on which knowledge is built: "experiences in order to be educative must lead out into an expanding world of subject-matter. . . . This condition is satisfied only as the educator views teaching and learning as a continuous process of reconstruction of experience" (p. 87).

An Arts-based Framework

Eisner (1994) developed a useful arts-based framework for conceptualizing forms of classroom resources in relationship to thinking. Like Dewey, he saw knowledge as built on sensory experience. Knowledge can be represented publicly through a variety of forms, such as discursive texts, poetry, painting, and dance. Propositional knowledge that appears in textbooks and tests does not substitute for sensory "real world" experience. Rather, it appeals to students' prior sensory experience for meaningful interpretation, or at least the ability of students to imagine the sensory experiences of the text's author. The greater the gap between students' experience and that presumed by the author of a text, the less meaning students will find in the text's words.

Classrooms that use only textbooks tend to reduce subject matter knowledge to words to memorize, thereby reducing possibilities for intellectual engagement, particularly if students do not share the sensory experiences of textbook authors. "Ironically, all of this is justified in the name of rigor, standards, and intellect" (Eisner, 1994, p. 81). Eisner argued further, "A culture or a school program that dulls the senses by neglect or disrespect thwarts the development of human aptitude and undermines the possibilities of the human mind" (p. 29). This is, in fact, an equity issue, since students differ in the sensory modalities through which they know the world the best (Shade, 1989). Below, I summarize Eisner's framework for expanding the range of sensory experiences used in the classroom. I created a diagram to illustrate it, shown in Figure 8.1. The framework differentiates among resources on the basis of form, mode, and syntax.

The first dimension is *form*, or sensory modality, in which knowledge is represented. Knowledge may be represented in visual, auditory, tactile, kinesthetic, gustatory, or olfactory forms. The forms teachers use matter greatly; whether one chooses words, pictures, textures, or sounds determines how students will experience a given concept. Any form through which experience is represented always reduces the experience itself; some aspects of human experience are represented better through one modality than another. For example, one can experience the concept of symmetry better through visualization than through verbal description. When I was reading about words jumping (related above), the children were able to both look at an illustration, move their bodies, and verbally give examples, in order to get the idea of rhythm in Duke Ellington's piano playing. Second-language learners or students with reading difficulties who gain little meaning from print they do not understand can still participate in learning through other modalities, such as pictures or video, if the teacher plans accordingly.

The second dimension of Eisner's curriculum framework is *mode* of representation. He identified three modes. The mimetic mode conveys knowledge by imitating reality; for example, pictures that look like the objects they represent use a mimetic mode along with a visual form. The

Figure 8.1. Expanding the Range of Sensory Experiences Used in the Classroom

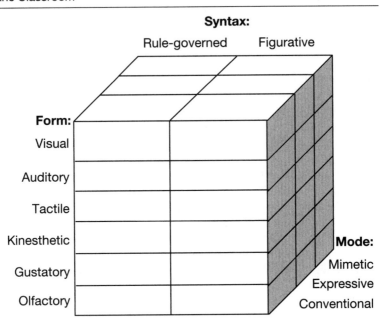

expressive mode conveys the "deep structure" or "essential properties" of phenomena—what is felt, what is below the surface. Literature and poetry are two forms of knowledge that are particularly useful at conveying expressive knowledge. The conventional mode consists of symbol systems that "stand in the place of something else" (Eisner, 1994, p. 54). Language and print operate as conventions; one needs to learn, for example, what *A* stands for, or what words mean, in order to access knowledge that is represented through these modes.

The third dimension of Eisner's framework is *syntax*, which refers to how parts of knowledge are arranged on a continuum that ranges from rule-governed at one end, to figurative at the other end. Spelling, for example, is highly governed by rules; poetry is not, although different kinds of poetry follow various rules. Eisner pointed out that a good deal of the elementary school curriculum consists of learning conventions of language, print, and numbers, and rule-governed syntax in order to access knowledge that is encoded in these conventions.

Thoughtful teachers can use a wide variety of resources to help students expand their understanding, ability to think, and ability to communicate ideas. Eisner (1994) emphasized that "forms of representation abound. . . . The most difficult task for educators may very well be relinquishing the yellow school bus mentality that conceives of both the purposes and the forms of schooling in terms conditioned by familiar and comfortable traditions" (p. 69).

An exercise for stretching one's ideas about classroom resources is to brainstorm resources or experiences for the big idea of a unit that would fit as many of the 36 boxes in Figure 8.1 as possible. For example, if we take Mona's unit on origins of the solar system (see Chapter 7), a resource that fits the box labeled *rule-governed–mimetic–visual* is the mechanical representation of the solar system that she used. It looks like the solar system, and performs regular revolutions around the sun when turned on. When Mona read to students the book *Earth Namer* (Bernstein & Kobrin, 1974), students experienced learning that was auditory-expressive-figurative. PowerPoint enabled students to work with all three modes of visual representation: mimetic, by using pictures that look like the object they depict; expressive, by using colors and decoration to express mood; and conventional, by using written names of objects. A teacher probably would not use resources from all 36 boxes. However, asking what might fit each box expands the range of possibilities. This range can then be mapped against the levels of thinking, discussed in Chapter 7, in order to select those that prompt a wide range of levels of thinking.

As Eisner (1994) argued, the arts can connect cognitive learning with affective learning by situating ideas in forms (such as visual) and syntax (such as figurative and imaginative learning) that engage students intellectually. Community arts draw on a wide range of forms that can engage students wonderfully in multicultural learning. For example, Cruz and Walker (2001) described a project in Tampa, Florida, in which a high-poverty school serving largely African American and Latino students developed an 8-week series of trips to local museums, alternating between an African American art museum and a museum dedicated to the history of Cubans and Spaniards. These trips broke down segregation among the students and, unexpectedly, to some extent among the parents. Some schools have developed active artist-in-residence programs (e.g., Bressler, DeStefano, Feldman, & Garg, 2000) or projects connecting students with local muralists (e.g., Conrad, 1994).

Community arts resources should not be ancillary to learning, but central to it. Below, Gina shows how she connects her classroom with community arts, which illustrates connections between Eisner's framework, Style's windows-mirror metaphor, transformative intellectual knowledge, and students' community culture.

Gina: Community as Central to Curriculum

As described earlier, Gina uses varied resources in her teaching. She regularly engages students through print, visual display, music, and movement. She teaches both conventional mode (conventions of English and Spanish language and of music and dance) and expressive mode extensively. She also teaches rule-governed syntax in relationship to dance and writing; as students gain mastery over rules, she encourages them to create and experiment. She sees the arts as greatly enriching how anything can be taught, enabling teachers to expand beyond a textbook approach to teaching. She also sees the community as a rich reservoir for resources that tap into transformative intellectual knowledge and students' community-based culture.

Gina teaches in a town that has a very active local arts community, particularly involving Mexican, Japanese, and Filipino dancers, musicians, poets, and artists. She regularly involves community artists in her curriculum, and has tried continually to persuade other teachers to do the same. Her master's thesis investigated possibilities for building an arts program that connects the school and the community (Rodriguez, 2002). Based on a survey and interviews with 59 students, she found almost half wanted to see more Mexican culture in the school's arts curriculum (curriculum as mirror). All but one saw her dance classes as both reflecting their own culture and teaching them about others (curriculum as both mirror and window). All 10 parents she surveyed believed that it is important for their children to learn about diverse cultural groups, and 9 of the 10 wanted their children to learn more about art that reflects their own cultural background.

Most teachers in her school, however, knew little about local community arts; they also tended to describe the parents in cultural deficiency terms, which reflected lack of knowledge about the community. Ironically, four of the six local artists she interviewed were school district employees, but had been invited by teachers only infrequently to contribute their knowledge because they lacked teaching credentials. The schools had censured three of them for not presenting "multicultural" and harmonious art: As authentic art, what they presented was grounded in the cultural community in which they worked, and some of it addressed controversial issues. Gina found teachers' lack of understanding of transformative knowledge embedded in community arts to be a major barrier to school–community collaboration. To build this collaboration over the long run, she is part of an activist coalition of parents of color, young progressive lawyers, Latino city council members, brown berets, and local educators.

Gina uses community-based resources in her own teaching extensively, for which she actively seeks grant money. For example, she had recently obtained a grant to bring a maestro from Michoacán, where many of her students came from, to teach indigenous dance. He is a Purépecha Indian whose father was the composer and choreographer for the Danza de los Viejos, the most widely known and representative dance from this region. In other words, he was really a folkloric treasure in its most humble form representative of the poorest class of Mexicans, the *indigenas*. Bringing him from Mexico would not only benefit her students, but also give something back to the community, since he would be able to teach members of the community more about the dances from Michoacán. In addition, her grant money allowed her to hire a local school bus driver who is an excellent mariachi musician to play music for the dance troupe show.

Gina also worked with parents in another project, called Café Literario, for which the parents were writing stories and poetry based on their own immigration experiences. In the process, they were learning to use computers. They had produced one book of stories so far, which Gina gave to a local muralist, who designed a mural on an outside wall of her school, and involved the parents and students in painting it. After the mural project they merged with another program that aims to decrease the digital divide and provides parents with free Internet access as well as loaner computers. Gina commented, "It's amazing to see parents with a third-grade education e-mailing each other! This has also been a great tool to organize people outside of district programs by creating listservs" (July 17, 2004).

These examples show how Gina creatively blends forms of knowledge, modes, and syntaxes, and engages both the students and the community in transformative knowledge that inspires more learning and literacy. Gina explained that teachers can do a lot with community resources if they are willing to learn: "Although teachers may not be experts in all of their students' cultures in anthropological-sociological terms, inviting students and their families to share their knowledge is essential to students feeling validated in the school curriculum" (Rodriguez, 2002, p. 85). She also emphasized that to do so authentically and transformatively, "one must become a member of the community. We have a large number of 'outside service providers' working in our schools with big hearts but they don't spend enough time here outside of work to really develop an understanding and respect for the fountains of knowledge in the community" (July 17, 2004).

LOCATING RESOURCES

There is no single strategy for locating good multicultural curriculum resources. The best teachers are not only ongoing learners themselves, but also inveterate collectors. Their classrooms (and often their garages) become well-stocked with materials over time, and they are usually actively involved in community and professional activities. While beginning teachers probably will not find all the resources they need the first year or two of teaching, with time they can assemble extensive resources.

Often the best teachers seek out other teachers and librarians with whom to share resources. Although I have met outstanding teachers who seem to have single-handedly developed extensive collections of resources over a period of years, more often such teachers attend multicultural and bilingual conferences, work with librarians to purchase multicultural materials for their school, exchange resources with other teachers, and subscribe to publications where they constantly learn about new resources.

Figure 8.2 offers a list of places to seek books, videos, and digital resources for multicultural curriculum. These sources offer articles and other information on multicultural topics, recommendations and reviews of books and other resources, catalogs of materials available for purchase, and Web links to other sources. All but three are online, and the most recent URL is given along with a description of the resource.

A wide range of resources is available to teachers who look for them. For example, some of the sources listed in Figure 8.2 contain actual curriculum resources. In addition, a rapidly growing proliferation of multicultural lesson plans is available online, but their quality ranges from excellent to superficial and stereotypic, so teachers should select carefully. Teachers with a clear sense of what they are teaching can even learn to identify and use the multiple and varied tools provided in the classroom for multicultural ends, including using very biased textbooks to examine social justice issues. Linda Christensen (2002), a high school teacher, explained:

> No matter what materials you're given, find a way to create social-justice units out of them. For example, if you're given *To Kill a Mockingbird*, take Charles M. Payne's book *I've Got the Light of Freedom: The Organizing Tradition and the Mississippi Struggle* and talk about the historical background necessary for understanding the context of the book.

Students themselves can be a source of curriculum resources, particularly through their involvement with youth popular culture. Popular culture includes the movies, music, 'zines, video games, fashions, and graffiti that young people consume and produce. As Giroux (2000) pointed out, for kids, popular culture "is one of the few places where they can speak

Figure 8.2. Sources for Multicultural Classroom Resources

Bilingual Books for Kids (*http://www.bilingualbooks.com/*) features bilingual books in Spanish and English.

Children's Literature and Disability (*http://www.nichcy.org/pubs1.htm*), by the National Dissemination Center for Children with Disabilities, lists children's books that feature various disabilities.

Cradleboard (*http://www.cradleboard.org/*) features a variety of Native American resources, particularly in science.

Cultural Arts Resources for Teachers and Students (*http://www.carts.org/*) features multimedia folk arts resources.

Frank Rogers' Multicultural Children's Literature page (*http://frankrogers.home. mindspring.com/multi.html*) contains a wealth of links to sources for books, organized by sociocultural group.

GLSEN booklink (*http://www.glsen.org/*) is a very helpful resource for gay/lesbian books for children and youth.

Lee and Low Books (*http://www.leeandlow.com/home/index.html*) is an excellent resource for multicultural children's literature.

Multicultural Books (*http://www.nal.net/sourceintl/*) focuses particularly on African American children's books.

Multicultural Education and the Internet (Gorski, 2005) is an excellent guide to using the Internet for multicultural teaching.

Multicultural Pavilion (*http://www.edchange.org/multicultural/index.html*) is a Web site loaded with information and links.

Multicultural Perspectives is a journal that offers reviews of books and other materials as well as feature articles and other curriculum resources.

Multicultural Resources for Young Readers (Muse, 1997) is a particularly outstanding and extensive annotated bibliography of children's literature.

MultiCultural Review (*http://www.mcreview.com*) is a journal that provides excellent reviews of an extensive amount of teaching materials, as well as feature articles and other curriculum resources.

National Women's History Project (*http://www.nwhp.org/*) and Women in World History (*http://www.womeninworldhistory.com*) both feature books and other resources for integrating women into the curriculum.

Oyate (*http://www.oyate.org/*) features Native American books, organized by age level; this Web site also offers guidance on popular books to avoid.

Public Broadcasting Service (PBS) (*http://www.pbs.org/teachersource/*) offers very helpful resources, although it is not specifically designed from a multicultural perspective.

Teaching for Change catalog (*http://www.teachingforchange.org/*) is excellent for multicultural social justice teaching resources for Grades K–12, in all subject areas.

for themselves, produce alternative public spheres, and represent their own interests" (p. 13). Using popular cultural forms, youth are able to talk back at the various forms of control over their lives and imagine public spaces in which ordinary people have the power to speak and create. Some teachers draw on popular culture, for example, by teaching literacy skills through music videos or poetry slams. More helpful than simply importing youth cultural forms into the classroom is guiding young people in critical analysis of them, such as examining power relations and identities that are inscribed in popular media, and who profits from their consumption of various media.

For her unit on West Coast Immigration (see Chapter 3), Christi sought resources that would serve as windows to the experiences of immigrants. The unit was full of short stories and videos, such as *El Norte* (Nava, 1983) (featuring Mexican and Central American immigrants) and *A Dollar a Day, Ten Cents a Dance* (Dunn & Schwartz, 1984) (featuring Filipino immigrants). She found video to be an especially powerful tool. I asked Christi where she found the rich pool of resources she was using. She explained that she had become very good at scavenging.

> Sometimes things just drop into my lap, and like, Wow! . . . I've actually been collecting over the last 7 years, because, you know, I've always wanted to do something like this. . . . So, I dedicated myself to just grabbing everything that I could, you know. If I found something that somebody was doing, or heard about something, um, the Internet's fabulous, I don't know what I would do without it. . . . I ended up with a lot of stuff, a lot of stuff! I mean, [pointing to a corner] these are just some of the huge file cabinets full of things. (February 24, 2004)

She also used electronic resources. Working in small groups, students were to create a character, based on guided background research using the Internet, such as *Encarta*, a Web-based encyclopedia, where students looked up information about the country from which specific groups came and information about those groups in the United States. They needed to gather enough information so that their characters would reflect accuracy and some degree of authenticity.

Students then created a Web page or PowerPoint presentation that used various narrative writing assignments they had completed throughout the unit related to their fictional character. In that way, like Juanita's and Mona's students (see Chapter 7), they not only learned through media, but also became authors of it.

POSSIBILITIES AND CHALLENGES

The teachers featured in this book emphasized that teachers can locate and use a variety of multicultural curriculum resources if they want to do so. A wide range of resources is available, and even within a state-standards context, teachers can locate and use them. That teachers do not see a reason to do so is the problem.

At the same time, cash-strapped schools and libraries have increasingly less revenue to invest in instructional resources. Despite the growing number of students from diverse language backgrounds and the fact that exposure to books in students' primary language helps them learn to read, libraries in many school districts have a paucity of books in primary languages of students from non-English-speaking homes, especially languages other than Spanish. For example, Lambson (2002) found that school libraries in the Phoenix, Arizona, area, where there are large numbers of students who speak a primary language other than English, were "seriously lacking in primary-language reading materials" (p. 240). With budget crises leading to library cuts and even closures (witness Salinas, California, where public libraries are being closed until revenues to reopen them are found), and with many states adopting measures opposing bilingual education and channeling money into materials to prepare students for testing in English, this situation is likely to get worse rather than better. And with school districts nationwide spending large sums on textbook-test packages, money available for alternative resources is diminishing.

Cheryl mentioned that she had bought much of her children's literature collection with her own money, reflecting a common experience among classroom teachers. Teachers are spending more and more of their own money for classroom materials: videos, software, learning kits, books, art supplies, and even basic supplies like paper and pencils. A survey by the National Education Association (2003) found that "overall, teachers' expenditures on students' needs averaged $443 for the previous school year (2000). This was up from the 1995 average of $408" (p. 2). The average elementary teacher spends $500 per year, and the average new teacher spends $700 per year. Over half of the money spent on classroom supplies comes from teachers; less than half is provided by school districts (Starr, 2002).

As corporate taxes have dropped over time, schools have become increasingly dependent on private sources to pay for education resources (Parenti, 2004). For example, People for the American Way (n.d.) reported an analysis of the escalation of corporate tax breaks in Illinois. Over the past 2 decades, the corporate share of state taxes dropped from 20 percent to 11 percent. This plus the more recent tax credit system "rob the state treasury of vital funds that are used to pay for the state's public schools." Hardest hit are districts serving poor communities. Lowering corporate taxes is a strategy states use to compete against each other to attract corporations, so this pattern has led to a loss in state revenue for schools nationwide. To compensate, schools are increasingly turning directly to corporations for financial help in forms such as corporate sponsorship of school programs and activities, appropriation of space, and corporately sponsored educational materials. These forms of corporate sponsorship, however, involve direct corporate advertising to youth—such as offering Coca-Cola drinks at lunch, and holding gym class in the ShopRight gym—or other direct forms of corporate influence on curriculum—such as Weyerhauser Lumber's science center, complete with brochures depicting "environmentally responsible clear cuts" (Molnar, 2002). Parenti (2004) investigated several teachers' perceptions of schoolhouse commercialism, and found the sample generally very critical of it but "willing to accept business arrangements out of desperation" (p. 63). Parenti's concern leads back to a major concern that prompted writing this book—schooling as a public resource for a diverse democracy—which I examine in Chapter 9.

Multicultural Curriculum, Democracy, and Visionary Pragmatism

The state/your school/your principal mandates that you teach the standards, and most of the standards treat academic knowledge as if it existed in a bubble separate from the realities of the world.
(Former high school math teacher, November 10, 2003)

A brand new teacher cannot implement multicultural curriculum as easily as a permanent one since the brand new teacher may face a firing situation much easier than the permanent teacher.
(Third-grade bilingual teacher, September 29, 2003)

I think deep down, this is why I have never been interested in teaching in a public school. The thought of having to teach something or in a way that I feel is boring to my students is absolute anathema to me; having to shove something down a student's throat and not having the freedom to find a balance WITH *my students so that we both feel that we are getting/giving the* MOST *that is possible out of a curriculum would be impossible for me day in and day out.*
(College ESL instructor, November 3, 2003)

This book has emphasized possibilities for multicultural curriculum design, elaborating on a framework that helps teachers deepen curriculum planning and teaching. As the comments above illustrate, however, teachers' agency as curriculum planners has been sharply circumscribed by the standards movement, leading some prospective educators to avoid public school teaching. Nevertheless, throughout this book, vignettes have illustrated teachers finding space to use the agency they still have, and using it with a sense of vision.

This chapter explores tensions between curriculum as framed by the standards movement and by multicultural movements, illustrating how these tensions play out in a sixth-grade classroom. The larger issue, however, is not how to plan curriculum, but rather what curriculum is for. I begin, therefore, by situating curriculum within a vision of participatory democracy.

CURRICULUM AND DEMOCRACY

Multicultural education, as well as related progressive movements, have long envisaged schools as servants of democratic life helping young people cultivate knowledge, intellectual tools, and experience, working across diverse viewpoints and identities to address shared social concerns. Now, perhaps more than ever before, it is vital to retain and act on this vision. Banks (2004a) emphasized, "Students must attain democratic values in school if we ever hope to change the political, social, and economic structures of stratified societies and nation-states because they are the future citizens and leaders" (p. 10). Parker (2003) echoed, arguing that "to lead a non-idiotic life is to lead the unavoidably connected and engaged life of the citizen, paying attention to and caring for the public household, the common good" (p. 11).

The standards movement is presented to the public as necessary for equipping young people with the skills they will need to enter the economy. Yet the economy, particularly at the upper levels, does not have room for everyone, and there is no evidence that closing achievement gaps will close opportunity gaps that have been widening for reasons unrelated to student achievement. According to the U.S. Census Bureau (2004), the share of income of the wealthiest one fifth of households jumped from 44 percent in 1973 to 50 percent in 2002. The share of the bottom one fifth dropped from 4.2 percent to 3.5 percent. Tax cuts that disproportionately favored the wealthy and elimination or outsourcing of jobs to reduce labor costs partially account for this widening gap. The upper one fifth, with increasing amounts of disposable income after the most recent tax cuts, are helping drive up housing costs through gentrification and purchase of second and third homes. Statewide in California, for example, the percentage of home buyers who were buying their first home has been dropping (Viega, 2004), and locally, affordable housing is a huge problem.

Middle- and low-income families increasingly find themselves downwardly mobile. According to the Economic Policy Institute (2004), between March 2001 and August 2004, 1.2 million jobs in the U.S. disappeared, representing a 0.9% contraction of the economy. Of people with at least

3 years tenure at their previous jobs, about one third took another job at lower pay, and another one third remained jobless. Average earnings of displaced workers who found another full-time job fell from $681 per week to $572 per week. While the fastest growing jobs (such as network systems communications analysts) require higher education, most new jobs that have been created (such as health aides) do not require high levels of skills, contrary to rhetoric often used to justify the standards movement. According to the Associated Press (2004), "The new jobs are concentrated in health care, food services, and temporary employment firms, all lower paying industries. Temp agencies alone account for about a fifth of all new jobs. Three in five pay below the national median hourly wage" (see also U.S. Department of Labor, 2003). So while the standards movement implies that raising test scores and closing achievement gaps will bring about equity, the context of widening gaps between rich and poor as well as economic restructuring belie that implied promise.

Testing and standardizing knowledge do not resolve such issues. Further, higher education is also facing a crisis in capacity to admit growing numbers of applicants. Private colleges and universities face shrinking publicly funded financial aid for student tuition, while family income for large segments of the population has either stagnated or fallen in real dollars (Enrollment Forecasting, n.d.). Public colleges and universities are also experiencing erosion of state support and find themselves needing to turn increasingly to corporations for funding, in the process shifting curricula toward corporate needs (Aronowitz, 2000).

All of this could be different. For example, using an economic cost-benefit analysis, Vernez, Krop, and Rydell (1999) showed how racial and ethnic gaps in educational attainment could be closed by investing monetary resources in education in order to increase its capacity; they showed further that "the added costs of providing more education may be recouped within a relatively short period 10 to 15 years" as a better educated population moves into the labor force (p. 97). But as a society, we have not chosen to invest resources in this way. As Aronowitz (2000) argued, "Ironically, the best preparation for the work of the future might be to cultivate knowledge of the broadest possible kind, to make learning a way of life that in the first place is pleasurable, and then rigorously critical" (p. 161). This kind of learning may be students' best defense against rapidly shifting job markets and unstable opportunities, and may be essential to reinvigorating an active citizenry around alternative social structural visions.

This kind of learning may also be necessary for our collective survival. As we humans increasingly acquire the ability to destroy ourselves through war or biological weapons, and as we see effects of our lives ravaging the biosphere, more and more we collectively need a citizenry that can think and act ethically and creatively. Rather than sugarcoating or avoiding such issues as racism or human greed, we must concentrate efforts on helping young people deal more constructively with these than have past generations. As Howard (2003b) argued, the sooner educators "can begin to facilitate discussions around race and racism, the quicker old wounds begin to heal, honest dialogue occurs, and a more meaningful discussion can begin to take place about what it means to be a democratic citizen. . . . our future as a nation is dependent upon it" (p. 39).

The standards movement, however, has framed curriculum largely as a commodity for individual consumption rather than as a resource for public good. It is ironic that school knowledge has become exceedingly prescribed and determined by states at a time when the United States is aggressively exporting its version of democracy and personal liberties. While politicians extol U.S. freedoms, teachers in the United States are being told what to teach and sometimes even given a script to follow. Emphasis on the "measured curriculum," constructs schools as factories in which "children are the products, moving passively along the assembly line, filling up with bits of subject matter and curriculum until they are inspected and certified to graduate to the next level" (Ayres, 2004, p. 137). Teachers are not supposed to think or question, but rather to act like clerks, checking to make sure that the requisite topics have been covered. And yet, "individual rights and freedoms come from the very communities that sustain such liberties," rather than those that suppress them (SooHoo, 2004a, p. 207). Meier (2002) asked, "If democratic habits can't flourish in school, and if they are viewed as utopian in the place we should have the most reasons for trusting each other, how much harder to believe their possibility in society at large?" (p. 181).

Further, the movement may well contribute to eroding the promise of public education for all. This would not be due to the work of those who are trying to improve public schools, but rather of those who are using the standards movement to press for privatization of public services. Based on an analysis of accountability legislation in Texas, after which No Child Left Behind was modeled, Valenzuela (2005) argued that, "the current accountability system serves as a handmaiden to the privatization agenda" (p. 264). She showed how a political and economic elite who had been pushing to privatize schools seized accountability as a tool of privatization. Under No Child Left Behind, schools that fail to meet achievement score targets ultimately are to be shut down or taken over by the state.[1] Accountability systems appear to be rational and efficient for detecting and dealing with failure. But such systems also serve the growth of private schools, particularly in a context in which few leaders are speaking out on behalf of public education. As Valenzuela remarked, "Woefully absent in our statewide educational leadership is a strong, democratic voice calling for an invigorated public sphere in which accountability is not to the state but to a citizen public" (p. 289).

Parker (2003) pointed out that "history gives democracy no advantages" (p. 52). Active democracies, historically, have been short-lived, at least those of European origin. If we were serious about sustaining and developing democracy and justice, we would need to "educate for principled activism" (Parker, p. 52). Educating students for principled activism in a multicultural democracy clearly places responsibilities on schools. These include the responsibility to expect the best from all students and teach to demanding expectations, and to prepare curriculum that engages students and respects who they are, what they know, and what they bring. It also includes continuing to deepen teachers' pedagogical skill with diverse populations, their transformative knowledge base, and the ideological clarity that grounds their work. I do not advocate simply handing the power to determine curriculum over to teachers without also engaging teachers very seriously in the work of teaching responsibly, and then supporting conditions that enable this work. It is true that in far too many classrooms, teachers teach poorly and curriculum is weak. But trying to solve that problem by prescribing what everyone should teach and learn undermines open inquiry and freedom of thought.

The curriculum design framework developed in this book offers a way to envision and create curriculum that fosters deep intellectual engagement and principled activism in a diverse society. There is no step-by-step process for doing this, however. The design framework, as mentioned in Chapter 1, is not linear, nor should it be. Readers will have noted that even though this book has offered many analytical tools and sets of questions to ask, it has not laid out a step-by-step process for designing multicultural curriculum. Although the book is constructed in a linear fashion, one can start almost anywhere in the framework. For example, a student-centered approach to curriculum starts with students and their questions rather than with teacher-identified central ideas. The teacher acts as facilitator, but not as principal determiner of curriculum. Or, one could start with transformative intellectual knowledge: planning an African-centered curriculum could start with research and theory in African American studies. One could also start planning with requirements for success in college.

However, all of the elements interrelate; multicultural curriculum design means working with all of them, recursively, rather than with some and not with others. For example, it means reading big ideas against ideology, assessment against transformative intellectual knowledge, and academic challenge in relationship to curriculum resources. Curriculum is not a static or finished product. It is always an ongoing intellectual endeavor, created, enacted, and re-created in specific contexts, involving specific teachers and specific students. And it is always a learning process on the part of the teacher, the students, and the school. Multicultural curriculum design, conceptualized this way, is not robotic, but rather living, organic, and (like the standards movement) political. As Fusarelli and Boyd (2004) argued, "Because the schools play a key role in influencing the beliefs of children, in conveying the history and traditions of a society, and in shaping its future, sensitive political issues invariably lurk around decisions about the curriculum the public schools shall follow" (p. 6).

Although this book has emphasized possibilities, many teachers feel caught between teaching content standards on which students will be tested and using their own autonomy as professional educators. All of the teachers in this book felt caught between their interest and commitment to multicultural–bilingual–social justice teaching and the demands of California's standards and accountability movement. Beginning teachers felt particularly vulnerable, a few fearing loss of their jobs if they questioned what the state and their schools were telling them to do. Terri's classroom showed these conflicts quite clearly. Below, I examine her experience in relationship to the four central curriculum questions discussed in Chapter 1, in order to illustrate possibilities that are being circumscribed when knowledge becomes standardized.

Terri: Participatory Democracy Versus Content Standards

Terri is a sixth-grade language arts–social studies teacher with over 20 years experience. The middle school in which she has taught for most of her career is located in a predominantly White, middle- to upper-class neighborhood that used to be largely Italian American. Over time, the school had become increasingly diverse by race, ethnicity, social class, and language mainly through a program that bused almost half of the students from low-income, very diverse neighborhoods. A White woman, Terri became interested in multicultural teaching many years earlier when student teaching, working as a bilingual teacher in the Los Angeles area for 2 years, and working for a humanitarian organization in Europe and the Middle East. After marrying, she started teaching in her current school. These experiences prompted her interest in enrolling in Multicultural Curriculum Design in fall 2001.

1. *What purpose should the curriculum serve?* As discussed in Chapter 1, the main stated purpose of curriculum in the standards movement is to increase measured achievement of students in order to make the United States more competitive globally. This purpose is articulated and elabo-

rated within a business model of increasing production, where quantifiable targets are set, efforts are aligned to them, and rewards and sanctions follow from the extent to which they are met. In contrast, while multicultural movements value equity in student academic achievement, they also conceptualize curriculum as preparation for participatory democracy.

Terri described her own goals as both developing academic learning and preparing for democracy. She strongly believes that schools should cultivate citizen participation. To that end, she works to build a classroom in which students speak up, debate, listen, and think. She has learned to open up controversial issues, encouraging debate without preaching her own point of view. By the time I met her, she had considerable experience learning to do this well. She is passionate about helping students learn to name and address problems they face collectively in their own lives. For her master's thesis, she worked with students in one of her classes to investigate a school problem regarding how students treat each other, and then generate solutions. She explained that she involved students in asking questions about equity "because I wanted to bring the issues of democracy and discrimination to the surface in my school environment. I involved my students because I believe, as Freire did, that, 'as they look at their environment, they will find the autonomy to become the problem solvers of institutional inequality'" (Pipes, 2002, p. 15).

Right after September 11, 2001, Terri described the personal and political power of students not only discussing issues, but also getting to know each other as people in the process:

> I was having a debate with my students about whether we should bomb Afghanistan. The majority of my students said, "No, we shouldn't, because we would be bombing innocent civilians, we would be doing what was done to us, it wouldn't solve anything," et cetera. But I had two boys who said, "Yeah, we just need to bomb them, look what they did to us, we just need to bomb them." And I let the kids dialog and talk, and all the different people tried to convince these boys that they didn't feel that this was right. Every day I try to create an atmosphere in the classroom where we can have this kind of discussion, where students feel free to disagree respectfully with one another as they explore their ideas. I'm not going to tell the students my own personal opinions . . . I want them to think for themselves. Finally one of the girls said, "Well, what about Ahmed?" (Ahmed was a Pakistani student who disappeared 2 days after September 11. I think he went back to Pakistan.) And so the students asked, "What about Ahmed? He's over

there. What will happen to him?" And those same two boys changed their minds and said, "Then we've got to come home. . . . We shouldn't bomb them." No great arguments, no amount of rationale would change their minds, only the human connection they had with their friend Ahmed. (October 19, 2001)

This story supported Terri's conviction that democracy requires people who can debate, speak their minds, and listen, and that young people can learn to build empathy and listen with their hearts as well as their minds.

She also believes that all students need an academically rich curriculum and should be taught in a way that builds access to college. "My job is to educate. They need to be able to read, they need to be able to write, they need to be able to analyze in order to become effective in society" (January 30, 2004). She explained:

I've got a curriculum that I want them to grasp, and that curriculum is about ancient civilizations, and understanding the major themes of those civilizations and what went on, and then being able to relate the past to the present, and looking at how that affects them, and where do we go from here. Also infusing quality literature in the program, not only to help their reading skills but also to help them just really connect literature with their lives, to see the beauty of literature, to see the applicability of literature to their experience and to inspire them to write and to read, to open their minds. (January 30, 2004)

Terri's convictions led her to continue to develop her skill as a teacher, and to seek ways to connect academic learning with inquiry, political participation, and work on social justice issues.

2. *How should knowledge be selected, who decides what knowledge is most worth teaching and learning, and what is the relationship between those in the classroom and the knowledge selection process?* A central conflict between the standards and multicultural movements revolves around the presumption of consensus over knowledge schools should teach, and beliefs about who should have the power to decide what young people will learn. The standards movement assumes consensus over knowledge in the disciplines, as defined by disciplinary experts. As a result, California has institutionalized a highly hierarchical structure of knowledge that builds conceptual knowledge and thinking on factual knowledge and skills in a fairly linear way; and it is anchored in a largely traditional, European American, Western, English-language knowledge base. In contrast, multicultural educa-

tors argue that there is no one definition of what everyone should learn, that school knowledge should be opened up to knowledge from historically marginalized communities, and that curriculum decision making should include bottom-up input. Further, what is taught in any given classroom should be culturally relevant and meaningful to the students who are there.

Terri's beliefs about knowledge resonate with those of multicultural educators. She believes that knowledge should be selected in a way that helps students learn to hear and understand multiple perspectives: "That's what I'm doing here, is helping to create, helping to motivate people to be responsible citizens" (January 30, 2004). She also believes that knowledge should come, in part, from the students themselves, as they ask questions and pursue interests that relate to broad curriculum goals. "It's a two-way street, we all learn from each other," she explained (January 30, 2004). Prior to passage of No Child Left Behind, Terri was used to working with textbooks and broad curriculum goals, along with additional resources, to build interdisciplinary thematic curriculum units that connect contemporary issues and students' questions with history and literature. Her 2-hour language arts and social studies block lent itself well to this.

For example, 2 years previously, she had designed and taught a unit related to ancient Egypt that examined hierarchical versus egalitarian social structures in history and currently, including the student social structure in her school. The unit was connected to the district's curriculum goals, and it used the adopted social studies and literature texts. But it placed in the forefront the analysis of social organization in various contexts and the role citizens can play to access political participation where they live; it used additional readings in literature and social studies and various activities to engage students in these issues.[2]

At the beginning of academic year 2003–04, I visited Terri's class of second-language learners, in which about half of the students were of Mexican descent and the rest were from countries around the world. As I listened to experiences students wrote about (such as war in the Balkans) in relationship to a literature assignment, I thought about linkages that could be made between their experiences and the upcoming social studies curriculum. The sixth-grade social studies curriculum in California focuses on history and geography of ancient civilizations, including Mesopotamia, Egypt, Kush, the Hebrews, Greece, India, China, and Rome. Given the diverse backgrounds of the students and knowledge some brought about the histories of countries from which they had come, I could envision lively inquiries into ancient civilizations, connecting past with present.

But Terri was being directed increasingly to adhere strictly to the state content standards, teaching the required content, in the prescribed sequence, without deviation. She commented, "I feel like the state would have us just, you know, go back to the traditional, OK, open your books, go to this page, we're hitting standard 122 today, subjects and verbs" (January 30, 2004). Since California's standards are quite detailed—listing names, places, dates, and concepts students are to learn—and since those for each discipline were written by different committees using different organizational structures, they limit possibilities for interdisciplinary curriculum. Although teachers in Terri's school were not yet expected to march students through all details of each set of standards, they were expected to show how everything they taught fit the standards. Terri explained:

> We used to have district goals and objectives that we were supposed to meet for the students that were, quote, standards-based. Now we have the standards. There are a lot more of them. And now we are asked to look at the standards, and on a daily basis we should be knowing which standard we're teaching each day. . . . I do give it more thought because I've been asked to do so, and I try to be more creative in doing the things that I think matter in the classroom. . . . I can't possibly teach all the standards like they want me to, if I use my creative side. (January 30, 2004)

For example, Terri usually ran a mock trial as part of her social studies curriculum. Although California's history–social science framework suggests using teaching processes like mock trials, the content standards do not specify studying trials at all except possibly in 12th grade, where students are to learn about their right to a fair trial. Since trials are not part of the sixth-grade curriculum, Terri was feeling increasing pressure to omit this unit.

More fundamentally, she was feeling pressure to adhere to a system in which concepts that are selected by "experts" are built on facts that have been selected from a fairly traditional perspective. As a result, she was feeling less and less able to respond to students' questions and interests, and less supported in her efforts to engage students with multiple perspectives about social issues, as the example below illustrates.

3. *What is the nature of students and the learning process, and how does it suggest organizing learning experiences and relationships?* As discussed in Chapter 1, the standards movement says fairly little about the nature of learning. However, to the extent that tests emphasize recall and basic skills, and content standards are numerous, the standards movement tends to con-

struct students as empty vessels or passive recipients of knowledge. No one actually says this, but it becomes the working reality when teachers feel pressured to "deliver" quantities of prescribed content to students.

Terri's view of students as inquirers who make meaning clashed with the institutionalization of learning as knowledge reception. For example, the standards for studying ancient Greece specify that students learn different forms of government, including tyranny, oligarchy, and democracy. Terri developed a unit in which small groups representing different Greek city-states would each choose their own form of government, then design and participate in Olympic games. I watched part of this process in her class of English-language learners and saw a clash in conceptions of learning play out.

Using an overhead projector, Terri reviewed with the class the definitions of *oligarchy, direct democracy, monarchy, tyranny*, and *representative democracy*. She assigned one form of government to each group and had the groups read passages in their textbook that discussed the form of government they were assigned, then construct a broader definition than the brief one they had just reviewed. (A girl from Japan had arrived earlier in the week, speaking little English. Terri paired her with a girl who had arrived from Taiwan several months previously to serve as a buddy.) After a few minutes, Terri asked for a volunteer from each group to stand and describe the form of government their group had discussed. Initially, she had to ask questions to draw out students' explanations; as they talked, she wrote their main ideas on the overhead to assist the class in taking notes and to assist students who were new to English in following the lesson. Occasionally terms needed to be clarified. For example, when explaining monarchy, Terri used the term *royal blood*. One student asked, "How do you get royal blood? I've never heard of royal blood, I have type-B blood." Terri explained that royal blood means that you come from a family in charge.

The term *tyranny* provoked lively discussion. Students were given the definition, "a leader who has power by force." A girl called out, "Arnold Schwarzenegger!" Several others agreed. Terri tried to steer them toward the fact that Schwarzenegger was elected to be governor; in the process students debated what forms of power he might have used to get elected. Then, when discussing representative democracy, a boy observed that President Bush's father had also been president, so was that a case of royal blood? Terri pointed out that the boy's observation was interesting, but that people had voted for him. She tried to get students to question why people vote as they do, and to see voting as something we have control over.

Afterward, Terri discussed with me the need for more time to go into depth, especially when some students bring up large questions, while others such as the new student from Japan, are trying to follow main ideas. "Just a little comment like Arnold Schwarzenegger, and you just realize, wow, there's a whole lesson there about political process and democracy, and you know, citizenship, and how we choose our leaders and why, and it's wonderful that that happens, and that they're thinking about it and talking about it" (January 30, 2004). While she would like to pursue such student-generated questions as the unit unfolded, she had standards-based content that needed to be covered and also made accessible to second-language learners, and she could not do all of this well in the time available. As she was pressed into content coverage, she was painfully aware that inquiry was being diminished.

4. *How should curriculum be evaluated? How should learning be evaluated? To whom is curriculum evaluation accountable?* By defining learning in terms of test scores, the standards movement has narrowed consideration of what curriculum is accountable for, and to whom. As Pinar (2004) wrote, "While curriculum as complicated conversation in the service of social and self-reflective understanding *will* transform the present, it will not do so in predicable ways," and it "makes no promises about raising test scores" (p. 207). Standardized tests do not measure cultivation of civic responsibility or caring individuals and communities (SooHoo, 2004a, p. 209). While teachers are being held accountable to the state on the basis of test scores, teachers are also adults trying to guide the broader development of young people.

Terri's students produced a good deal of written work, which she used to evaluate their learning. As she explained,

> I see great strides in their reading, in their writing, in their verbalization, like literature and analysis. When I look at that, I see that their skills are getting much better, much, much better. And I've had comments from people, you know, who, when they took their CELDT [California English Language Development Test] test, never had seen students write so much or care so much. And so I see it's happening, in that way. (January 30, 2004)

But her concurrent work helping students become better people was outside the accountability system.

After one of my visits, Terri mentioned, "You may have heard one person say, Can't we talk about the other thing? 'Cause that's where their hearts are right now." I asked what was happening. She replied, "The boys want to talk about how the girls treat them. The girls want to talk about how the boys treat them. And the marginalized girls in the class want to talk about how the girls who have power treat them." Then she shared a specific incident that had just happened involving sexual harassment. "A good thing is, they tell me. And they are now comfortable, if I say, well let's talk about it, they will talk about it. There's no code of silence with them, they'll let me in. We'll talk about it, and that's probably good, because then it's out there" (January 30, 2004).

This openness placed responsibility on her to help students work through problems in their relationships with each other, to the extent that she could do so ethically and with respect to privacy issues. She kept class time as space for academic work, but during lunch, between classes, and sometimes before or after school, helped students work with problems they experienced on the school bus and in school corridors. But under the accountability system, Terri's work as an adult guiding young people in social living went unacknowledged. The deeper the engagement teachers have with young people, the more they run up against schools organized increasingly to reduce engagement, which Terri explained is emotionally draining. Meier (2002) observed that the United States is "perhaps the only civilization in history that organizes its youth so that the nearer they get to being adults the less and less likely they are to know any adults" (p. 13).

ADMINISTRATIVE SUPPORT

While teachers have varying degrees of agency to construct multicultural curriculum, teachers also work in systems that institutionalize particular concepts of curriculum, learning, teaching, and relationships. In this book, while I have emphasized what teachers can do, I am mindful of constraints teachers face.

Pressure to follow curriculum standards and textbooks reverses efforts that some teachers and schools have made to develop culturally and linguistically relevant programs that work for their students. McCarty (2002) returned in 2000 to Rough Rock, Arizona, to find out how the Navajo language arts program described in Chapter 8 was faring. She found teachers struggling with the new state standards. One teacher said, "Should I be teaching Navajo or teaching the standards?" Another said, "We don't have time for Navajo. We've been told to teach to the standards" (p. 198). In other words, a culturally relevant curriculum that had been helping students achieve, even as measured through traditional tests, was being dismantled to conform to state standards.

The teachers whose classrooms I visited emphasized the importance of their principals supporting their work and protecting authentic learning in their schools. Although this book is not a study of principals, it does point toward the value of administrative support of teachers, and of administrators being able to link a vision of schooling with a rich understanding of classroom practice. Principals, however, are also caught in an institutionalized flow of top-down power that places students and communities on the bottom, and teachers only one or two rungs up from the bottom. What principals do in that context may well exacerbate inequities.

No Child Left Behind authorizes money to low-performing schools to bring up test scores. Some administrators work constructively with their teachers and communities, using resources primarily to help teachers more effectively teach the students they have, but many others quickly hire outside education consultants, a move that does not necessarily improve student learning over the long run (Iatarola & Fruchter, 2004). Indeed, as one of the teachers pointed out in an e-mail message to me, principals may be directed by the district administration to spend money only on such consultants. She said, "Many of these companies preach a prescriptive, basal-style curriculum with increased time for the basics" (July 21, 2004). Any school that receives Title I funding must have a school site council. Local stakeholders, including parent groups, the Migrant Education Program, and school site councils, are supposed to approve how school dollars are allocated. But often they are brought in after decisions have been made, then asked to rubber-stamp decisions, such as whether or not they approve one particular program, or whether they want their children's achievement scores to go up. The teacher commented that "parents rarely question anything because of the way information is presented. The constant misinformation and exclusion of the parents from the actual creation of school site plans in marginalized communities is a major barrier to any curriculum being transformative. Culturally responsive curriculum must include the involvement of parents in its very conception" (July 21, 2004).

A circular loop becomes institutionalized when children's low academic performance is attributed to poverty and cultural deficiencies. Their parents are then viewed as lacking knowledge that would be of value to educators, so prescriptions are adopted for raising achievement that may well ignore students' strengths, identities, and interests. If these prescriptions fail to bring up test scores significantly, the community's poverty, culture, and language is seen as the main problem.

VISIONARY PRAGMATISM IN A TIME OF STANDARDIZATION

Engaging students in democratic decision making appealed to most of the teachers in Multicultural Curriculum Design. But learning to do this takes time and is not part of most standards-based curricula. Most teachers cannot simply shift from teacher-centered to student-centered, democratic pedagogy without help or support. An experienced elementary teacher in Multicultural Curriculum Design, for example, asked for additional reading over the semester to help her visualize better what democratic pedagogy might look like in her own third-grade classroom. She explained that her school often had events like food drives, in which everyone participates, but when the event ends, so does participation. She wanted to help students to see themselves as able to make a difference in authentic and ongoing ways. She, as well as several other teachers, found articles in *Rethinking Schools* particularly helpful illustrations of democratic teaching at the K–12 level and connecting it to political issues. But the teachers repeatedly pointed out that they were being held accountable for raising test scores rather than for preparing citizens for democratic life.

Democracy in the United States is under attack, reflected in the erosion of teachers' control over curriculum. As Apple (2004b) pointed out, the United States (as well as many other countries) is facing an "odd combination of marketization on one hand and centralization of control on the other" (p. 615). This means that education increasingly is being viewed as a market product to be consumed by individuals for their own private use (such as to get a job), rather than as a public resource that develops a citizenry who can act on behalf of the good of both their own communities and others with whom they share space and resources. Budget discussions that refer to education as a "special interest" rather than a public resource reflects this pattern.

Teachers who are aware of the growing centralized control over education, coupled with erosion of democracy, are finding themselves caught in the middle. While they can often visualize exciting curricula that engage their students in important questions, they may not see much space in their teaching day to use such curricula, particularly if they are expected to follow a script. And, since their students are being held accountable through testing systems, ultimately students are the ones who are most affected by what teachers decide to do. If teachers deviate from following the standards and texts, their students end up paying a price if test scores drop. What, then, is possible?

I find Collins's (1998) notion of *visionary pragmatism* to be a useful concept for considering agency in this context. Collins explained, "A creative tension links visionary thinking and pragmatic action. Any social theory that becomes too out of touch with everyday people and their lives, especially oppressed people, is of little use to them. . . . At the same time, being too practical, looking only to the here and now—especially if present conditions seemingly offer little hope—can be debilitating" (p. 188). Visionary pragmatists recognize what is possible to accomplish in a specific context, but at the same time, see beyond that context. Visionary prag-matists reach for what may seem unattainable, seeking ways to turn the impossible into the possible.

Ethically, teachers need to decide what is in the best interests of the students they teach, the students' communities, and the larger society. On the one hand, to what extent is it in students' best interest to ignore what they will be tested on? On the other hand, to what extent is it in their best interest to reduce knowledge to test preparation? How should educators conceptualize student achievement more broadly? How should teachers work with curriculum that reflects dominant ideologies? The process of curriculum design and teaching is rooted in these ethical questions. While doing our best by students in the context of possibilities now, I hope we maintain and nurture a vision of a participatory democracy for tomorrow.

NOTES

1. Schools that fail to meet targets for 2 consecutive years are to notify parents of the option to transfer to another school. Schools that fail to meet targets for 4 consecutive years are to be reconstituted with a new faculty, and those that fail for 5 years can be closed or taken over by the state.

2. This lesson plan can be found in Grant & Sleeter (2003), pp. 319–324.

References

Action Learning Systems. (2002). *Addressing the components of high achieving schools.* Sacramento, CA: Author.

Ada, A. F. (1999). *The lizard and the sun,* New York: Dragonfly Books.

Agbo, S. A. (2001). Enhancing success in American Indian students: Participatory research at Akwesasne as part of the development of a culturally relevant curriculum. *Journal of American Indian Education, 40*(1), 31–56.

Allende, I. (2002). *La cuidad de las bestias.* New York: Harper Collins.

Amrein, A. L., & Berliner, D. C. (2002). High-stakes testing, uncertainty, and student learning. *Education Policy Analysis Archives, 10*(18). Retrieved January 15, 2003, from http://epaa.asu.edu/epaa/v10n18/

Anderson, J. M. (2002). Toward a post-colonial feminist methodology in nursing research: Exploring the convergence of post-colonial and black feminist scholarship. *Nurse Researcher, 9*(3), 7–27.

Anderson, T. (1996). The national standards for arts education: A (multi)cultural assessment. *Studies in Art Education, 38*(1), 55–60.

Anyon, J. (1979). Ideology and United States history textbooks. *Harvard Educational Review, 49*(3), 361–366.

Anyon, J. (1981). Elementary schooling and distinctions of social class. *Interchange, 12*(2&3), 118–132.

Apple, M. W. (1977). The process and ideology of valuing in educational settings. In A. A. Bellack & H. M. Kliebard (Eds.), *Curriculum and evaluation* (pp. 468–494). Berkeley: McCutchan.

Apple, M. W. (1999). *Power, meaning and identity.* New York: Peter Lang.

Apple, M. W. (2001). *Education the "right" way.* New York: RoutledgeFalmer.

Apple, M. W. (2004a). *Ideology and curriculum* (3rd ed.). New York: RoutledgeFalmer.

Apple, M. W. (2004b). Schooling, markets, and an audit culture. *Educational Policy, 18*(4), 614–621.

Aronowitz, S. (2000). *The knowledge factory.* Boston: Beacon Press.

Associated Press. (2004). Income gap of poor, rich, widens. *CBSNEWS.com.* Aug. 18, 2004. Retrieved August 18, 2004, from http://www.cbsnews.com/stories/2004/08/13/national/main635936.shtml

Athanases, S. Z. (1996). A gay-themed lesson in an ethnic literature curriculum: Tenth graders' responses to "Dear Anita." *Harvard Educational Review, 66*(2), 231–256.

Au, K. H. (1990). Changes in a teacher's views of interactive comprehension instruction. In L. C. Moll (Ed.), *Vygotsky and education* (pp. 271–286). Cambridge, UK: Cambridge University Press.

Au, K. H., & Carole, J. H. (1997). Improving literacy through a constructivist approach: The KEEP demonstration classroom project. *The Elementary School Journal, 97*(3), 203–221.

Ayers, W. (2004). *Teaching the personal and the political.* New York: Teachers College Press.

Bae, Y., Choy, S., Geddes, C., Sable, J., & Snyder, T. (2000). Trends in educational equity of girls and women. *Education Statistics Quarterly, 2*(2), 115–120.

Bailes, C. N. (2002). Mandy: A critical look at the portrayal of a deaf character in children's literature. *Multicultural Perspectives, 4*(4), 3–9.

Banks, C. A. M. (2005). *Improving multicultural education.* New York: Teachers College Press.

Banks, J. A. (1991a). Multicultural education: Its effects on students' racial and gender role attitudes. In J. P. Shaver (Ed.), *Handbook of research on social studies teaching and learning* (pp. 459–469). New York: Macmillan.

Banks, J. A. (1991b). *Teaching strategies for ethnic studies* (5th ed.). Boston: Allyn & Bacon.

Banks, J. A. (1993). The canon debate, knowledge construction, and multicultural education. *Educational Researcher, 22*(5), 4–14.

Banks, J. A. (1996). The African American roots of multicultural education. In J. A. Banks (Ed.), *Multicultural education, transformative knowledge, and action* (pp. 30–45). New York: Teachers College Press.

Banks, J. A. (1998). The lives and values of researchers: Implications for educating citizens in a multicultural society. *Educational Researcher, 27*(7), 4–17.

Banks, J. A. (1999). *An introduction to multicultural education* (2nd ed.). Boston: Allyn & Bacon.

Banks, J. A. (2003). *Teaching strategies for ethnic studies* (7th ed.). Boston: Allyn & Bacon.

Banks, J. A. (2004a). Introduction: Democratic citizenship in multicultural societies. In J. A. Banks (Ed.), *Diversity and citizenship education* (pp. 1–16). San Francisco: Jossey-Bass.

Banks, J. A. (2004b). Race, knowledge construction, and education in the United States. In J. A. Banks & C. A. M. Banks (Eds.), *Handbook of research on multicultural education* (2nd ed., pp. 228–239). San Francisco: Jossey Bass.

Baron, R. M., Tom, D. Y. H., & Cooper, H. M. (1985). Social class, race, and teacher expectations. In J. B. Dusek (Ed.), *Teacher expectancies* (pp. 251–269). Hillsdale, NJ: Lawrence Erlbaum.

Barton, P. E. (2003). *Parsing the achievement gap: Baselines for tracking progress.* Princeton, NJ: Educational Testing Service.

Bartolomé, L. I., & Trueba, E. T. (2000). Beyond the politics of schools and the rhetoric of fashionable pedagogies: The significance of teacher ideology. In H. T. Trueba & L. I. Bartolomé (Eds.), *Immigrant voices* (pp. 277–292). Lanham, MD: Rowman & Littlefield.

Bellack, A. A., & Kliebard, H. M. (Eds.). (1977). *Curriculum and evaluation.* Berkeley: McCuthchan.

Berlak, A. (2003). Who's in charge here? Teacher education and 2042. *Teacher Education Quarterly, 30*(1), 31–40.

Berliner, D. C., & Biddle, B. J. (1995). *The manufactured crisis: Myths, fraud and the attack on America's public schools.* Cambridge: Perseus Books.

Bernstein, M., & Kobrin, J. (1974). *Earth namer.* New York: Scribner.

Beyer, L., & Liston, D. (1996). *Curriculum in conflict.* New York: Teachers College Press.

Bigelow, B., & Peterson, B. (1998). *Rethinking Columbus.* Milwaukee: Rethinking Schools.

Bigler, R. S. (1995). The role of classification skill in moderating environmental influences on children's gender stereotyping: A study of the functional use of gender in the classroom. *Child Development, 66,* 1072–1087.

Bigler, R. S. (1999). The use of multicultural curricula and materials to counter racism in children. *Journal of Social Issues, 55,* 687–705.

Bigler, R. S., Brown, C. S., & Markell, M. (2001). When groups are not created equal: Effects of group status on the formation of intergroup attitudes in children. *Child Development, 72,* 1151–1162.

Bloom, A. C. (1989). *The closing of the American mind.* New York: Simon & Schuster.

Bloom, B. S. (1956). *Taxonomy of educational objectives: Classification of educational goals.* New York: Longman, Green.

Bracey, G. W. (2003). The No Child Left Behind Act, a plan for the destruction of public education: Just say no. *EDDRA.* Retrieved December 16, 2004, from http://www.america-tomorrow.com/bracey.EDDRA/EDDRA32.htm

Brandt, G. L. (1986). *The realization of anti-racist teaching.* Lewes, England: Falmer Press.

Brenner, M. (1998). Development of mathematical communication in problem solving groups by language minority students. *Bilingual Research Journal, 22* (2, 3, & 4), 103–128.

Bressler, L., DeStefano, L., Feldman, R., & Garg, S. (2000). Artists-in-residence in public schools: Issues in curriculum, integration, impact. *Visual Arts Research, 26*(1), 13–29.

Britton, F., Lumpkin, M., & Britton, E. (1984). The battle to imprint citizens for the 21st century. *The Reading Teacher, 37,* 724–733.

Britzman, D. P. (1995). Is there a queer pedagogy? Or, stop reading straight. *Educational Theory, 45*(2), 152–165.

Brophy, J., & VanSledright, B. (1997). *Teaching and learning history in elementary schools.* New York: Teachers College Press.

Burris, C. C., Heubert, J., & Levin, H. (2004). Math acceleration for all. *Educational Leadership, 61*(5), 68–71.

Business Roundtable. (1997). *A business leader's guide to setting academic standards.* Retrieved July 7, 2004, from http://www.brtable.org/TaskForces/TaskForce/

Business Roundtable. (1999). *Transforming education policy: Assessing ten years of progress in the states.* Washington, DC: Business Roundtable.

Byrne, M. M. (2001). Uncovering racial bias in nursing fundamentals textbooks. *Nursing and Health Care Perspectives, 22*(6), 299–303.

Cabazon, M. T., Nicoladis, E., & Lambert, W. L. (1998). *Becoming bilingual in the*

Amigos two-way immersion program (Research Report #3, Center for Research on Education, Diversity, and Excellence). Retrieved June 1, 2001, from http://crede.org/pdf/rr03.pdf

Cacoullos, A. R. (2001). American feminist theory. *American Studies International, 39*(1), 72–117.

California Department of Education. (2001). *History–social science framework and standards for California public schools.* Sacramento, CA: Author.

California Department of Education. (2003). *Science content standards for California public schools.* Sacramento, CA: Author.

Casteñeda, O. (1993). *Abuela's weave.* New York: Lee & Low Books.

Center for Educational Policy Research. (2003). *Standards for Success.* Eugene, OR: University of Oregon. Retrieved June 1, 2004, from http://www.s4s.org

Center for Research on Education, Diversity & Excellence. (2002). Five Standards. Retrieved May 5, 2003, from http://www.crede.org/standards/standards.html

Chow, R. (1987). New schoolbooks. *China News, 48*(329), 12.

Christensen, L. (2002). Teach the kind of skills they will need to overcome injustice themselves. *Rethinking Schools Online, 17*(1). Retrieved November 20, 2003, from http://www.rethinkingschools.org/archive/17_01/Advi171.shtml

Churchill, W. (2002). *Struggle for the land.* San Francisco: City Lights.

Clawson, R. A. (2002). Poor people, black faces: The portrayal of poverty in economics textbooks. *Journal of Black Studies, 32*(3), 352–361.

Codjoe, H. M. (2001). Fighting a "public enemy" of black academic achievement: The persistence of racism and the schooling experiences of black students in Canada. *Race Ethnicity and Education, 4*(4), 343–375.

Cohen-Scali, V. (2003). The influence of family, social, and work socialization on the construction of the professional identity of young adults. *Journal of Career Development, 29*(4), 237–249.

Collins, P. H. (1998). *Fighting words.* Minneapolis: University of Minnesota Press.

Comer, J. P. (1988). Educating poor minority children. *Scientific American, 259*(5), 42–48.

Connell, R. W. (1985). *Teachers' work.* Boston: Allen & Unwin.

Conrad, D. R. (1994). Educating with community murals. *Multicultural Education, 2*(1), 7–9.

Cooney, T. J., & Hirsch, C. R. (1990). *Teaching and learning mathematics in the 1990s.* Reston, VA: National Council of Teachers of Mathematics.

Cooper, H., & Moore, C. J. (1995). Teenage motherhood, mother-only households, and teacher expectations. *Journal of Experimental Education, 63*(3), 231–248.

Cornbleth, C., & Waugh, D. (1995). *The great speckled bird: Multicultural politics and education decision-making.* New York: St. Martin's Press.

Cortés, C. E. (2000). *The children are watching: How the media teach about diversity.* New York: Teachers College Press.

Cortés, C. (2002). *The making and remaking of a multiculturalist.* New York: Teachers College Press.

Crocco, M. S. (2001). The missing discourse about gender and sexuality in the social studies. *Theory Into Practice, 40*(1), 65–72.

Cruz, B. C., & Walker, P. C. (2001). Fostering positive ethnic relations between African American and Latino children: A collaborative urban program using art and history. *Multicultural Perspectives, 3*(1), 9–14.

Cruz-Jansen, M. I. (2001). ¿Y tu abuela a'onde está? *Sage Race Relations Abstracts, 26*(1), 7–24.

Cummins, J. (1986). Empowering minority students: A framework for intervention. *Harvard Educational Review, 15,* 18–36.

Danziger, K. (1990). *Constructing the subject.* New York: Cambridge University Press.

Darder, A. (1991). *Culture and power in the classroom: A theory for a critical bicultural pedagogy.* New York: Bergin & Garvey.

Darling-Hammond, L. (1994). Performance-based assessment and educational equity. *Harvard Educational Review, 66*(1), 3–30.

Denbo, S., & Beaulieu, L. M. (2002). *Improving schools for African American students: A reader for educational leaders.* Springfield, IL: C. C. Thomas.

Derman-Sparks, L. (1989). *Anti-bias curriculum.* Washington, DC: National Association for the Education of Young Children.

Desmond, C. T. (1996). *Shaping the culture of schooling: The rise of outcome-based education.* Albany: State University of New York Press.

Dewey, J. (1938). *Experience and education.* New York: Touchstone.

Diamond, J. B., Randolph, A., & Spillane, J. P. (2004). Teachers' expectations and sense of responsibility for student learning: The importance of race, class, and organizational habitus. *Anthropology & Education Quarterly, 35*(1), 75–98.

Diamond, B. J., & Moore, M. A. (1995). *Multicultural literacy: Mirroring the reality of the classroom.* New York: Longman.

"Don't turn back the clock!" (2003). *The Education Trust.* Retrieved July 17, 2004, from   http://www2.edtrust.org/NR/exeres/F3232B52-86C1-4792-94A5-13270E4B7D29

Dunn, G. (Producer), & Schwartz, M. (Producer). (1984). *A dollar a day, ten cents a dance* [Film]. [Independent feature]

Easton, J. Q., Forrest, E. P., Goldman, R. E., & Ludwig, L. M. (1985). National study of effective community college teachers. *Community/Junior College Quarterly, 9*(2), 153–163.

Economic Policy Institute. (2004). *Job watch: Tracking jobs and wages.* Retrieved August 18, 2004, from http://www.jobwatch.org/

Education Trust. (2003). *Achievement in America.* Retrieved August 19, 2004, from http://www2.edtrust.org/edtrust/achievement+in+america.html

Enrollment forecasting. (n.d.) *Hardwick day: Strategic competitive advantage for private colleges.* Retrieved July 17, 2004, from http://www.itsacademic.com/trends/forecasting/default.asp

Eisner, E. W. (1994). *Cognition and curriculum reconsidered* (2nd ed.). New York: Teachers College Press.

Feiner, S. F., & Morgan, B. A. (1987). Women and minorities in introductory economics textbooks: 1974–1984. *Journal of Economic Education, 18*(4), 376–392.

Ferguson, R. F. (2003). Teachers' perceptions and expectations and the black-white test score gap. *Urban Education, 38*(4), 460–507.

Feshbach, N. D. (1975). Empathy in children: Some theoretical and empirical considerations. *Counseling Psychologist, 5,* 25–30.

Feshbach, N. D., & Feshbach, S. (1987). Affective processes and academic achievement. *Child Development, 58,* 1335–1347.

Fine, M., Weis, L., & Powell, L. C. (1997). Communities of difference: A critical look at desegregated spaces created for and by youth. *Harvard Educational Review, 67*(2), 247–285.

Flores, J. (2003). *Dismantling the master's house: using whose tools? A critical analysis of the experiences of University Service Advocates at the Service Learning Institute of California State University, Monterey Bay.* Unpublished master's thesis, California State University, Monterey Bay.

Foley, C. L., & Boulware, B. J. (1996). Gender equity in 1990 middle school basal readers. *Reading Improvement, 33*(4), 220–223.

Ford, D. Y., & Harris, J. J., III, (2000). A framework for infusing multicultural curriculum into gifted education. *Roeper Review, 23*(1), 4–10.

Foster, M. (1995). African American teachers and culturally relevant pedagogy. In J. A. Banks & C. A. M. Banks (Eds.), *Handbook of research on multicultural education* (pp. 570–581). New York: Macmillan.

Foster, S. J. (1999). The struggle for American identity: Treatment of ethnic groups in United States history textbooks. *History of Education, 28*(3), 251–278.

Foucault, M. (2000). *Power/knowledge: Selected interviews and other writings.* New York: Pantheon Press.

Franklin, M. E. (1992). Culturally sensitive instructional practices for African-American learners with disabilities. *Exceptional Children, 59*(2), 115–122.

Freire, P. (1998). *Pedagogy of freedom.* Boulder, CO: Rowman & Littlefield.

Friedrich, A. (2004, August 17). School testing shows mixed results. *Herald.Com.* Retrieved August 19, 2004, from http://www.montereyherald.com/mld/montereyherald/9434751.htm?template-contentmodules/printstory.jsp

Fuller, E. J., & Johnson, J. F., Jr. (2001). Can state accountability systems drive improvements in school performance for children of color and children from low-income homes? *Education and Urban Society, 33*(3), 260–283.

Fusarelli, B. C., & Boyd, W. L. (2004). Introduction: One nation indivisible? *Educational Policy, 18*(1), 5–11.

Gallegos, B. P. (1998). Remembering the Alamo: Imperialism, memory, and postcolonial educational studies. *Educational Studies, 29*(3), 232–247.

Gándara, P., Rumberger, R., Maxwell-Jolly, J., & Callahan, R. (2003, October 7). English learners in California schools: Unequal resources, unequal outcomes. *Education Policy Analysis Archives, 11*(36). Retrieved October 8, 2003, from http://epaa.asu.edu/epaa/v11n36/

Garland-Thomson, R. (2002). Interrogating disability, transforming feminist theory. *NWSA Journal, 14*(3), 1–33.

Gay, G. (1983, April). Multiethnic education: Historical developments and future prospects. *Phi Delta Kappan, 64,* 560–563.

Gay, G. (1995). Curriculum theory and multicultural education. In J. A. Banks & C. A. M. Banks (Eds.), *Handbook of research on multicultural education* (pp. 25–43). New York: Macmillan.

Gay, G. (2000). *Culturally responsive teaching.* New York: Teachers College Press.

Gibbons, P. (2002). *Scaffolding language, scaffolding learning.* Portsmouth, NH: Heinemann.

Gillborn, D., & Youdell, D. (2002). *Rationing education.* Philadelphia: Open University Press.

Ginsburg, M. (2004, February 15). Educated buyers: Test scores, school ratings drive decisions as much as floor plans and city services. *San Francisco Chronicle.* Retrieved August 22, 2004, from http://www.sfgate.com

Giroux, H. A. (2000). *Stealing innocence.* New York: St. Martin's Press.

Glickman, C. D. (2000/01). Holding sacred ground: The impact of standardization. *Educational Leadership, 58*(4), 46–51.

Gordon, E. (1990). On the other side of the war. In S. Watanabe & C. Bruchac (Eds.), *Home to stay: Asian American women's fiction.* Greenfield Center, New York: Greenfield Review Press.

Gordy, L. L., & Pritchard, A. M. (1995). Redirecting our voyage through history: A content analysis of social studies textbooks. *Urban Education, 30*(2), 195–218.

Gorski, P. (2005). *Multicultural education and the Internet* (2nd ed.). Boston: McGraw-Hill.

Grant, C. A. (2004). Oppression, privilege, and high-stakes testing. *Multicultural Perspectives, 6*(1), 3–11.

Grant, C. A., & Sleeter, C. E. (2003). *Turning on learning* (3rd ed.). New York: Wiley.

Greenfield, E. (1977). *Mary McLeod Bethune.* New York: Crowell.

Grumet, M., & Stone, L. (2000). Feminism and curriculum: Getting our act together. *Journal of Curriculum Studies, 32*(2), 183–197.

Gutiérrez, R. (2000a). Advancing African-American, urban youth in mathematics: Unpacking the success of one math department. *American Journal of Education, 109,* 63–111.

Gutiérrez, R. (2000b). Is the multiculturalization of mathematics doing us more harm than good? In R. Mahalingam & C. McCarthy (Eds.), *Multicultural curriculum* (pp. 199–219). New York: Routledge.

Haberman, M. (1995). *Star teachers of children in poverty.* West Lafayette, IN: Kappa Delta Pi.

Hahn, C. L., & Blankenship, G. (1983). Women and economics textbooks. *Theory and Research in Education, 2,* 67–76.

Hake, R. R. (2004). Direct science instruction suffers a setback in California—Or does it? *AAPT Announcer, 34*(2), 177: Retrieved September 14, 2004, from http://www.physics.indiana.edu/~hake/DirInstSctback-041104f.pdf

Hamilton V. (1997). *Drylongso.* San Diego: Harcourt Brace.

Haney, W. (2000). The myth of the Texas miracle in education. *Educational Policy Analysis Archives, 8* (4). Retrieved August 15, 2004, from http://epaa.asu.edu/cpaa/v8n41

Hankes, J. E. (1998). *Native American pedagogy and cognitive-based mathematics instruction.* New York: Garland.

Hankes, J. E., & Fast, G. R. (2002). *Perspectives on indigenous people of North America.* Reston, VA: National Council of Teachers of Mathematics.

Hauser-Cram, P., Sirin, S. R., & Stipek, D. (2003). When teachers' and parents' values differ: Teachers' ratings of academic competence in children from low-income families. *Journal of Educational Psychology, 95*(4), 813–820.

Havill, J. (1990). *Jamaica Tag-Along*. Boston: Houghton Mifflin.

Haycock, K. (2001). Closing the achievement gap. *Educational Leadership, 58*(6), 6–11.

Haycock, K. (2003). A new core curriculum for all. *Thinking K–16, a publication of the Education Trust, 7*(1), 1–2.

Haycock, K., & Craig, J. (2002). Closing the achievement gap. *Principal, 82*(2), 20–23.

Hayibor, B., & Peterat, L. (1995). Gender equity and secondary school home economics textbooks. *Canadian Home Economics Journal, 45*(3), 102–108.

Heath, S. B. (1983). *Ways with words: Language, life, and work in communities and classrooms*. Cambridge, UK: Cambridge University Press.

Hillocks, G. (2002). *The testing trap; How state writing assessments control learning*. New York: Teachers College Press.

Hogben, M., & Waterman, C. K. (1997). Are all of your students represented in their textbooks? A content analysis of coverage of diversity issues in introductory psychology textbooks. *Teaching of Psychology, 24*(2), 95–100.

Hood, S. (1998). Culturally responsive performance-based assessment: Conceptual and psychometric considerations. *Journal of Negro Education, 67*(3), 187–196.

Horn, R. A., Jr. (2003). Developing a critical awareness of the hidden curriculum through media literacy. *The Clearing House, 76*(6), 298–300.

Howard, T. C. (2003a). Culturally relevant pedagogy: Ingredients for critical teacher reflection. *Theory Into Practice, 42*(3), 195–202.

Howard, T. C. (2003b). The dis(g)race of the social studies. In G. Ladson-Billings (Ed.), *Critical race theory perspectives on the social studies* (pp. 27–43). Greenwich, CT: Information Age Publishing.

Hulpach, V., & Zwadsky, M. (1996). *Ahaiyute and Cloud Eater*. San Diego: Harcourt Brace.

Humphreys, J. T. (1997, Winter). Sex and geographic representation in two music education history books. *Bulletin of the Council for Research in Music Education, 131*, 67–86.

Hunt, J. B., Jr. (2003). Unrecognized progress: Today's schools are undeniably better than the schools of 1983, and a trio of recent reforms makes them even better. *Education Next, 3*(2), 24–28.

Iatarola, P., & Fruchter, N. (2004). District effectiveness: A study of investment strategies in New York City public schools and districts. *Educational Policy, 18*(3), 491–512.

Irvine, J. J., & Armento, B. J. (2001). *Culturally responsive teaching: Lesson planning for elementary and middle grades*. Boston: McGraw-Hill.

Jackson, P. (1968). *Life in classrooms*. New York: Holt, Rinehart, & Winston.

Jackson, S. A., Logsdon, D. M., & Taylor, N. E. (1983). Instructional leadership behaviors: Differentiating effective from ineffective low-income urban schools. *Urban Education, 18*(1), 59–70.

Jacobs, D. (1981). Teaching the Arab world: Evaluating textbooks. *Social Studies, 72*(4), 150–153.

Jhally, S. (1995). Image-based culture: Advertising and popular culture. In G. Dines & J. M. Humez (Eds.), *Gender, race and class in media* (pp. 77–87). Thousand Oaks, CA: Sage.

Johns, J. R. (2003). *Dance as identity, resistance and power.* Unpublished master's thesis, California State University–Monterey Bay.

Johnson, D. L., Maddux, C. D., & Liu, L. (1997). *Using technology in the classroom.* New York: Haworth Press.

Jones, M. A., Kitetu, C., & Sunderland, J. (1997). Discourse roles, gender and language textbook dialogues: Who learns what from John and Sally? *Gender and Education, 9*(4), 469–490.

Jones, M. G., Jones, B. D., & Hargrove, T. Y. (2003). *The unintended consequences of high-stakes testing.* Lanham, MD: Rowman & Littlefield.

Jordan, C. (1992). The role of culture in minority school achievement. *The Kamehameha Journal of Education, 3*(2), 53–66.

Jussim, L., Eccles, J., & Madon, S. (1996). Social perceptions, social stereotypes, and teacher expectations. In M. P. Zanna (Ed.), *Advances in experimental social psychology* (Vol. 28, pp. 281–388). San Diego, CA: Academic Press.

Katzenberger, E. (Ed.). (1995). *First world, ha, ha, ha!* San Francisco: City Lights Books.

Kauffman, D., Johnson, S. M., Kardos, S. M., Liu, E., & Peske, H. G. (2002). "Lost at sea": New teachers' experiences with curriculum and assessment. *Teachers College Record, 104*(2), 273–300.

King, J. E. (1992). Diaspora literacy and consciousness in the struggle against miseducation in the black community. *Journal of Negro Education, 61*(3), 317–340.

King, J. E., Hollins, E. R., & Hayman, W. (Eds.). (1997). *Preparing teachers for cultural diversity.* New York: Teachers College Press.

Kliebard, H. M. (1982). Education at the turn of the century: a crucible for curriculum change. *Educational Researcher, 11*(1), 16–24.

Kliebard, H. M. (1995). *The struggle for the American curriculum* (2nd ed.). New York: Routledge.

Knapp, M. S. (Ed.). (1995). *Teaching for meaning in high-poverty classrooms.* New York: Teachers College Press.

Kohn, A. (2002). Poor teaching for poor kids. *Language Arts, 79*(3), 251–255.

Kornhaber, M. L. (2004). Assessment, standards and equity. In J. A. Banks & C. A. M. Banks (Eds.), *Handbook of research on multicultural education* (pp. 91–109). San Francisco: Jossey-Bass.

Koza, J. E. (1994). Females in 1988 middle school music textbooks: An analysis of illustrations. *Journal of Research in Music Education, 42*(2), 145–171.

Kumashiro, K. K. (2002). Against repetition: Addressing resistance to anti-oppressive change in the practices of learning, teaching, supervising, and researching. *Harvard Educational Review, 72*(1), 67–92.

Kumashiro, K. K. (2004). *Against common sense: Teaching and learning toward social justice.* New York: RoutledgeFalmer.

Ladson-Billings, G. (1994). *The dreamkeepers.* San Francisco: Jossey Bass.

Laduke, W. (1999). *All our relations: Native struggle for land and life.* Minneapolis, MN: Honor the Earth.

Lambson, D. (2002). The availability of Spanish heritage language materials in public and school libraries. *International Journal of Bilingual Education and Bilingualism, 5*(4), 233–243.

Lee, C. D. (1998). Culturally responsive pedagogy and performance-based assessment. *Journal of Negro Education, 67*(3), 268–279.

Lee, J. (in press). Reducing school segregation and closing achievement gap: Cross-state trends of within-school and between-school racial segregation and math achievement gaps. In G. Orfield & E. Frankenburg (Eds.), *Can we make a rainbow? From segregation to integration.* Charlottesville: University of Virginia Press.

Lei, J. L., & Grant, C. A. (2001). Multicultural education in the United States: A case of paradoxical equality. In C. A. Grant & J. L. Lei (Eds.), *Global constructions of multicultural education* (pp. 205–238). Mahwah, NJ: Erlbaum.

Leonard, S. (2002). Children's history: Implications of childhood beliefs for teachers of Aboriginal students. *Australian Journal of Indigenous Education, 30*(2), 20–24.

Lepore, J. (1999). *Encounters in the new world: A history in documents.* Oxford: Oxford University Press.

Levine, D. P. (1995). *Rethinking schools: An agenda for change.* New York: New Press, distributed by W.W. Norton.

Lewis, A. (2000). *Figuring it out: Standards-based reforms in urban middle grades.* New York: McConnell Clark Foundation

Linn, R. L., Baker, E. L., & Betebenner, D. W. (2002). Accountability systems: Implications of requirements of the No Child Left Behind Act of 2001. *Educational Researcher, 31*(6), 3–16.

Lipman, P. (2004). *High stakes education.* New York: RoutledgeFalmer.

Loewen, J. W. (1995). *Lies my teacher told me.* New York: New Press.

Loutzenheiser, L. W., & MacIntosh, L. B. (2004). Citizenships, sexualities, and education. *Theory Into Practice, 43*(2), 151–158.

Lowell, S. (1996). *Los tres pequeños jabalies.* Flagstaff, AZ: Northland.

Lucey, H., & Reay, D. (2000). Identities and transition: Anxiety and excitement in the move to secondary school. *Oxford Review of Education, 26*(2), 191–205.

Macedo, D. (1994). *Literacies of power.* Boulder, CO: Westview.

Madaus, G., & Clarke, M. (2001). The adverse impact of high-stakes testing on minority students: Evidence from one hundred years of test data. In G. Orfield & M. L. Kornhaber (Eds.), *Raising standards or raising barriers? Inequality and high-stakes testing in public education* (pp. 85–106). New York: Century Foundation Press.

Mahari, J. (1998). *Shooting for excellence.* New York: Teachers College Press.

Manset-Williamson, G., & Washburn, S. (2002). Administrators' perspectives of the impact of mandatory graduation qualifying examinations for students with learning disabilities. *Journal of Special Education Leadership, 15*(2), 49–59.

Marquez, S. A. (1994). Distorting the image of "Hispanic" women in sociology: Problematic strategies of presentation in the introductory text. *Teaching Sociology, 22*(3), 231–236.

Marzollo, J., & Pinkney, J. B. (1993). *Happy birthday, Martin Luther King.* New York: Scholastic.

Mbandaka, H. V. (1995). The influence of colonial ideology on schoolbooks in the Belgian Congo. *Paedagogica Historica, 31*(2), 355–405.

McCarty, T. L. (1994, Winter). Bilingual education policy and the empowerment of American Indian communities. *The Journal of Educational Issues of Language Minority Students, 14,* 23–41.

McCarty, T. L. (2002). *A place to be Navajo.* Mahwah, NJ: Erlbaum.

McNeil, L., & Valenzuela, A. (2001). The harmful impact of the TAAS system of testing in Texas: Beneath the accountability rhetoric. In G. Orfield & M. L. Kornhaber (Eds.), *Raising standards or raising barriers? Inequality and high-stakes testing in public education* (pp. 127–150). New York: Century Foundation Press.

Meier, D. (1998). Can the odds be changed? *Phi Delta Kappan, 79*(5), 358–362.

Meier, D. (2002). *In schools we trust.* Boston: Beacon Press.

Mestre, J. P., & Gerace, W. J. (1986). A study of the algebra acquisition of Hispanic and Anglo ninth graders: Research findings relevant to teacher training and classroom practice. *NABE: The Journal for the National Association for Bilingual Education, 10*(2), 137–167.

Meyer, R. J. (2002). *Phonics exposed.* Mahwah, NJ: Erlbaum.

Milligan, J. K., & Bigler, R. S. (in press). Addressing race and racism in the classroom. In G. Orfield & E. Frankenburg (Eds.), *Can we make a rainbow? From segregation to integration.* Charlottesville: University of Virginia Press.

Mitchell-Powell, B. (1995). Standards and practices: Children's literature and curricula reform for the twenty-first century. *Social Studies and the Young Learner, 8*(1), 19–21.

Moll, L. C., & Gonzalez, N. (2004). Engaging life: A funds of knowledge approach to multicultural education. In J. A. Banks & C. A. M. Banks (Eds.), *Handbook of research on multicultural education* (2nd ed., pp. 699–715). San Francisco: Jossey-Bass.

Molnar, A. (2002). The corporate branding of our schools. *Educational Leadership, 60*(2), 74–79.

Moore, D. S. (1982). Reconsidering Bloom's taxonomy of educational objectives, cognitive domain. *Educational Theory, 32*(1), 29–34.

Moses, R. P., & Cobb, C. E., Jr. (2001a). Organizing algebra: The need to voice a demand. *Social Policy, 31*(4), 4–12.

Moses, R. P., & Cobb, C. E., Jr. (2001b). *Radical equations.* Boston: Beacon Press.

Murrell, P. C., Jr. (2001). *The community teacher.* New York: Teachers College Press.

Murrell. P. C., Jr. (2002). *African-centered pedagogy.* Albany: State University of New York Press.

Muse, D. (Ed.). (1997). *Multicultural resources for young readers.* New York: The New Press.

National Commission on Excellence in Education. (1983). *A nation at risk.* Washington, DC: U.S. Government Printing Office.

National Education Association. (2003). *Status of the American public school teacher 2000–2001.* Washington, DC: Author.

Natriello, G., & Pallas, A. (2001). The development and impact of high-stakes testing. In G. Orfield & M. L. Kornhaber (Eds.), *Raising standards or raising barriers? Inequality and high-stakes testing in public education* (pp. 19–38). New York: Century Foundation Press.

Nava, G. (Director) (1983). *El norte.* Artisan Entertainment.

Neill, M., Bursh, P., Schaeffer, B., Thall, C., Yohe, M., & Zappardino, P. (1995). *Implementing performance assessments.* Cambridge, MA: FairTest.

Neill, M., & Gayler, K. (2001). Do high-stakes graduation tests improve learning outcomes? Using state-level NAEP data to evaluate the effects of mandatory graduation rates. In G. Orfield & M. L. Kornhaber (Eds.), *Raising standards or raising barriers? Inequality and high-stakes testing in public education* (pp. 107–126). New York: Century Foundation Press.

Neuman, S. B. (1999). Books make a difference: A study of access to literacy. *Reading Research Quarterly, 34*(3), 286–311.

Nochlin, L. (1971). Why are there no great women artists? In V. Gornick & B. K. Moran (Eds.), *Woman in sexist society* (pp. 480–510). New York: Basic Books.

Noguera, P. (2003). *City schools and the American dream.* New York: Teachers College Press.

Oakes, J. (1985). *Keeping track.* New Haven, CT: Yale University Press.

Oakes, J., Blasi, G., & Rogers, J. (2004). Accountability for adequate and equitable opportunities to learn. In K. Sirtonik (Ed.), *Holding accountability accountable: What ought to matter in public education.* New York: Teachers College Press.

Orfield, G., & Kornhaber, M. L. (Eds.). (2001). *Raising standards or raising barriers? Inequality and high-stakes testing in public education.* New York: Century Foundation Press.

Ortiz-Franco, L. (1990). Interrelationships of seven mathematical abilities across languages. *Hispanic Journal of Behavioral Sciences, 12*(3), 299–312.

Osler, A. (1994). Still hidden from history: The representation of women in recently published history textbooks. *Oxford Review of Education, 20*(2), 219–235.

Owens, E. W., & Waxman, H. C. (1994). Comparing the effectiveness of computer-assisted instruction and conventional instruction in mathematics for African-American postsecondary students. *International Journal of Instructional Media, 21*(4), 327–336.

Palmaffy, T. (1998, March–April). The gold star state: How Texas jumped to the head of the class in elementary-school achievement. *Policy Review,* No. 88, 30–38.

Pang, V. O., & Sablan, V. A. (1998). Teacher efficacy. In M. E. Dilworth (Ed.), *Being responsive to cultural differences* (pp. 39–58). Washington, DC: Corwin Press.

Parenti, O. (2004). *Commercialization of public education: Voices of academics and educators on corporate involvement in the schools.* Unpublished master's thesis, California State University–Monterey Bay.

Parker, W. C. (2003). *Teaching democracy.* New York: Teachers College Press.

People for the American Way. (n.d.). Inequity in Illinois. Retrieved July 13, 2004, from http://www.pfaw.org/pfaw/general/default.aspx?oid=15547

Peritt, D. C. (1997). Can technology increase course opportunities for migrant students? *NASSP Bulletin, 81*(No. 587), 15–18.

Perry, T., Steele, C., & Hilliard, A., III. (2003). *Young, gifted and black.* Boston: Beacon Press.

Peterson, B. (2002). Advice to new teachers from teachers who have been there:

"We need to teach for global justice." *Rethinking Schools Online, 17*(1). Retrieved November 20, 2003 from http://www.rethinkingschools.org/archive/17_01/Advi171.shtml

Peterson, B. (2000/01). Planting seeds of solidarity. *Rethinking Schools Online, 15*(2). Retrieved March 10, 2005, from http://www.rethinkingschools.org/archive/15_02/Seed152.shtml

Pierson, F. R., Schellenberg, A., Runningfox, J., Cardinal, T., Bedard, I., & Brave Bird, M. (1994). *Lakota Woman*. Atlanta: Turner Home Entertainment.

Pinar, W. F. (2004). *What is curriculum theory?* Mahwah, NJ: Erlbaum.

Pinkney, A. D. (1998). *Duke Ellington*. New York: Hyperion Books for Children.

Pipes, T. (2002). *Beneath the surface: Middle school students and diversity*. Unpublished master's thesis, California State University–Monterey Bay.

Pohan, C. (2000). Practical ideas for teaching children about prejudice, discrimination, and social justice through literature and standards-based curriculum. *Multicultural Perspectives, 2*(1), 24–28.

Potter, E. F., & Rosser, S. V. (1992). Factors in life science textbooks that may deter girls' interest in science. *Journal of Research in Science Teaching, 29*(7), 669–686.

Powell, R. R. (1996). Epistemological antecedents to culturally relevant and constructivist classroom curricula: A longitudinal study of teachers' contrasting worldviews. *Teaching and Teacher Education, 12*(4), 365–384.

Powell, R. R., & Garcia, J. (1988). What research says about stereotypes. *Science and Children, 25*, 21–23.

Ravitch, D. (1990). Diversity and democracy: Multicultural education in America. *American Educator, 14*(1), 16–20, 46–68.

Reyes, P., Scribner, J. D., & Scribner, A. P. (Eds.). (1999). *Lessons from high-performing Hispanic schools*. New York: Teachers College Press.

Reyhner, J. (1986). Native Americans in basal reading textbooks: Are there enough? *Journal of American Indian Education, 26*, 14–21.

Roderick, M., Jacob, B. A., & Bryk, A. S. (2002). The impact of high-stakes testing in Chicago on student achievement in promotional gate grades. *Educational Evaluation and Policy Analysis, 24*(4), 333–357.

Rodriguez, G. (2002). *Building effective arts programs that reflect and include our community*. Unpublished master's thesis, California State University–Monterey Bay.

Romanowski, M. H. (1996). Problems of bias in history textbooks. *Social Education, 60*(3), 170–173.

Roth, J., & Damico, S. B. (1999). Student perspectives on learning and instruction: Differences by race/ethnicity and gender. *Journal of At-Risk Issues, 6*(1), 32–39.

Ruggieri, C. A. (2003). Rethinking standards-based reform. *English Journal, 92*(4), 15–17.

Ruiz de Velasco, J. (2005). Performance-based school reforms and the federal role in helping students that serve language-minority students. In A. Valenzuela (Ed.), *Leaving children behind* (pp. 33–56). Albany: State University of New York Press.

Russell, D. (1998). *Black genius and the American experience.* New York: Carroll & Graf.

Sale, K. (1991). *The conquest of paradise: Christopher Columbus and the Columbian legacy.* New York: Knopf.

Sambell, K., & McDowell, L. (1998). The construction of the hidden curriculum: Messages and meanings in the assessment of student learning. *Assessment & Evaluation in Higher Education, 23*(4), 391–402.

Sanchez, T. R. (2001). "Dangerous Indians": Evaluating the depiction of Native Americans in selected trade books. *Urban Education, 36*(3), 400–425.

Schall, J., & Kauffmann, G. (2003). Exploring literature with gay and lesbian characters in the elementary school. *Journal of Children's Literature, 29*(1), 36–45.

Schaufele, C., & Srivastava, R. (1995). Earth algebra: Real-life mathematics in Navajoland. *Journal of Navajo Education, 12*(2), 12–15.

Scheslinger, A. M., Jr. (1992). *The disuniting of America.* New York: Norton.

Schoenfeld, A. H. (2004). The math wars. *Educational Policy, 18*(1), 253–286.

Schommer, M. (1998). The role of adults' beliefs about knowledge in school, work, and everyday life. In M. C. Smith & T. Pourchot (Eds.). *Adult learning and development: Perspectives from educational psychology* (pp. 127–143). Mahwah, NJ: Erlbaum.

Schommer, M., Calvert, C., Gariglietti, G., & Bajaj, A. (1997). The development of epistemological beliefs among secondary students: A longitudinal study. *Journal of Educational Psychology, 89*(1), 37–40.

Schon, I., Hopkins, K. D., & Davis, W. A. (1982). The effects of books in Spanish and free reading time on Hispanic students' reading abilities and attitudes. *NABE Journal, 7,* 13–20.

Schultz, T. (1998). History of development of California science content standards. Retrieved September 14, 2004, from http://www.sci-ed-ga.org/standards/history.html

Segarra, J. A., & Dobles, R. R. (1999). *Learning as a political act: Struggles for learning and learning from struggles.* Cambridge, MA: Harvard Educational Review.

Shade, B. J. R. (1989). *Culture, style, and the educative process.* Springfield, IL: Charles O. Thomas.

Sherman, W. L., & Theobald, P. (2001). Progressive Era rural reform: Creating standard schools in the Midwest. *Journal of Research in Rural Education, 17*(2), 84–91.

Shepard, L. A. (2000). The role of assessment in a learning culture. *Educational Researcher, 29*(7), 4–14.

Shor, I. (1992). *Empowering education.* Chicago: University of Chicago Press.

Shorish, M. M. (1988). The Islamic revolution and education in Iran. *Comparative Education Review, 32*(1), 58–75.

Short, E. C. (1986). A historical look at curriculum design. *Theory Into Practice, 25*(1), 3–9.

Singer, J. Y., & Smith, S. A. (2003). The potential of multicultural literature: Changing understanding of self and others. *Multicultural Perspectives, 5*(2), 17–23.

Singh, K., & Granville, M. (1999). Factors that affect enrollment in eighth grade algebra for African-American students. *Research in Middle Level Education Quarterly, 22*(2), 57–73.

Skilton-Sylvester, P. (2003). Less like a robot: A comparison of change in an inner-city school and a Fortune 500 company. *American Educational Research Journal, 40*(1), 3–41.

Skrla, L., Scheurich, J. J., Johnson, J. F., Jr., & Koschoreck, J. W. (2001). Accountability for equity: Can state policy leverage social justice? *International Leadership in Education, 4*(3), 237–260.

Sleeter, C. E. (1992). *Keepers of the American dream.* London: Falmer Press.

Sleeter, C. E. (1995). An analysis of the critiques of multicultural education. In J. A. Banks & C. M. Banks (Eds.), *Handbook of research on multicultural education* (pp. 81–94). New York: Macmillan.

Sleeter, C. E. (2001). *Culture, difference, and power.* New York: Teachers College Press.

Sleeter, C. E. (2004). Standardizing imperialism. *Rethinking Schools, 19*(1), 26–27.

Sleeter, C. E., & Grant, C. A. (1991). Textbooks and race, class, gender, and disability. In M. W. Apple & L. Christian-Smith (Eds.), *Politics of the textbook* (pp. 78–110). New York: Routledge, Chapman, & Hall.

Sleeter, C. E., & Grant, C. A. (2003). *Making choices for multicultural education: Five approaches to race, class and gender* (3rd ed.). New York: Wiley.

Sleeter, C. E., & Stillman, J. (2005). Standardizing knowledge in a multicultural society. *Curriculum Inquiry, 35*(1), 27–46.

SooHoo, S. (2004a). We change the world by doing nothing. *Teacher Education Quarterly, 31*(1), 199–211.

SooHoo, S. (2004b). Woman warrior liberating the oppressed and the oppressor: Cultural relevancy through narrative. In J. J. Romo, P. Bradfield, & R. Serrano (Eds.), *Reclaiming democracy* (pp. 258–280). Upper Saddle River, NJ: Merrill Prentice-Hall.

Soto, G. (1992). *Too many tamales.* New York: Putnam.

Soto, G. (1995). *Chato's kitchen.* New York: Putnam.

Stanton-Salazar, R. (2004). Social capital among working-class minority students. In M. A. Gibson, P. Gándara, & J. P. Koyama (Eds.), *School connections* (pp. 18–38). New York: Teachers College Press.

Starr, L. (2002). Dear Santa: A holiday wish for schools. *Education World.* Retrieved July 13, 2004, from http://www.education-world.com/a_issues/issues366.shtml

Stecher, B. (2001). The effects of the Washington reform policies on school and classroom practices, 1999–2000. *Politics of Education Bulletin, 25*(1), 5–14.

Style, E. (1996). Curriculum as window and mirror. The S.E.E.D. Project on Inclusive Curriculum. Retrieved November 20, 2003, from http://www.wcwonline.org/seed/curriculum.html

Su, Y. (1997/98). Changing minds: How elementary social studies textbooks both reflect and change society. *International Journal of Social Education, 12*(2), 76–104.

Taba, H. (1962). *Curriculum development theory and practice.* New York: Harcourt, Brace & World.

Taub, D. E., & Fanflik, P. L. (2000). The inclusion of disability in introductory sociology textbooks. *Teaching Sociology, 28*(1), 12–23.

Tetreault, M. K. T. (1983). Integrating women's history: The case of United States history high school textbooks. *History Teacher, 19,* 211–262.

Tetreault, M. K. T. (1984). Notable American women: The case of United States history textbooks. *Social Education, 48,* 546–550.

Tetreault, M. K. T. (1989). Integrating content about women and gender into the curriculum. In J. A. Banks & C. A. M. Banks (Eds.), *Multicultural education: Issues and perspectives* (pp. 124–144). Boston: Allyn & Bacon.

Tettegah, S. (1996). The racial consciousness attitudes of white prospective teachers and their perceptions of the teachability of students from different racial/ethnic backgrounds: Findings from a California study. *Journal of Negro Education, 65*(2), 151–163.

Thompson, S. (2001). The authentic standards movement and its evil twin. *Phi Delta Kappan, 82*(5), 358–362.

Titchkoski, T. (2000). Disability studies: The old and the new. *Canadian Journal of Sociology, 25*(2), 197–224.

Townsend, B. L. (2002). Testing while black. *Remedial & Special Education, 23*(4), 222–230.

Tupper, J. (2002). Silent voices, silent stories: Japanese Canadians in social studies textbooks. *Alberta Journal of Educational Research, 48*(4), 327–340.

Tyler, R. W. (1969). *Basic principles of curriculum and instruction.* Chicago: University of Chicago Press.

U.S. Census Bureau. (2004). Historical income tables—Households. Retrieved August 22, 2004, from http://www.census.gov/hhes/income/histinc/h0201.html

U.S. Department of Education. (1994). *High standards for all students.* Washington, DC: U.S. Government Printing Office.

U.S. Department of Education. (2001). *No Child Left Behind.* Retrieved September 18, 2003, from http://www.ed.gov/nclb/overview/intro/execsumm.html

U.S. Department of Labor. (2003). *Tomorrow's jobs.* Retrieved August 25, 2004, from http://www.bls.gov

Valadez, J. R. (2002). The influence of social capital on mathematics course selection by Latino high school students. *Hispanic Journal of Behavioral Sciences, 24*(3), 319–339.

Valenzuela, A. (2005). Accountability and the privatization agenda. In A. Valenzuela (Ed.), *Leaving children behind* (pp. 263–294). Albany: State University of New York Press.

Vernez, G., Krop, R. A., & Rydell, C. P. (1999). *Closing the education gap: Benefits and costs.* Santa Monica, CA: Rand Education.

Viega, A. (2004, August 21). Home haves and have-nots. *Monterey County Herald,* pp. E1–2.

Vygotsky, L. (1930). *Mind and society.* Retrieved May 5, 2004, from http://www.marxists.org/archive/vygotsky/works/mind/chap6.htm

Walford, G. (1983). Science textbook images and the reproduction of sexual divisions in society. *Research in Science & Technology Education, 1*(1), 65–72.

Walker, D. F. (2003). *Fundamentals of curriculum design* (2nd ed.). Mahwah, NJ: Erlbaum.

Wang, D. (2002). Stories told from different perspectives. *International Journal of Curriculum and Instruction, 4*(1), 25–41.

Wang, F. (2002). A "textbook solution" to curing our country's education woes: How textbooks and the considerable economic resources of textbook publishers can be used to improve student achievement. *EducationNews.org*. Retrieved April 6, 2004, from www.educationnews.org/a.htm

Wang, J., & Odell, S. J. (2002). Mentored learning to teach according to standards-based reform: A critical review. *Review of Educational Research, 72*(3), 481–546.

Ward, C. (2001). Under construction: On becoming a constructivist in view of the "standards." *Mathematics Teacher, 94*(2), 94–96.

Warren, S. R. (2002). Stories from the classroom: How expectations and efficacy of diverse teachers affect the academic performance of children in poor urban schools. *Educational Horizons, 80*(3), 109–116.

Watahomigie, L. J., & McCarty, T. L. (1994). Bilingual/bicultural education at Peach Springs: A Hualapai way of schooling. *Peabody Journal of Education, 69*(2), 26–42.

Watkins, W. H. (1993). Black curriculum orientations: A preliminary inquiry. *Harvard Educational Review, 65*(3), 321–338.

Wertsch, J. V. (1999). Revising Russian history. *Written Communication, 16*(3), 267–295.

Wexler, P. (1992). *Becoming somebody: Toward a social psychology of school.* London: Falmer Press.

Wharton-McDonald, R., Pressley, M., & Hampston, J. M. (1998). Literacy instruction in nine first-grade classrooms: Teacher characteristics and student achievement. *The Elementary School Journal, 99*(2), 101–128.

White, B. C. (2000). Pre-service teachers' epistemology viewed through perspectives on problematic classroom situations. *Journal of Education for Teaching, 26*(3), 279–305.

Wiggins, G., & McTighe, J. (1998). *Understanding by design.* Alexandria, VA: Association for Supervision and Curriculum Development.

Wiley, T. G., & Wright, W. E. (2004). Against the undertow: Language-minority education policy and politics in the "Age of Accountability." *Educational Policy, 18*(1), 142–168.

Wineburg, S. (2001). *Historical thinking and other unnatural acts.* Philadelphia: Temple University Press.

Wixson, K. K., & Dutro, E. (1999). Standards for primary grade reading: An analysis of state frameworks. *The Elementary School Journal, 100*(2), 89–110.

Woodson, J. (1995). *From the notebooks of Melanin Sun.* New York: Blue Sky/Scholastic.

Wynter, S. (1992). *Do not call us Negroes: How multicultural textbooks perpetuate racism.* San Jose, CA: Aspire Books.

Zimmerman, J. (2002). *Whose America? Culture ward in the public schools.* Cambridge, MA: Harvard University Press.

Index

About the Author

Christine E. Sleeter is Professor Emerita in the College of Professional Studies at California State University, Monterey Bay, where she teaches courses in multicultural education. In 1995, she came as a planning faculty member to start California State University in Monterey Bay and in 2003, she was awarded the University's President's Medal for her work. She lectures nationally and internationally on antiracist multicultural education and teacher education. Dr. Sleeter has received several awards for her work, including the National Association for Multicultural Education Research Award, and the AERA Committee on the Role and Status of Minorities in Education Distinguished Scholar Award. She is currently Vice President of Division K (Teaching and Teacher Education) of the American Educational Research Association. She has published over 90 journal articles and book chapters. Her journal articles appear in publications such as *Review of Research in Education, Curriculum Inquiry, Journal of Teacher Education, Teacher Education Quarterly,* and *Social Justice.* Her most recent books include *Culture, Difference, and Power; Multicultural Education as Social Activism;* and *Turning on Learning* with Carl Grant.